WHEN I FIRST CAME TO THIS COUNTRY

WHEN I FIRST CAME TO THIS COUNTRY

Another Immigrant Story

Özcan Tuncel, Ph.D.

To order additional copies of this book, contact:
Xlibris Corporation
1-888-795-4274
www.Xlibris.com
Orders@Xlibris.com
38990

I dedicate this book to my mother*[1], wife, children and their children.

---

[1] *Deceased on March 18, 2005.

To:

Industrialist Tonguç Ösen*[2], CEO of CMS Group,

And

Kemal Baysak, the former Mayor of Karşıyaka, CEO of TERBAY Corp., Hon. Consul General of Bosnia and Herzegovina

For being my lifelong friends

And

Dr. Nihat Önderoğlu,

For always being a big brother to me.

---

[2]   *Deceased on December 29, 2005.

Contents

Preface

On August 23, 2003, Doğan, "my beautiful son" (*güzel oğlum benim*) as I call him, and his lovely bride Bernadette got married in Gloucester, Massachusetts. At their wedding I was asked to say a few words:

"Dear friends, relatives and guests. Welcome, *wellkommen* and *hoşgeldiniz*. Thanks for coming here tonight, especially those of you who came from far distances. We very much appreciate it.

In my family, from time to time I tell stories which begin with the phrase "When I first came to this country". My kids right away, somewhat jokingly and sarcastically, would say "there goes Baba again telling one of his stories about when he first came to this country". No, I am not going to tell you any of those stories tonight. I have strict instructions!

I cannot help but think back however, to some 48 years ago when I was 18 years old, leaving Turkey and coming to New York City harbor by boat via Italy. In that misty, foggy, early morning when my boat was passing in front of the Statue of Liberty, my heart was full of excitement, joy, hope and great expectations for the future. I did not know what lay ahead. All I was hoping for was to get a good education.

Years later, I married my lovely and caring wife İlkay who gave me three wonderful children: Nükhet, Doğan and Müge. Through her I gained an extended family, my in-laws Nilüfer and Cemal Ramadan, and of course Tim and my granddaughter little Molly Ayla.

There are many immigrants in this room tonight like myself who came to this country at one time for varied reasons. We all have done very well through hard work and perseverance. We also raised some wonderful families. In our life travels I am glad our roads crossed and I got to know you.

I am now at a certain stage in my life, at a new chapter and a new page where my son Doğan is getting married to his lovely bride Bernadette whom we love very much. I have always been very proud of Doğan and tonight is no exception. My good friend Ronnie, who is in this room tonight, paid me the ultimate compliment when he said, "If I had a son I would have liked him to be just like Doğan". I think that says it all about Doğan.

Today Doğan and Bernadette are starting their lives' journey together. I know their hearts are full of excitement, joy, hope and great expectations for the future, just like mine was 48 years ago "when I first came to this country".

I wish them bon voyage, best of luck and may God bless. Thank you".

This tells my story briefly, but there is more to tell. President Bill Clinton in a television interview, talking about his autobiography, urged everyone to write his or her life story to pass on to future generations. As immigrants to this country, we all have many stories to tell going back to the "old days". Our unique backgrounds, separation from our families, our strengths, and adaptation to the new country, our successes and yearnings for the old homeland in many respects are very similar. No matter how many years we live in another country, apart from the one we were born into, the reality is that the nostalgia, the childhood memories and love for one's homeland never seems to die out. We think we have gotten adjusted to the new country and would not dream of ever living anywhere else, but our homeland still draws us back. In their nostalgic moments you hear immigrants reminisce their old stories. My story is no more unique than the next one but it is one story to tell. With my family's encouragement I decided to attempt to share my life story. I owe my life story to two wonderful women who shaped my being: my mother Naciş and my beloved wife Ilkay. I dedicate this book to my mother who was my guiding light, a tower of strength and full of determination even at her golden age of 87, and to my lovely wife, companion and friend whose care and affection for her family never faltered.

As I was writing my memoirs I realized I had to include a lot of technical terminologies and technical stories related to my job. Since I was an engineer working mostly on technical matters, my stories involved technical subjects that might seem somewhat boring. But I was educated to be an engineer and that is what I did during my forty year career at General Electric. I was blessed to live in a period when engineering was highly regarded as the cornerstone of our developing world and I had the opportunity to practice my skills with a long engineering career in one of the industry's giants. I therefore could not avoid but refer to many engineering subjects I worked on, mostly turbines and jet engines. If you can overcome the initial dullness of the technical matters, I hope you will find them different and interesting.

Özcan Tuncel
August 26, 2003

Homesickness transforms the objects of
our memories into poetic ideals.

George Sands

1

The Beginning

Historical Background

My family's roots trace back to the Balkans. More specifically to the two important cities of the Ottoman Empire in the Balkans: Janina (*Yanya*) of Macedonia where my father was from and Salonica (*Selanik*) of Thrace where my mother was from. Both of these cities are now part of Greece.

My parents were born and lived in a period where their lives were affected by the Balkan wars, the First World War, the end of the Ottoman Empire, the Turkish Independence War and the beginning of the Turkish Republic. It was a period of the end of a once mighty empire and birth of a great new nation, a period of wars, devastation, misery, and later hopes for a bright future in the new Republic.

The mighty Ottoman Empire, which had once stretched its borders in Europe to the gates of Vienna, found itself declining in the 19th century and losing grounds. The Ottomans were gradually driven out of Europe with only the Balkans left under their ruling. It was centuries of history that was courageous, turbulent and tragic. With strong support and direct involvement of the European nations and especially Russia, the Balkan states were revolting against the Ottomans and fighting for their independence. The second half of the 19th century in the Balkans witnessed the military battlegrounds and political maneuverings of the English, French, Italians, Austrians, Germans and Russians against the Ottomans. Friendships and treaties among the nations would not last long. Countries would switch sides even for small self-interests. At every opportunity the

Western powers would instigate and manipulate the Christian minorities in the Balkans to uprisings within the Ottoman borders.

The Russian-Ottoman War in 1877-1878 was the last major attack by the Russians to gain a foothold in the Straits and take over Istanbul to establish the center of the Orthodox Church. The Ottomans found themselves fighting the Russians on two fronts; in the Balkans as well as in northeastern Anatolia. In spite of the heroic resistance shown by the Ottomans, especially by *Gazi Osman Pasha* in *Plevne*, the Russians were making significant gains on both fronts. The Ottomans were further hindered by the need to divide their forces to fight the British occupation of Egypt, the French occupation in Tunisia, the Austrian involvement in Bosnia-Herzegovina and against the revolts of the Greeks, Bulgarians, Albanians and Armenians. They had no choice but to agree to a devastating peace treaty.

On July 13, 1878, the Congress of Berlin gave rise to the beginnings of new, independent nations of Bulgaria, Romania, Bosnia and Herzegovina, Montenegro and Serbia. The Treaty of Berlin ended the Ottoman Empire as a significant European power and created many Balkan states, whose internal rivalries caused ongoing turmoil even to the present day.

The Ottoman Sultan was left in Europe with a strip of territory south of the Balkan Mountains extending from the Black Sea to the Adriatic including Macedonia, Thrace and Albania. This included the provinces of Adrianople (Edirne), Salonica, Kosova, Janina and Manastir, the area where my ancestors were living. Autonomy and independence however was hardly satisfying to the emerging Balkan states. Each soon aspired for more territory and started constant aggression against what was left of the Ottoman Empire. At the beginning of the 20th century the Ottomans were engulfed with civil revolts in every corner of the Balkans.

During the period of 1911-1912, the Italians attacked the Ottoman armies in Tripoli and Benghazi in North Africa. Britain and France had already taken most of the northern African territories and only Tripoli was available for the Italians to expand their dream of an old glorious Roman Empire. The Italians were not, however, successful in the battlegrounds against the Ottoman garrison, led by a young officer named Mustafa Kemal Bey. The Italians, being humiliated, decided to attack with their Navy at various Turkish port cities. They later began sending arms and ammunition to Montenegro and Albania encouraging new rebellions and attacks against the Ottomans in the Balkans.

The Balkan Wars (1912-1913)

The Italian attack on Tripoli convinced the Balkan leaders to take advantage of the Ottoman preoccupation in North Africa. With the support of Austria and other European nations, Greece, Serbia, Montenegro and Bulgaria reached alliances to overthrow the Ottomans from the Balkans. Russia also had a significant involvement in this plot. Montenegro started the First Balkan War by moving into northern Albania on October 8, 1912. Soon after, its allies participated in the war fighting the Ottoman army on many fronts. The Ottomans were in no position to fight this war. Communications between Macedonia and Thrace were cut, making the two Ottoman armies ineffective. The Ottomans were losing the battles on all the fronts. Bulgarians advanced to Adrianople (Edirne). Soon after, the Greeks took over Salonika (*Selanik*) on November 8, 1912 and put Janina (*Yanya*) under siege. Taking advantage of the horrific conditions of the Ottomans, Albania declared its independence in 1912 and the Greeks took over all the Aegean islands. The Ottoman soldiers in Edirne and *Yanya* continued defending their cities very bravely. The Bulgarians, not being able to capture Edirne against strong and relentless Turkish defenses, began a campaign of slaughtering thousands of Turkish peasants in Thrace (*Trakya*). On March 28, 1913 Edirne was starved to submission to the Bulgarians. On March 6, 1913 *Yanya* had already fallen to the Greeks. For the Ottoman Empire the First Balkan War was an unimaginable disaster. In just six weeks in the autumn of 1912 a coordinated effort by the Balkan states with the backing of the western nations resulted in the loss of almost all the European territories that was Turkish. This finally ended 500 years of Ottoman Turkish rule in Europe.

At the end of the First Balkan War which ended in April 1913, Greece and Serbia benefited with large portions of the Ottoman Macedonia leaving very small enclaves in Thrace to Bulgaria. Bulgarians, feeling cheated, prepared to fight for a larger share of the spoils of their victory. Bulgaria always had its sights on Salonica and there were ongoing incidences between the Greek and Bulgarian soldiers that created animosities between them. On June 29, 1913 the Second Balkan War started because the Balkan States got greedy and were not willing to share Macedonia with their own partner Bulgaria. Bulgarians initiated an attack on the Serbs. Soon after, the Bulgarians found themselves fighting against Greece, Macedonia, Serbia and Romania. In this civil infighting, this time the Bulgarians were losing the war in all the fronts. "The Young Turks" at this point took advantage of the situation by attacking the Bulgarians with a small army and restoring Edirne back into Turkish territories. The Second Balkan War which lasted barely a month ended with significant losses for the Bulgarians.

The Balkan wars were some of the most devastating battles in history. Not only did the Ottomans lose all their territories in Europe, but also millions of people died and 6.5 million Moslem residents were left behind, their lives devastated in these lost territories. All Ottoman subjects were given 4 years to decide if they wished to remain under Christian rule or to emigrate. The Ottomans were left with a small enclave of land in Europe bordering with the Greeks and Bulgarians, which remained as today's borders of the new Turkish Republic in Eastern Thrace.

Father's Family in Janina

My paternal grandfather Sadık Bey (no family surnames during the Ottoman Empire) was the Commander of the Ottoman Gendarmes (*Jandarma Komutanı*) in Janina (*Yanya*). *Yanya* was a very cosmopolitan city at the time. It was located close to the western borders of Greece next to Albania. Because of its geography, the city was populated with the Albanians (*Arnavut*), Greeks (*Yunanlı*), Italians, Serbs (*Sırb*), Bosnians (*Boşnak*), Bulgarians, Jews and Turks. There was a large number of Sephardic Jews who immigrated to the Ottoman Empire when Philip II exiled them from Spain during the Spanish Inquisition. Sultan Bayezıt II and later Sultan Süleyman the Magnificent (*Kanuni Sultan Süleyman*) had agreed to accept them into Ottoman lands and had them settle in these parts of the Balkans. *Selanik* and Istanbul were two major cities where the Jews brought a lot of capitol to contribute to the Empire's banking and commerce business. The Jews were very well accepted and adopted into the Turkish society. After the Turks, the Jews were the Empire's most loyal citizens. During the rise of Balkan nationalism the Jews increased the intensity of their identification with the Ottoman Turkish state. Those close ties, friendship and harmony between the Turks and the Jews continued for years, even to this day. In those days the main occupation of the Moslem Ottomans was either farming or the military. The non-Moslem citizens were mostly involved in trade and commerce.

Being in the military, Sadık Bey had moved his family to various locations within the Ottoman territories in the Balkans. His last duty in *Yanya* was being in charge of the gendarme (military police) forces. His family was large with five children and other relatives living in *Yanya*. My father Ali Riza was born in *Yanya* in 1910 as the fourth child after Malik, Mclek and Aliye. Cevat was born next and added to the family as the fifth child. Specific birth dates were not known since midwives delivered the babies at home. Two other children had died during infancy or childbirth. In those days soldiers were assigned to high-ranking military officers to help with their domestic needs. My grandmother Şakire Hanım would not have been able to raise her children without the help from these soldiers.

When the First Balkan War started, life in this happy but struggling military family got disrupted. For years, with the ongoing wars and revolts all around *Yanya*, they knew sooner or later that the Greeks would attack *Yanya*. Before long, the Greek army laid siege to Janina against an overwhelming Turkish resistance. Sadık Bey and the soldiers in his command took part with the other Ottoman garrisons in the defense of the city. The Turkish soldiers tried to protect *Yanya* with admirable heroism. They fought with valor and determination. The defense of *Yanya* lasted for a long time and the soldiers and commanders were heartily recognized for their bravery. The Sultan awarded Sadık Bey two Balkan War medals. On March 6, 1913 *Yanya* eventually fell to the Greeks. My father Ali Riza was three years old then. At this young age he contracted typhoid, an infectious disease, which was all around. If the war had not killed the people, then plague, cholera or malaria was going to. Father, however, recovered from typhoid with some after effects such as the loss of hearing in one ear and being short tempered.

At the end of the First Balkan War, with the Treaty of London, the remaining Ottoman lands were given to the Balkan states. With this treaty the Moslem citizens had the choice of staying behind or immigrating to Turkey. Sadık Bey, with his wife Şakire Hanım and their five children, had to leave *Yanya* and travel to Istanbul to report to duty there. Being a military family, the army was their "home". The family endured fires, epidemic and hunger, bombardments and military defeat.

Their trip to Istanbul was very arduous, with war and devastation happening at every corner of the lost empire. They travelled on oxen driven carts part of the mountainous roads through a divided and ruined land until they arrived in Thrace. After Thrace they completed the journey by train all the way to Istanbul. The soldiers assigned to Sadık Bey were a great help during the long journey. Without their support the family would have never made it to their destination. One of the soldiers carried my sickly father Ali Riza in a basket all the way to Istanbul. During this trip they witnessed the ending of a once mighty empire. The land was crumbling and the people were dying everywhere. With the peace treaties the bloodshed had not stopped. The Christian population was randomly attacking homes, killing or driving the Muslims out of their homes to avenge the 500 years of Ottoman occupation.

Being in Istanbul was a great relief for the family because they were now in secure Ottoman lands. This did not last too long however, because the First World War had just started.

The First World War

In 1914 the First World War started in Europe. At the beginning of the war, England, France and Russia were fighting against the Germans and Austrians. The Germans badly needed the Ottomans to support them in this war. The Ottomans however, were in no position to get involved with this one after so many devastating wars that had left the country in ruins. However, some of the leaders of the government, led by Enver Pasha, Talat Pasha and Cemal Pasha believed the Germans could win this war while public opinion was strongly against it. The "leadership" however, was under constant pressure by the Germans to take part against Russia. At this time, two German cruisers, the Goeben and the Breslan, which were running away from the British Navy, passed the Dardanelles and sailed to Istanbul to get protection. The Ottoman government informed the British that they had bought these ships, which they named *Yavuz* and *Midilli*, respectively, and they now belonged to the Ottoman government. During this period the German attacks against the French on the Western Front were meeting with strong resistance and their advance was halted. In order to reduce the burden on the Eastern Front against the Russians, the Germans insisted that the Ottomans should enter the war. Although the Ottoman public, the government and even the Sultan did not agree about taking part in the war, the Germans planned to use these two destroyers to pull the Ottomans in. The three pashas who were secretly negotiating with the Germans somehow got the permission from the Government for the ships to sail under the Turkish flag into the Black Sea. The ships, without approved authority, attacked the Russian fleet and some major Russian ports. On November 16, 1914 the Ottomans once again were in a state of war against the Russians, the English and the French. Not much later Bulgaria took its place in the war on the side of the Germans.

The entrance of the Ottomans into the war changed the entire geographic spectrum. While the war was initially being fought in Europe, the battlegrounds were now extended to a much larger landscape of the Ottoman territories. Turkish forces were fighting the Russians, the English and the French at far corners of Ottoman lands. In addition, the Turks had to help the Bulgarian and Austrian armies on the Romanian front. The Russians were not doing well against the Germans on the Eastern Front. In order to help the Russians from the sea, the British and the French had to pass through the straits. They therefore attacked the Dardanelles. A major force composed of the English, Australian and New Zealand soldiers landed on the Gallipoli coast to open up the Dardanelles Strait. One of the most spectacular and successful defenses of the Turkish soil took place at Gallipoli (*Gelibolu*). The Ottoman troops, commanded by Mustafa Kemal, heroically defended this coast, caused significant enemy losses and pushed the allied forces back. This was a welcomed and much needed victory for the Turks. Mustafa Kemal became the great hero of Gallipoli in the hearts of every Turk.

For the Ottomans the war on the Northeastern Front against the Russians was not going well. The Russians had taken several Turkish cities including Erzurum. After the Dardanelle campaign, Mustafa Kemal once again was in the Eastern Front driving the Russians back. The battles continued in Arabia, Egypt and Iraq with most of the Middle Eastern lands that were once Ottoman-controlled, being lost. At the end of the First World War in 1918, the Ottoman Empire had collapsed and its territories were divided. The Allied forces occupied Anatolia and began parceling the once glorious and powerful empire. The British controlled Istanbul and the Straits; the French and Italians landed on different parts of Anatolia; the Greeks, who entered the war much later towards the end without any effort, landed in Izmir and occupied the surrounding areas. The division of the country by the Allies was ruthless, excessive and unjustified. All that was left for the Turks was the central terrain of Anatolia. This was a major devastation, which generated strong nationalistic reaction from the Turks who vowed to save the country from the enemies.

The Turkish War of Independence (*İstiklal Harbi*)

Once again it was the same scenario, with the Ottoman Empire devastated by war and lying in ruins. The Sultan yielded to all the wishes of the Allied forces and the enemy occupied every corner of the empire. The three pashas that caused the collapse sneaked out of the country but were later caught in different locations and killed. At the end of the war, Turks were dealt very unfairly by the Allied powers. At this point, there was no other choice but to start the resistance movement, the Independence War (*İstiklal Harbi*). Once again the people put their hopes in their new hero Mustafa Kemal, who on 19 May 1919, by leaving Istanbul and landing in Samsun, started the Independence movement. His close associate Kazım Karabekir was now the Commander of the Eastern Army at Erzurum. By this time my grandfather Sadık Bey was assigned to Kazım Karabekir's army on the Eastern Front. Once again he was on the move, traveling to Erzurum. By now his family included two more additions, Ayşe and Tevfik making it a total of seven children. Since Istanbul was under British occupation, the entire family fled to Erzurum. During the train ride one of the children Cevat, had an accident and lost his left arm below the elbow. He remained with only one hand and a bitter, arrogant personality the rest of his life.

Mustafa Kemal and his associates started the national movement against the occupation by gathering consensus inside Anatolia (*Anadolu*). A Grand National Assembly *(Büyük Millet Meclisi)* was formed and a new Constitution *(Anayasa)* was drawn in 1921. A new Turkish Government was established in Ankara and the Sultan's Government in Istanbul was no longer recognized. At the same time a new Turkish Army was being prepared for war. The Greeks by now had advanced much beyond Izmir into the Aegean district approaching towards the new capital Ankara causing bloodshed and atrocities to the local Muslims along the way. The Greek offensive continued until Ismet Inönü stopped them. The second offensive of the Greeks once again was stopped in *Sakarya* with Mustafa Kemal and Ismet Inönü commanding the troops. After fighting with the Russians and Armenians on the Eastern Front, my grandfather was assigned to the army on the Western Front, once again fighting the Greeks. Finally, the Great Offensive (*Büyük Taarruz*) started on 26 August 1922 when the Turkish army drove the Greek army into the Aegean Sea. As they were fleeing from the Turkish forces, the Greek soldiers burned the towns to the ground and plundered everything in their path. What the Greeks left behind was shear devastation. The Greek Army however, did not last more than two weeks under the onslaught of fierce Turkish forces. On September 9, 1922 the Turkish cavalry marched into Izmir and went directly to the Konak Government Building and raised the Turkish flag. The main army followed the cavalry forces and Izmir was liberated. My grandfather was among those soldiers who first entered the city. On September 13 a suspicious fire broke out in the city's Alsancak district and spread rapidly burning half of the city. The hot flames of the big fire raced furiously through the city with the "*imbat*" wind coming from the sea feeding the fire further, devouring all the buildings in its path. The dark black smoke cloud had blanketed the city and could be observed with terrible anxiety across the bay in the neighborhood of Karşıyaka. By the time the fire subsided, half of the city was burned to the ground leaving behind smoke filled rubbles of buildings piled up in a huge open field. We called this burned out field "*yangınlık*". Although the "great fire" was started intentionally in the Greek and Armenian quarters where the Greek and Armenian partisans were suspected, the responsible parties were never found.

After Izmir was liberated, other parts of the country were cleared of the enemy as well. The Turkish War of Independence was won and the new Turkish Republic was recognized by the entire world. As part of the peace settlement with the Treaty of Lausanne, the Greeks and the Turks agreed to exchange populations. Over one million Greeks and a half a million Turks were forced to leave their homes and move to their new countries. Although most of the people left their homes, there were a few that chose to stay behind. After the Greeks emigrated, Izmir turned into a ghost city. The vacant houses were given to the Turkish immigrants. The military personnel, however, had the first choice of selecting from some lovely properties. Instead of choosing a nice, big house in a better section of Alsancak, my grandfather Sadık Bey somehow chose a very small, five-room house deserted by the Greeks on a narrow side street. The house was built on a forty square meter lot, a foot below street level, with an entry, living room, a dark kitchen and a tiny bathroom on the first floor. Upstairs there were three small bedrooms and a ladder leading to the terrace. The house had no electricity or running water. There was a hand-operated pump in the kitchen pulling the water from a ground well. This house was not much but it was home for the family. The address was 1457 Sokak No.36 Alsancak, an address where I would end up growing up in and an address that would be carved in my memory with happy and sad memories. The house was only half a block from "*yangınlık*", the burned part of the city where all the neighborhood children would play.

At the end of this long journey, which was full of battles, devastation, misery and finally victory, Sadık Bey was again awarded a gold Independence War Medal (*İstiklal Madalyası*) given only to the brave soldiers of the new Turkish Republic. Sadık Bey now had three medals to his name to be proud of: two Balkan War Medals and one Independence War Medal. The long ordeal for the military family was finally over and

Sadik Bey retired from the army with a pension. The Turkish Republic was now fully established and the country was at peace. As one of the first reform movements, the Turkish Republic adopted the surname rule and Sadık Bey randomly chose "Tuncel" as his family last name. At this time Mustafa Kemal was bestowed by the grateful Turkish nation the last name of "Atatürk" which meant "the father of the Turks".

Mother's family in Salonica

Salonica *(Selanik)* was a beautiful city on the northern shores of the Aegean Sea. The city surrounded the bay like a pearl necklace with views over the sea to Mount Olympos. For centuries the Greeks and the Turks coexisted in this city in harmony and trust under Ottoman rule. Over the years, with European influence *Selanik* prospered, grew and changed its appearance more radically towards a western city with an Ottoman character. After Istanbul, *Selanik* was the second most important city to the Ottoman Empire in Europe. The port city of *Selanik*, with many ethnic nationalities, flourished in commerce, agriculture, art and cultural activities, and it was always sought after by everyone as the ideal city to live in. Its military academies trained some of the brightest officers for the Ottoman army. Mustafa Kemal (Atatürk) Bey, who was born in *Selanik*, was one of those officers. In the summertime the stores and outdoor cafes, tavernas, coffee-houses, casinos, restaurants and cabarets around the bay were full of people strolling around and enjoying the beautiful weather and lovely views of the bay. There was joy, friendship and harmony in the air. The Christian, Moslem and Jewish citizens of the city were always intermingled. They shopped from each other's stores, worked together and even had intermarriages. In this very cosmopolitan city great tranquility prevailed. This harmony however, got interrupted as the Ottoman Empire started collapsing and as Greek nationalism started rising. This reversal gained momentum when the Greeks attained their independence and the Ottomans were driven out of the Balkans.

When the First Balkan War had started on October 8, 1912 *Selanik* was the primary target of the Greeks. The Greek forces quickly attacked *Selanik* and the city fell to them on November 8, 1912. Although the city was defended very feverishly, the Ottomans were not able to save it. Once the Greeks took over the city, the old neighborly friendship was all forgotten. Muslim homes were looted, burned and the people were tortured and killed. Millions of Muslims and Jews because of their support of the Ottomans were uprooted from their homes. It was now their turn to avenge the 500 years of Ottoman occupancy. With the reversal of power Greeks started a systematic eradication of the Ottoman traces from the city by converting the mosques into churches, tearing down the minarets which had been a defining feature of Salonica's skyline for 500 years and other Ottoman landscapes, requisitioning and ransacking all the Muslim and Jewish properties including the cemeteries. Life in Salonica and its surrounding territories became impossible for the Muslims and the Jews. A state of terror prevailed over the Muslim population when the Greek troops, irregulars and bandits continued their torture, massacres and looting of their properties. Local authorities would not protect them. There was constant humiliation and a pattern of violence in all the corners of the city.

My maternal grandfather, Üzeyir Bey and my maternal grandmother Pembe Hanım lived at the outskirts of *Selanik* in an area called Kalamaria (*Geremerya*). Kalamaria, a suburb of Salonica with villas and tree-lined streets was located to the east of the city, beyond the old city walls and the cemeteries. They were wealthy property owners and a prominent family in *Selanik*. After the Balkan wars the large Muslim population living in *Selanik* and its surroundings were given the permission to remain in their homes if they chose to and live under the Greek rule. Üzeyir Bey and his family did not want to leave their beautiful home at that time and move to Turkey since they could not transfer their properties and belongings. They were also deeply attached to their birthplace and to the neighborhood where they lived all their lives. Furthermore, they had no family in Turkey and had no place to go to in a land that was foreign to them. They were well established in *Selanik* and there were still many Turkish families and relatives in the area. This was their home and the only land they had ever known. They had two beautiful daughters, Ayşe and Firdez, and they were a very happy family. When the Balkan Wars came to an end in 1913 the situation in *Selanik* was calm. This did not last too long however, since in 1914 WWI had begun abruptly in Europe. Once again the Ottomans were at war and during the next four years they would again be fighting with the allied powers and the Greeks. This period witnessed the collapse of the Ottoman Empire and the occupation of Turkey by the allied powers. Between 1917 and 1923 the Greek-Turkish relationship was at its lowest with the Greek landing and occupation of Izmir, the invasion of Anatolia and the climaxing into another war. This was followed by the catastrophic defeat of the Greek army at the hands of Mustafa Kemal's new Turkish army and a forced exchange of populations without any precedent in history. The Independence War during 1919-1922 gave the Turks a new Turkish Republic after the allied powers and the Greeks were driven out of Turkey. The Greeks had suffered the worst disaster in their history. At the end of 1922 Greek and Turkish delegates meeting in Lausanne negotiated an end to the war and agreed to a comprehensive exchange of populations. Although there had been so-called voluntary exchanges before, this time it was a compulsory exchange of Greek and Turkish populations. Although some Jews left their homes and moved to France, Italy, United States and Palestine, most of the Jews remained in Salonica. Their stay in Salonica was not well received by the Greek society which harboured deeply rooted prejudices and discrimination against the Jews. They were also gradually thrown out of Salonica with their final demise happening by the Nazis during World War II. The end of 1924 was set as the final date for the Muslims to leave the country. In 1916 my mother Fatma (middle name Naciye) was born and Hanife was the fourth daughter born soon after. The four daughters of Üzeyir Bey and Pembe Hanım were the most beautiful blond children in Selanik. Üzeyir himself was so blond that he had a nickname "*Sarî*" (blond) Üzeyir. Pembe Hanım was busy managing her house while raising her four lovely daughters with proper Muslim values and yet instilling European culture in them as well.

After the disastrous Greek defeat in Anatolia, life in *Selanik* for the Turks became unbearable. Muslim homes were constantly being looted, burned and the people were tortured and killed by the Greeks as a revengeful reaction for their terrible defeat in Turkey. Üzeyir Bey was desperately trying to protect his beautiful family from the onslaught that was happening all around. It was not long before the Greek irregulars, mostly neighborhood men who knew the family, were at his door demanding money and gold from him. He tried to guard his family and his wealth but they knew he was a wealthy man and they wanted everything he owned. Although Üzeyir Bey kept them away for a while by giving them some of his gold, they eventually demanded everything. They wanted to know where the rest of his gold was hidden and to make him talk, they decided to torture him. They squeezed his head with a metal ring and clamp. Ongoing and repeated tortures left Üzeyir Bey crippled. For as much as they did not want to, the sense of desperation was so overwhelming that the family had no other alternative but leave *Selanik* right away. They frantically hid whatever gold they had remaining in the well in the backyard garden of their house with the hope of returning to their home someday. But that would never happen.

They were among the first exodus of people from *Selanik* who left by steamship to sail to Izmir. This was the historic immigration of millions of Muslim refugees from their homes. People were not allowed to sell those goods they could not take with them and were forced to leave everything they owned behind because they were carefully searched and controlled. They could only take what they could carry in their hands and that was not much. Their pride and dignity however was still intact. Chaos, hunger and disease were widespread and throughout this period the family had suffered a lot. Once a wealthy landowner, Üzeyir Bey's family was now poor and destitute immigrants.

As the steamship was leaving *Selanik* Bay slowly, the immigrants were all leaning over the side of the boat and straining themselves to look back and get a last glance of their homeland with tears in their eyes. None of those eyes would ever see *Selanik* again. They could feel the heavy pulsating beat of their heart and they did not speak a word between them, but accepted this as their fate or "*alın yazısı*" (written on forehead). Their hopes of returning to their home to reclaim their past would never materialize. The steamship sailed on the Aegean Sea passing by many beautiful islands. Once the proud sailing waters of the Ottoman Navy, the sea of our great admirals Turgut Reis and Barbaros Hayrettin Pasha, was now taken over by the Greeks completely. On the boat, the second daughter Firdez died as a result of German measles and she was buried at sea.

When the family landed in Izmir in 1922, Üzeyir Bey and Pembe Hanım still had their three lovely daughters; Ayşe, Fatma (Naciye) and Hanife. My mother Naciye was six years old at the time.

2

The Early Years

Father's Youth

After Colonel Sadık Tuncel retired from the army and settled in Alsancak, Izmir with his family, on 29 October 1923 the new Turkish Republic was established and the Grand National Assembly (*Büyük Millet Meclisi*) elected Mustafa Kemal Atatürk to be the first President of the Republic. Ismet Inönü became the first Prime Minister. The last Sultan, Abdülmecit and all his family members were exiled out of the country and the Ottomans were no more. The country however, was war torn and decimated and the people were poor and desperate. They did not know if there would be a next meal or where it would come from. When the Greeks were driven out of Turkish lands not only did they leave behind burned out villages and towns but stories of atrocities and murders that they induced would be told for many years. There were only bitter memories in the minds of everyone that witnessed or experienced those days, but now they knew the future was secure and bright under Atatürk's leadership. The country needed a complete renewal and this miracle would not happen by itself. It required sweat and hard work. Turks were never afraid of hard work and they were ready to build a new nation and a new country from the ashes of the old torn down empire.

Even though half of the city was burned, Izmir was still an enchanting place. The remaining unburned section of Alsancak had small row houses as single family dwellings on narrow cobblestone streets. On some streets there were beautiful mulberry (*dut*) and acacia (*akasya*) trees. A few houses had gardens with beautiful plants and rose and jasmine bushes climbing up the stone walls. In the hot summer days sweet fragrances coming from the jasmine, honeysuckle and rose bushes would spread around the neighborhood flowing into the houses from the open windows. In the evenings people would pull out their chairs and sit in front of their houses to feel the cool breezes carried by "*imbat*" winds coming from the bay. Ladies would collect the jasmine petals and string them into necklaces or bracelets while other family members sat enjoying their evening tea (*çay*). Children would be running around the barren streets from dawn until dusk playing ball or hide and go seek and many other basic games they had made up while neighbors would indulge in friendly conversations and sometimes gossip about each other's affairs. This was their only quality time.

Alsancak, which was a unique neighborhood, was very cosmopolitan with some Italian, Greek, and Jewish families still remaining behind in their homes. This was part of the final war agreement. Among the neighbors, Sadık Bey was better off then most since he had a nice military pension. He and Şakire Hanım had their little house in Alsancak with all the family members settled around them. Malik was the oldest of the seven surviving children. He was tall and very good-looking. In the family, he had the most opportunity for some education. The other children, especially the girls had very little or no education. For his times, Malik was very courageous and adventurous since he had married an Italian girl named Sophia. Although the family reluctantly accepted the Italian bride, Madam Sophia, as she was referred to, was never warmly welcomed into the family. Malik got a job in the Municipal Water Works (*Devlet Su İşleri*) and the couple settled in a rented flat one street over from his parents. The second child Melek married a barber named Cemal. They were also living very near to her parents' house. Neither of these two couples had any children. Aliye, who was number-three child, married a National Railroad Company (*Devlet Demir Yolları*) employee. They were also living close by in *Kahramanlar*. They had three children; Cavit, Suat and Yılmaz. The family was expanding and settling close to their parents in Alsancak.

My father Ali Riza, who was 12 years old when the family came to Izmir, was a difficult child. He showed no interest in education. During the war days, since the family was always on the move, education was not a priority, survival was. When education was available, Ali Riza would not have anything to do with schooling. After trying different odd jobs for a few years, he showed an interest in shoe making. He was built very muscular with broad shoulders, strong and big hands. He was growing into a good looking young man with fair skin, keen black eyes, and thick dark hair neatly combed back. He was of medium height with a very athletic appearance. By the time he was eighteen years old, he found no occupation or excitement in Izmir and decided to try his luck in Istanbul.

His uncle was living in *Çengelköy*, a quaint town of Istanbul, on the Anatolian coast of the Bosphorus and he went to stay with him. He was overwhelmed with the village-like atmosphere of *Çengelköy*. He loved walking along the shores of the Bosphorus lined with huge oak trees. He was very idle and felt he had to do something with his life. He joined the boxing club in Üskűdar and started practicing. To support himself financially however, he got jobs doing the only thing he knew which was making shoes. In boxing he relied on his wild strength and powerful arms. Swinging the hammer all day long, while making shoes developed his hands and arms further. He was doing well in the rings against his opponents because they were small time boxers. To get into the professional league however, he had to work much harder with full dedication. He dreamt of being like Jack Dempsey or Joe Lewis. What he lacked in technique, he made up in shear strength and bravery. After a few fights in the ring, he decided boxing would not be an ultimate career for him. He had to do something else with his life. He had no education and he was completely illiterate until his dying days. He could only write numbers in Arabic which was helpful in his shoemaking profession. He quit boxing and turned his full attention to being a good shoemaker. In Istanbul he worked with various shoemakers improving his craft. Not only could he repair old worn out shoes, but he could also make new custom shoes from scratch. After a few years of apprenticeship in Istanbul he was ready to go on his own, but Istanbul was too big, too competitive and difficult to start anew. He did not have enough resources so the next best thing he could do was to return to Izmir where all his family was located.

After exploring a few opportunities in Izmir, Ali Riza rented a store in Alsancak to start his custom shoemaking business. His store's front window displayed a beautiful sign with the name of "*Altın Kundura*" (Golden Shoe). The store was very close to his sister Melek's house and not far from his father's house. All he now needed were some good customers. Since Sadık Bey's family had spent a large portion of their lives in *Yanya* among the Greeks, they were all fluent in speaking Greek as well as Turkish. In the household, the Greek language was used as often as the Turkish. The Tuncels were now an established family in Alsancak and people knew about Ali Riza's shoemaking business. Customers started bringing their shoes to him mostly for repairs. For custom made shoes, however, Greek and Italian neighbors were the main customers. Ali Riza had pictures of different shoe models he had collected from various popular English magazines that he would show his clients. He would make a pattern of the feet on a piece of paper with widths measured on two locations and record them with his Arabic numerals next to the pattern. These dimensions would be used in preparing the wooden mold. He would then cut the upper leathers in a pattern chosen by the customer. At this point a trip would be required to *Çankaya* where the "shoe sewers" were located. In a couple of days the upper sole was ready to be nailed with very small thin nails over the wooden mold. The mold was conveniently held over his legs next to his knees and nailing was done against his legs. Nailing shaped the upper leather sole around the wooden mold very tightly. The next step would be sewing of the innersole against the leather surface while the bent nails were removed one by one. The lower sole, the heavy thick bottom was further sewn by hand with stitches imbedded into the leather. Small holes were opened with a sharp pin and the thread was pulled through these holes with a pig's hair attached at the end. The process continued until the entire lower sole was sewn all around and the heels were finally attached. Custom shoemaking was tidious, time consuming and a difficult art. Once it was finished, however, you were a proud owner of a pair of beautiful shoes. Ali Riza took pride in his craft and he produced some perfect looking shoes. As his business improved he hired an assistant. He was now getting to be an established shoemaker in Alsancak.

Mother's Youth

When Pembe Hanim arrived in Izmir in 1922 with her three lovely daughters and handicapped husband Üzeyir Bey, she was scared of the uncertainty but was determined to make a new life for her family. She was forced to leave her beautiful home and all the other worldly belongings behind in *Selanik* and come to this unknown land. The new Turkish government had just come out of a devastating war, while picking the ruins left behind by the Greeks. Nevertheless, the government made all the arrangements for these desperate, displaced people and had prepared a hope for the future. The government officials met the immigrants at the Izmir Port and took them to the Alsancak train station where they were all boarded on the train for Bayındır, a small town about 50 Km. from Izmir. My mother had just started her life's journey in this new land at the age of six at the Alsancak train station and she would end up living the rest of her life in her own house very close to this train station.

In Bayındır they were settled in a small, two-story house located on a parcel of land with a few olive trees on it. It did not take them long to start working the land. Pembe Hanım was able to manage her family with very little money she had. Üzeyir Bey however was in no shape physically to be able to do much for his family. He was not well because of the injuries he had sustained to his brain from the tortures by the Greeks and not long after he got sick and died. His loving family quietly buried him in Bayındır. Pembe Hanım was left a widow with three young children to take care of. She had a broken home where she had lost one daughter and a husband but she still possessed the will to work and the spirit to live. It is an accepted fact that no matter which country they are from, immigrants are always hard working people. This must be due to a desperate need, fear of failure and a drive to succeed. In the case of my mother's family they had no other choice but to work hard. In Bayındır, with the new law of the Turkish government, they adopted a new family surname of "Toku".

All the immigrants who had settled in Bayındır were now busily working and making a life for themselves. The small lands they were cultivating were flourishing with abundant produce, which was enough for their families, as well as to sell in the market place. Bayındır started getting a reputation as a fertile and productive farmland. Merchants from Izmir frequently came to Bayındır to buy their produce to market in the big city. One day a merchant from Izmir, Lütfü Önderoğlu met Pembe Hanım and her three daughters. Lütfü Bey realized Pembe Hanım was not a farmer type and was not doing that well in farming. He offered to help and have them move to Izmir. Since his oldest daughter Nevzat was my mother's age, he suggested having my mother live in their house and grow up together with Nevzat. This seemed like a good plan. The Toku family once again was on the move back to Izmir. Pembe Hanım bought a house on the hills of Izmir known as *Hatay* and got settled in this small house with her daughters Ayşe and Hanife. The house had a little back yard and a fountain at the corner known as *çeşme* being fed from a spring coming from the hills above. The *Hatay* neighborhood was very isolated then with very few houses around the hillside. There was no transportation to *Hatay* and the only way to reach there was with a streetcar on the lower land along the shore and then by climbing the hill on foot. Today *Hatay* is one of the most crowded sections of Izmir with noisy traffic and apartment buildings which look like a concrete jungle. My grandmother's house was at the heart of *Hatay* located at the "*Çeşme*" Bus Stop, named after the fountain she once had at the corner of her house. Today in this very crowded section of town everybody refers to the *Çeşme* bus stop but nobody really knows how the name was derived.

To support her family, Pembe Hanım got a job at the National Railroad (*Devlet Demir Yolları*) and worked in the service department where the steam locomotives were being repaired and maintained. She would get up early in the morning and walk down the hill to *Çankaya* and pass by the International Fair and continue to walk to the Alsancak train station where her job was. The commute was over four miles each way and she did this every day for many years until she retired at an old age.

My mother moved in with the Önderoğlu family and started living in their home near the *İki Çeşmelik* neighborhood. Besides Nevzat, the family had three other children: Nihal, Ahmet and Nihat. My mother and Nevzat were always together, playing on the streets and going to the local stores to buy candies. Since they were the same age, they were growing up together as if they were twin sisters. When Lütfü Bey's business improved, he moved his family to a very nice three-story house in Alsancak. As my mother was growing older she started looking after the youngest child in the family, Nihat. Nihat grew up in my mother's hands. As the years followed one another my mother was growing up to be a gorgeous blond with blue eyes. When she walked by people would stop and take a second look at the curvaceous young woman with beautiful, naturally curly blond hair. Her beauty was known all around Alsancak.

The Marriage

My father's "*Altın Kundura*" shoe store was on 1460 Sokak in Alsancak on the same street as the Önderoğlu family residence. His shoe making business was improving with time and he and his assistant were keeping busy. When he was not working, my father would spend most of his time in front of his modest store monitoring this beautifully proportioned young woman with lustrous blond hair walk by to go to go to the corner grocery store. He himself was a very well built, lean, good looking young man with dark hair and keen dark eyes. It did not take him long before he decided he was ready to get married, hopefully to this blond beauty. The only way that could happen was to have his family go and ask for her hand from her family. In those days this was the only proper way for two young people to be able to get together. He anxiously urged his family members to go and knock on Pembe Hanım's door. Without much scrutiny the two families agreed to join these two young people in matrimony. The marriage quietly took place on 21 November 1935 as a simple civil ceremony with no reception or big celebration. My mother was slender and beautiful in her white wedding gown. She was only nineteen years old. Without much fanfare, the marriage got finalized hurriedly and the young couple moved in together with my father's family into the small house at 1457 Sokak No. 36. They were given the dark bedroom in the back of the house under the terrace. My mother started her married life living together with her in-laws and she would soon discover that her husband's family was not the most pleasant people to live with. They were difficult and inconsiderate, but my mother had married into this family and she could do nothing but hope for the best in the future.

Özcan Is Born

I was born in 1937, a little over a year after the wedding. My father and mother were still living with my paternal grandparents. My youngest uncle Tevfik was also living in the same house in the small front bedroom. According to my mother, I was born on a "cold wintry day". My exact birth date is not known. Years later we stipulated, with my mother's questionable reassurance, my birth date to be January 20th. My birth certificate (*nüfus*), however, which was a little book at that time, showed my birth date to be August 26, 1937. I might have been born in the wintertime but the official registration and obtaining the actual birth certificate must have been done on August 26. In western countries where birth dates are known to the exact minute of the day, I was haunted with dismay the rest of my life not knowing what my exact birth date was. For convenience we substituted and accepted January 20th as my birthday. Officially however I had to use August 26 for all my legal and business transactions the rest of my life. I am the only person I know who had two birth dates and always had to explain the situation in embarrassment.

When my mother was ready to deliver me, my grandmother Pembe took her to Aunt Ayşe's house in *Hatay* where a midwife performed the delivery at home. After staying at my aunt's house for a few days, mother and I went back to Alsancak. Because my mother's milk was not sufficient to nurse me, Aunt Ayşe participated in breast feeding me also. Six months earlier she had given birth to her second son Metin and had plenty of milk to spare. She thus became my milk mother (*süt anne*). Lucky beginning, everything was happening to me in doubles, two birth dates and two milk mothers!

My father was still working in his *Altın Kundura* shoe store but business was now very slow. Mustafa Kemal Atatürk and his Republican People's Party (*Cumhuriyet Halk Partisi*) were in power and running the country. Although there had been considerable improvements in the economy since the beginning of the Turkish Republic, most people were still at poverty level. There was some progress made in industry and agriculture but the rate of growth was so slow that the government found it necessary to bring almost everything under state control. This limited the growth of private enterprise. Capitals were not available and the loans secured from the western countries were being used by the State very properly in developing major industries. Factories were being built, ports and railroads were being developed, power plants were generating electricity and new banks including the new Central Bank (*Merkez Bankası*) were being established. The birth of a new nation was being followed by the birth of a new reverberate economy. During that period, state controlled monopolies performed significant roles in developing the country's economy. One industrial enterprise that started in 1933 was *Sümerbank*, which controlled the textile business, shoe industry, cement mills and steel and iron industries. Little did I know that my fate would be tied to Sümerbank in later years when I would receive a full scholarship to study in America. Although Atatürk's economic policies and five-year plans showed progress, living conditions were still very difficult. Besides the economic difficulties, the majority of the people were illiterate and not fully ready to manage themselves in a full democracy. During Atatürk's period, rebellions, discontent and opposition to the government necessitated firm measures to enable the country to survive. Atatürk had to use autocratic means to achieve his goals of modernizing Turkey.

A year after I was born, on November 10, 1938, Atatürk died at the young age of 57 in the Dolmabahçe Palace in Istanbul. The Turkish nation had lost their father and their leader. There would never be anyone similar to him again. Under the Kemalist guidelines the country continued to flourish even to this day. Atatürk's wartime partner Ismet Inönü, who was the Prime Minister at the time, became the President. When Inönü took over the government, the Nazi power in Germany was at its peak and the war atmosphere could be felt all around. The Germans were again pushing for Turkish alliance. Inönü however knew too well how the Ottoman Empire had been dragged into its destruction. The Turkish nation was in many treaties and economic developmental programs with the British and the French. When the Second World War started in 1939, Inönü's biggest accomplishment was keeping Turkey out of the war. Communist Russia, who initially was in sympathy with the Nazis, once again started threatening Turkey. Inönü, while maintaining good ties with England and France and still concerned about the Communist and Nazi invasions, maintained Turkey's neutrality with brilliant diplomacy. As the war expanded all the way to the Turkish borders, Inönü had to mobilize the Turkish army putting over one million men under arms. Under these conditions Hitler and Stalin would think twice before they would consider attacking Turkey. The war conditions were a very heavy burden to an already weak Turkish economy. Unemployment was high, shortages of food and other goods were taking its tolls on the civilian population. In spite of all these difficulties, the conditions were still better than most European nations that were being decimated by the war.

The Little House

After I was born, Sadık and Şakire's house became too crowded and uncomfortable. My grandfather Sadık Bey was not an easy person to live with. His bad nature and ill temper were attributed to his military career. The family was not pleasant and considerate towards my mother either. She was treated more like a maid than a daughter-in-law. The time had come to move to our own house.

On the same street of 1457 Sokak, No. 6 was available. Father rented this house for us. It was a very little house indeed but this was enough for us to be independent and a happy family. The house was only one level with a living room, a small bedroom, a small yard in the back and a kitchen and bath adjacent to the yard. Like my grandparents' house, it had no electricity or running water but it was home to us. Ropes attached to two big nails hammered into opposite walls were used to make a makeshift crib. A blanket was used to make a hammock type of a swing. As was the custom at the time, I was swaddled to make me immobile. People in those days believed that swaddling a baby would keep the baby's bones straight. My mother was the most attentive and loving mother anyone could have. With two milk mothers feeding me, I was a chubby baby. My hair was blond and my eyes were blue, just like my mother's and Grandpa Üzeyir's.

As World War II continued, life became more difficult for everyone. Food, especially bread was being distributed with coupons. Every morning long lines formed in front of the corner bakery to get the rationed bread. Bread has always been the most important staple of the Turkish meal. The large army that the country was supporting was a further drain to minimal resources of the government. Businesses were folding and unemployment was high. My father's shoe store was also feeling the crunch. It was not long before my father had to close the store because he could not pay the rent. He got a job in a textile factory, *Şark Sanayi*, as a laborer. He, however, was not happy in his new job because it was difficult for him to be a subordinate when all this time he had been his own boss. Because of his work-related stress as well as his childhood illness, he was short-tempered and very difficult at home. About this time, grandfather Sadık passed away leaving behind a large family including many grandchildren and his prized three war medals.

As I was growing up in our little house at No.6, I remember playing with neighborhood children on high steps in front of their homes. When you are little, even small steps seem high. I used to sit on the windowsill and wait for my father to return from his job at the factory. One day my father told me a story: A Jewish man told his little boy to jump from the window. The little boy said to his father that it was too high. The father responded assuredly that he would catch him. When the little boy jumped, the father moved away and the child fell down. The father's advice to his child was "don't always take things for granted. Sometimes you cannot even trust your own father". I do not know why my father's story got stuck in my mind. I somehow did not take his only advice to me in full value, since I grew up being a trusting and caring person.

Life went on in our little house eventhough we did not have much to live on. Every morning my mother was at the bread line waiting for our ration. She could now claim me for a half loaf of bread. She was happy that at least we had bread. My mother was an excellent cook. Turkish meals always used fresh ingredients because nothing was ever frozen. Plenty of vegetables were always used with very little meat added since meat was very expensive. My mother was very ingenious creating different dishes with very little meat. In Turkish cuisine there are also many vegetable dishes which are served cold and cooked with olive oil. My mother somehow always managed to put some deliciously cooked food on our table.

My mother always dreamed of my growing up to be a "great man" (*büyük adam*) one day. She did not want me to become a shoemaker, which my father thought was the best he could offer me. In 1942, as the war was raging on, my mother decided to register me in the first grade at Gazi Elementary School *(Gazi İlk Okulu)*. I was only 5 ½ years old, too young in Turkey for a child to start elementary school. Although the school administration did not accept me, her persistent plea with the principal got me into the school. She was a determined young woman and she was not going to give up that easily.

Gazi Elementary School (*Gazi İlk Okulu*)

When I started elementary school in September 1942, my mother was the happiest woman in the world. She dressed me with the required black smock uniform with a detachable white collar. I was wearing short pants and knee-highs socks with beautifully polished black shoes. Every morning she held my hand firmly and walked me to school. I could sense in her presence next to me that this young woman was very proud of the moment. She had a thin erect body and her wavy blond hair was flowing in the air. This was her exultation. She did not want me to be illiterate like herself or my father. She was very resolute and determined to make certain that her little boy would get a good education.

I started reading the first alphabet book:

> *AT AT TUT*
> *BABA AT AL*
> . . .

It was a standard beginner's book used throughout the country, approved by the Ministry of Education. My mother would take me to *Konak* to buy me notebooks, pencils, pencil sharpener and eraser. We covered my books and notebooks with blue book covers and this was an overwhelming experience for her. Each class was assigned to a teacher who stayed throughout the entire five grades. My teacher, Fazıl *Öğretmen* (teacher) was an aging, gray haired, very stern but well experienced educator. In later years when we were not learning our arithmetic lessons well, he would resort to hitting us with a wooden ruler. Sometimes he used the sharp edges of the ruler which would hurt terribly when it landed on our soft and tender palms. In those days, fear of our teacher and ensuing punishment were good reasons for us to learn our lessons. During this period families were very anxious to have their children get a good education. It seemed like they would accept any liberties given to the teachers. Although I never heard my mother say it, *"eti senin kemiği benim"* (his flesh is yours, his bones are mine) the general mentality reflected the leniency of the families towards the teachers. Everyone regarded a good education very highly at almost any cost.

The classroom was divided almost equally with boys and girls handsomely uniformed in their black and white outfits. Since we were the first generation of Ataturk's children, Turkish nationalism was being expounded in our classrooms:

> *Ben bir Türküm, soyum ırkım uludur*
> *Göğsüm millet sevgisiyle doludur*
> *Tuttuğum yol Atatürk'un yoludur*
> *Hep o yoldan yürümektir dileğim*

> I am a Turk, my ancestors are great
> My heart is full of national love
> I follow Atatürk's footsteps
> I wish to walk that path always

At school assemblies, we were taught to support our country's new economic development program by singing:

> *Yerli malı*
> *Yurdun malı*
> *Her Türk onu*
> *Kullanmalı*

This meant that every Turk must use the country's own products.

School was fun and our teachers were educating us very attentively. I was managing my schoolwork all by myself. I had no mentor or anyone that could help me with my assignments. When I completed my elementary school, Gazi İlk Okulu had given me a good basic education.

Besides attaining a good education, Turkish nationalism with Kemalist doctrines were principals that we were taught. These important principals of building and protecting our own land, and being loyal to our country would stay with us for the rest of our lives. One of the important principals adopted in the Kemalist doctrines was secularism (*layıklık*) which was the separation of state and the Islam religion. Accordingly, our elementary education in those years did not include religion classes. Any basic prayer

I could recite in Arabic without knowing its meaning was taught to me by my *Babaanne* (father's mother). My grandmother never missed her daily prayers and. during these prayers I sometimes would follow her movements and recite a few verses from the Koran I had learned from her. Although I was taught in believing in Allah, the Prophet Mohammed and Islam's holy book the Koran, my religious education was very limited.

3

Alsancak

The House at Number 36

In 1944 the Second World War was still raging and approaching towards its final year. The circumstances at home were not pleasant. Father had lost his factory job and he was trying to survive by repairing shoes at home. That did not bring much or a steady income. About this time we were being evicted from our little house. For me and my mother that was a sad day. We had nowhere to go but to grandmother's house on the same street at Number 36. When I was seven years old, we moved back into the dark room again. The mattress was spread on the floor for all three of us to sleep together. My grandmother and Uncle Tevfik were in the two front rooms. The dark room was located underneath the terrace that was made out of galvanized sheet metal. In the summer time the metal would heat up with the intense Aegean sun so much that our dark room would be like a furnace. After the war, in the hot summer nights, we would venture upstairs to sleep on the terrace. The steep stairs going to the terrace was covered with a door that had a broken glass window. During the war, fearing any air attacks, we were told to cover the glass so no light would be seen from above. There was not much light inside the house anyway. We used kerosene lamps for light. The lamp base was filled with kerosene and the wick that was saturated with the fuel, would give off a dim light through the glass top chimney. We would adjust the intensity of the light by turning the knob or blow it from the top to completely put it out. Our liquid lamp became a multipurpose tool. The ceiling in our dark bedroom was just below the galvanized metal terrace and it was made of wooden boards. During Izmir's frequent rains, the terrace was always leaking and the wooden ceiling had rotted away. This was an ideal thriving ground for little red bed bugs known as *tahta kurusu*, termite-like blood suckers with creepy round and flat bodies which feasted on people's blood. During the hot nights when we were sleeping, swarms of these bed bugs would come out of the wood cracks and assault us by sucking our blood. When we turned on the kerosene lamp we could see these ugly creatures creeping all around. My father would clear the ceiling of these bed bugs by holding the top opening of the lamp chimney underneath of these creatures. The heat from the lamp would burn them and they would fall inside the lamp. Every night the battle with *tahta kurusu* would rage on, ending with the intense burning smell of the bloody bugs. The three of us would then try to go to sleep. Eradicating the *tahta kurusu* would be another function of our multipurpose kerosene lamp.

We would get some relief from the *tahta kurusu* in the wintertime when cold, rainy and damp weather would dominate. When the rains started, the galvanized roof would leak heavily into our dark room and small hallway where the staircase was. Sometimes there were not enough buckets or cooking pans to collect the leaking water. These utensils were scattered on the crowded floor so much that there was not enough room to walk let alone sleep. I used to love to listen to the constant periodic sound of raindrops as they were impinging on the sheet metal up above. I would then go to sleep.

The kitchen was located in the back of the house below our dark bedroom and it also was dark since there was no window. Most of the time we would need to use the kerosene lamp in the kitchen when cooking or taking baths. The house water came from a single source, pumped with a hand pump located in the kitchen. Below the pump we could see a heavy lead pipe penetrating all the way into the ground well. In those days no one knew or even suspected that lead was dangerous to human health. Lead poisoning was never heard of. The bathroom was just a toilet, which was located at the far corner of the house under the stairs. The toilet consisted of a single round hole in the ground. Among the people this type of toilet was labeled as *"alla turka"* toilet, while the western style toilet with a bowl was called *"alla franca"*. The *alla turka* toilet consisted of a stone slab with two landings for the feet located on both sides of the hole. Squatting on this type of toilet was extremely hard on the knees! The house had a sewer connection in the middle of the street and frequently when the sewer needed repairs the municipal workers would dig a long trench in front of the house with their picks and shovels. The repairs would last for days with the trench remaining open all of this time. Adults used the toilet room also to take their baths. My mother however, used a wash basin to wash me in. She always scrubbed me very hard as if she was peeling off my skin while using a very large, hard and not so foamy "green soap" which always burned my eyes. As I was growing older, I kept both hands on my front private parts while my mother bathed me. This went on for some time until I was old enough to wash myself inside the toilet room.

Cooking was done on a kerosene stove (*gaz ocağı*). The stove consisted of a brass alloy base with a hand pump attached. Pumping the base would pressurize the fuel that would be sprayed through a very small hole above the ignition. The housewives knew well how to operate the stove properly. Two conditions were necessary: proper pressure inside the base and a clean small hole for spraying the fuel out. Turkish women were very creative and capable. They could cook some of the best recipes in their kitchen with equipment that required technical handiwork and ingenuity. Since our house had no electricity, there was no refrigeration either. A screened cupboard (*tel dolap*) was used to store the food safely from flies and insects. Everyday we bought fresh meat and vegetables and cooked them right away. Very little food was kept in the cupboard. In the summertime, I used to go to buy ice from the ice depot in large chunks to keep the food in a cool screened cupboard.

Like other foods, milk was also bought periodically. Our milkman brought fresh milk daily from the farm in two large containers tied to either side of his skinny little donkey. We did not buy milk everyday because we could not afford it. Drinking milk everyday, especially cold milk, was not done. The milk we bought, maybe once a week, would be used after it was boiled to make yogurt and rice pudding (*sütlaç*). Sometimes I would be given a glass of warm sweetened milk to drink. After raw milk was boiled to pasteurize, there was a thick layer of cream on top. I loved to eat this cream with a spoon.

In Izmir as the damp and cold winter months approached, homes needed to be heated. Izmir did not get any snow, but frequent winter rains would cause penetrating dampness and body aches. We used a brazier (*mangal*) to heat up the house. The brazier was made out of galvanized metal or brass that held the charcoal fire. The charcoal, processed out of wood pieces, was piled on a layer of ashes, which was placed inside the brazier. Ashes basically were insulation between the fire and the metal. As a little boy, starting at age seven, I was put in charge of getting the fire started every evening. I would start the fire by burning a few pieces of pinewood over the coal. A little metal chimney placed over the coal and pine pieces would help to generate a draft to accelerate the burning once it had started. I would have to fan the fire continuously to get it started and going. I did not like to fan because it was tiring. For me it was also embarrassing trying to start a coal fire in front of our house. Luckily our neighbors were in the same situation. This process went on until all the black charcoal turned red and no blue flames were coming out of the newly started fire. This was a very rudimentary evaluation of the coal's burning to avoid carbon monoxide poisoning. The *mangal* was then taken inside the house and was located in the middle of the living room. Besides warming the house, the fire was used to brew the late afternoon tea with a kettle placed on a three-legged support over the fire. Periodically Turkish coffee was made on the "slow burning" fire when the coffee maker (*cezve*) was pushed against the hot ashes. It was important for the foam to develop and rise very slowly. Turks like their coffee with thick foam on it. For me the best thing was placing chestnuts inside the hot ashes to roast. We had to make sure that the chestnuts were slit cut so that they would not burst and scatter the ashes all around. As I mentioned before, Turkish people are creative individuals. The *mangal* was also utilized as multipurpose equipment. Unfortunately, the *mangal* warmed only the living room and the rest of the house was still damp and cold. We would sleep in the cold bedrooms upstairs with heavy quilts covering us. I always pulled the quilt over my head to keep my entire little body warm.

Since we were living in my grandmother's house for free, my aunts and uncles felt that my mother should do all the housework. Mother took on the responsibilities of cleaning the house, doing the laundry, and cooking very seriously. After boiling the water on the kerosene stove, she had to wash the clothes by hand then climb the steep stairs to the terrace to hang them to dry. She would then cook for the family in a very creative way with very little money we had. She had to go out and buy the produce and the meat every day. Cleaning the house, especially the rooms with wooden floors was another task she had to deal with. Periodically the wooden floors had to be scrubbed with a hard bristle brush to look clean and shiny. The wood was already old, split and nothing to look at. But somehow this cleaning was expected and had to be done. At home, besides my mother, father and me, my grandmother, a great aunt and uncle Tevfik were living. As if this was not enough, everyday late in the afternoon, the rest of the family members, uncles and aunts would come to visit their mother. After the front of the house was nicely swept and watered to cool the hot cobblestones, the chairs would be pulled out for everyone to sit in front of the house. This was the family's only social togetherness. Again my mother was expected to serve coffee and tea to all those visiting family members. The family spoke some incomprehensibles in Greek when my mother and I were around; in spite of the fact they knew we did not understand them. Uncle Cevat periodically came to visit from Ayvalık and stayed at his mother's house also. When he was visiting, he most inconsiderately expected my mother to wash and iron his clothes and serve him fried eggs for breakfast every morning. All my father's family members were treating my mother like a maid. Mother did not have any other choice but to put up with this type of inconsiderate, rude and selfish behavior. Her only thought was protecting her little boy and giving him a secure and loving home.

All this time my father was making shoes at home. He had set up his small workbench and work stool at the entrance of the house. Early in the morning he would put on his apron and start either repairing or making new shoes. All day long he would be banging his hammer on the shoes resting on his knees. When the shoes were completed they looked nice. At this time, I was now taking on my first job responsibilities. I would take the shoes to the customer's homes hoping to get some tips. When my father was making new shoes, he would be using a lot of thin long nails by bending them over the sole. When he was finishing the sole by sewing it with string attached to pig's hair he would pull the bent nails out. Another job of mine was to straighten these nails to be used again. I would sit in front of the house on the narrow pavement and with a hammer in my hand I would straighten these nails for hours. Initially I would hit my fingers very often, but in time I got very good at it. As the clan members gathered at our house in the afternoon, my father would quit for the day and join his mother and others for a cup of coffee. After the job was done, he would always put his tools away properly and sweep his work area before closing shop. This was a good work habit I learned from my father, which I continued to practice the rest of my life.

The Neighborhood (*Mahalle*)

Izmir in Turkish is known as "*Güzel İzmir*" (Beautiful Izmir). It is located on the eastern shores of the Aegean Sea, on the midpoint of Anatolia (Asia Minor). The city lies at the end of a long and narrow gulf and surrounds the bay completely. The mountains rise all around as if trying to protect the beauty of the city. The climate is mild and in the summer the constant and refreshing sea breeze gives much needed relief to temper the sun's heat. The palm trees are all lined along the boulevards and the seashore promenade which is known as "*Kordon*" (Cordone). It is a cosmopolitan and lively city with activities all year round with the International Fair highlighting the summer jubilation.

Izmir had the most exciting and long history beginning in the Third Millennium BC sharing its culture with Troy. By 1500 BC it had fallen under the influence of the Hittite Empire. Later Izmir, then known as Smyrna, became one of the most advanced and important cities in the Ionian Federation. During this period the city experienced brilliant cultural activities and economic growth. Smyrna was known as the birthplace of Homer where he continued to live and wrote his epic story the Odyssey and made many significant cultural contributions. The Lydian conquest of the city, around 600 BC and subsequently the Persian rule in the 6th century BC brought this glorious period to an end. It was not until the conquest of the city by Alexander the Great in the fourth century BC that a new city was built on the slopes of Mt. Pagos (*Kadifekale)*. Even today, the castle built by Alexander still dominates the city from the peak of *Kadifekale*. The city started rejuvenating and continued its expansion into a new importance and greatness during the following Roman and Byzantine periods. Smyrna became an important trading post joining the West to the far reaches of the East. The Seljuks, who were expanding their newfound empire in the 11th century, conquered this crown city, and subsequently with the transformation of the Seljuk Empire into Ottoman Empire in 1415, Sultan *Mehmet Çelebi* made Izmir a significant part of the Ottoman Empire. Many remnants and impressive ruins remaining from these great empires are scattered around the city for the locals and tourists to enjoy and appreciate the historical greatness of this city. The *Agora*, or the market place, aqueducts, various temples and rich archeological museums remained proud survivors and went on to create the beautiful cosmopolitan city that greets the visitors today as it reminds them the glorious past of Izmir. Izmir has always been loved and admired by everyone for her ambiance and charm, her culture and gentility. The modern symbol of Izmir is the Clock Tower (*Saat Kulesi*) standing at the center of *Konak* Square in the heart of the city. It was a gift from Sultan Abdulhamid in 1901 and it is decorated in the most elaborate Ottoman style. *Konak* Square is the gateway leading to the city's lively shopping center known as *Kemeraltı* market.

Alsancak, where I grew up, was one of the exclusive neighborhoods of the city with a large Greek population. After the Independence War in the great fire of Izmir, half of Alsancak was burned. Our house was only one block from the burned section, which we called "*yangınlık*", and it was all open, empty, dirt-covered hills and trenches. It was like a scar on the face of this old, tired, worn-out city. For a long time this area did not get developed and it became our playground. Because of the vast open space, we could play ball or fly our kites here. We made our own kites by tying three sticks together in the middle to form a hexagonal shape which was then covered with a very thin paper. The tail of the kite was made very decoratively out of thin strips of paper with bright colors tied into a long string. On windy afternoons, we would all take our homemade kites with long tails and fly them proudly enjoying the fluttering of our kites in the breeze. This joy sometimes got interrupted by older and bigger sadistic kids from other neighborhoods who with razor blades attached to the tails of their kites would cut our lines and have our kites drift away into far distances. We would then resort to a safer game of soccer or what we called "*futbol*". We did not have rubber balls to play with but instead we improvised by making a nice hard ball stuffed and sewn from rags. This was an excellent alternative except when we hit the ball with our heads and it would hurt very badly. But no real soccer player would avoid hitting the ball with his head!

There was no shortage of kids in the neighborhood and we all knew each other and our families. We would always start a game instantly when a few of us got together. Games were very basic with no expensive toys. We would make two teams and play jumping over each other, or use a long stick to hit the short stick to far distances known as "*çelik-çomak*". Our games became a little more expensive when we had to buy marbles or tops to play with. Some kids were experts in hitting the marbles or spinning the tops. I somehow did not develop those skills too well. In the evenings when we played hide and seek with the girls included, I always enjoyed those games more. I was now getting to an age where I was appreciating being around girls. Our streets were completely empty of vehicles for us to play games and for the families to sit in front of their houses. There were even a couple of big trees on our street. An acacia tree in front of our house, with its beautiful blue-white flowers, filled the air with its sweet scent. I would dream of having a car one day with a girl sitting next to me. I had built a "car" made out of heavy wires. I bent the wires to make the two wheels attached with a middle shaft section, and then a long wire with a steering wheel at one end was attached to the shaft and the wheels. I would walk behind the two wheels rolling and steering my wire car. The most interesting aspect of this experience was my making the corresponding noises of the car's starting, gears shifting and tires squeaking while turning the corner or stopping. Driving my own wire car was most enjoyable, if only I had a girl sitting next to me.

Metin was my close friend and neighbor living across the street. His father had passed away and his mother Canan Hanım and sister Ayşe were supporting the family by working in a tobacco-processing factory in Alsancak. Metin later became a medical doctor in Izmir. Aydoğan was another boy living across the street. Instead of going to school he chose to work in an iron foundry and later went to Germany as a guest worker. Teresa lived next door to Aydoğan's house. Her father, Monsieur Andon was Italian and her mother, Madam Ulumya was Greek. All the boys had a crush on Teresa because she was a beautiful girl. She eventually got married to an Italian and moved to Milan. Monsieur Andon was a movie projector operator at *Lale Sinema*. Betul, Berta and Berna were the three beautiful daughters of our teacher neighbor Ülkiye Hanım and Esat Bey. Berta was the closest to my age and our families were already making plans that I would marry Berta when we grew up. Sevim, the daughter of Süleyman Bey and Seher Hanim living at the corner house, was very well developed physically. She was very popular with older boys who were always coming from far distances to see her. Leman Abla was another blond beauty on our street. It seemed like all the beautiful girls of Alsancak were concentrated on our street. All these people living in our neighborhood were warm, kind and sincere friends and neighbors. We did not have much but we had a lot of trust, deep feelings and kindness towards each other. When in need, everyone would run to help each other. It was a poor but happy neighborhood.

Baha Bey operated the corner grocery store (*Bakkal*). Our *Bakkal Baha*, as we called him had a very small store filled with all the household needs. Baha Bey usually let me fill my glass bottle with kerosene, which we bought one liter at a time for our cooking and light lamp. We would buy what we needed from him in very small amounts and have it charged to our account. When we had some money we would then pay him towards our debt. I could never understand how he could keep track of the entire neighborhood's debts in his greasy, torn out notebook. In the hot summer nights our entertainment was going to the outdoors open-air cinemas. Families and friends would all gather together at the cinemas, sitting on hard wooden chairs, eating nuts, sunflower and squash seeds and eyeing each other. At other times, we would all stroll along the *Kordon*'s seaside promenade, walking aimlessly while trying to observe the neighborhood girls and still enjoy the cool breeze coming from the Aegean Sea.

In 1948, I was 11 years old and approaching towards the end of my elementary school days. My mother was happy that her little boy was finishing the elementary school and could read and write, something she and my father could not do. They had given me a warm and protective family life that I cherished. I also cherished my friends and neighbors for giving me a happy and memorable childhood in what was then a beautiful neighborhood.

The Middle School

After completing *Gazi İlk Okulu*, my elementary school, I continued into the middle school at Inönü Lycee (*İnönü Lisesi*) that was part of the high school. There was no separate middle school at that time. Our school was located next to the Izmir International Fair grounds and it was a long walk for me every day. Our school was not co-educational. At that time the girls had only two choices for school, Izmir Girls High School (*İzmir Kız Lisesi*) or The Republic's Institute for Girls (*Cumhuriyet Kız Enstitüsü*) to study arts and crafts. In the Middle School we were expected to take a variety of subjects including Introductory English. Middle School was difficult for me because there was no one at home who could help me with my homework. I had problems figuring things out on my own and throughout my Middle School years I was an average student. Although I did not fail any classes, I was not a super performer either. I liked playing games on the street with my friends. My mother, however, persistently made sure that I came into the house every day on time to do my homework. At times I tried to resist going inside while I was in the middle of a fun game. My mother would then put my father to task who was always conveniently at home to fetch me inside either by giving me a fierce look or by using a brute force, which I did not like. During this period my great aunt and uncle Malik had passed away. Uncle Malik's wife, Madam Sophia, who was never well received by the family, left for Italy to be closer to her own people. My uncle's demise was due to a dispute with his management at his work place, the Municipal Water Works, where he had informed the authorities of some wrong doings by the management. Although he was being honest, he lost his job and was never able to resolve it in the Turkish courts. A good, educated man ended up jobless, broke, desolate and desperate until he died. Uncle Tevfik meanwhile got married and lucky for me he moved out. I was now too old to share a bed with my mother and father so I moved to the front bedroom to share with my grandmother.

My grandmother would pray five times a day, as any devout Moslem would. She had taught me how to pray and recite a few verses from the Koran in Arabic. Although I did not know the meanings of the prayers, they were very moving and emotional experiences for me. My young mind would soak up these prayers very readily. Although I had not received any formal religious education in school, my limited experience and knowledge would provide me with strong religious beliefs the rest of my life. During Ramadan (*Ramazan*) I went to Eid (*Bayram*) prayers with my father in the courtyard of the iron foundry close to our home. Alsancak did not have a mosque and we would pray at any large gathering place. The chanting of prayers in large groups lifted me to a higher level of emotions where I felt I was closer to Allah. I knew that Allah would hear my prayers for me to succeed and pull me and my family out of these difficult circumstances. Even today I still reach to the same emotional levels when I am in a mosque praying and reciting verses from the Koran. When religious beliefs and feelings are instilled in you at a young age, they remain with you the rest of your life. I continued to pray to Allah even in my privacy to help me and show me the right path so I could achieve on my own. I have always been a private person keeping my thoughts and prayers to myself. I was shy but not an introvert. I made friends easily and opened up to them after I got to know them better. Those people whom I care about became my lifetime friends. Since I was an only child my good friends became an important part of my life filling the emptiness of not having any brothers or sisters.

In 1949 when I was 12 years old, Ramadan came in the summertime. Almost all the family members were fasting during the month of Ramadan. Fasting is done between sunrise and sunset. In the summer months, since the days are longer, the fasting period is much longer. As a good Moslem I felt I should also fast. I woke up with the rest of the family for a predawn "*sahur*" feast and ate enough to keep me going the rest of the day. I was happy that I was a part of this ritual. As Izmir's blazing hot summer sun started heating all around I started feeling weak. The cobblestones on the street had heated up as if they were in a barbecue. I did not attempt to play with my friends on the street. As the day advanced into early afternoon, although I was not hungry, I needed water very badly. It was too hot and I was very weak. I felt like a lost man in the middle of a hot desert looking for an oasis. My oasis was in the kitchen but I could not have it. I was told to lie down and rest. By mid afternoon I started getting real fainting spells and my head was spinning. I had to have water and unfortunately had to break my fasting before I got too sick. After that experience I did not attempt to fast ever again. To us as children, Ramadan was a very festive occasion. The muezzin's prayers would fill the entire valley resonating from the surrounding hills. We would spend the last minutes of the days during Ramadan watching the *Kadifekale* hill from the open space of *"yangınlık"* for the firing of the cannon, announcing the time to break the fast. In those days you could hear the roar of the cannon all through the city. We would then run home informing our families that it was time to eat the *"iftar"* dinner. This ritual continued during the entire month of Ramadan. I always wondered why the sound coming from the cannon was always much later than the smoke I saw right after the firing. During Ramadan friends and families gathered at each other's homes every evening to break the fast. Multi-course dinners were served beginning with soup. The first morsel of food eaten was always either an olive or a date. This would be followed with hot soup to coat the empty stomach, then the main course, fruits and dessert.

The following winter, as the New Year of 1950 was approaching, the stores in Alsancak had beautiful displays of snow and Saint Nicholas (*Noel Baba*) in their windows. I had never seen snow in Izmir, but the cheerful and smiling face of *Noel Baba* with his big fat belly located among snow-like cotton balls reflected joy and happiness. Although Saint Nicholas, known as Santa Claus in the Christian world, brings gifts to children during Christmas with his sleigh from the North Pole, he is originally from Turkey. More than a thousand years ago Saint Nicholas was born in Turkey in the town of Myra, today known as *Demre* and became a bishop of Myra of Asia Minor. Nicholas was born to wealthy parents who died when he was still a boy. They left their fortune to their only son but they also helped him understand that the family's money was for making the world a better place. Nicholas gave away much of his wealth and devoted himself to his religious studies. He became a bishop at a young age and travelled the world, and everywhere he journeyed, he offered help and kindness. He brought much happiness even to those who never expected his help. I decided to make a little New Year's *Noel Baba* stand of my own similar to what I had seen in the store windows. I went to the park in front of *Tekel* tobacco factory and broke off two pieces of pine branches and placed them on a table in our living room. I then drew a big picture of *Noel Baba* on cardboard similar to the ones on the storefronts, and colored it. I scattered the cotton around the stand, which made it look wintry and very pretty. There were no gifts but the entire family enjoyed my *Noel Baba*.

At times we travelled to *Hatay*, which was on top of one of the hills overlooking Izmir Bay. This is where my entire mother's family was now living. Both of my aunts were married and living in their own houses with their husbands and children. Aunt Ayşe was married to Abdullah Enişte who was a carpenter and bricklayer. They had three children: Necdet, Metin (my milk brother) and Meral. Aunt Hanife was married to Ihsan Abi who was also a shoemaker. They had three children also: Özten, Bülent, and Asuman. I certainly had no shortage of cousins. In the winter months when we got together in my Aunt Ayşe's house, the house where I was born, the entire family would play a game of *Tombala*, a game similar to Bingo. For my mother and me these were always fun times to be together with her family. Although I did not get to see them as much, I enjoyed my mother's side of the family much more than my father's.

The Circumcision

In the summer of 1948 when I was 11 years old, I still had not been circumcised. Most children were circumcised between the ages of 5 and 7. Age of 11 was very late but my family did not have the means and kept on postponing this urgent matter at my expense as if they were going to improve their financial circumstance anytime soon. Moslem boys, at an early age, are circumcised in a very festive celebration beginning with religious prayers and ending with music, entertainment, lots of food and sometimes even drinking. These days, rich families find this occasion of the circumcision of their sons as a good excuse to have elaborate parties spending a fortune. On the other extreme, poor families who cannot afford it have mass circumcisions provided by the City Board of Health. The Moslem circumcision is very similar to the Jewish bris. It is done for the reason of cleanliness and health. Jews have the bris when the baby is a newborn and have a celebration also. Judaism views circumcision as a religious ceremony, therefore a Mohel performs the circumcision. A Mohel is a Jew who is trained in the physical procedures of circumcision and understands the religious significance of the ritual. During the ceremony the baby is given his Hebrew name. A Moslem circumcision, on the other hand, does not have to be performed by a religious man and is done at a later age.

For weeks our house was cleaned and prepared for the big event of my circumcision. My mother and some relatives rolled out dough and made trays of *böreks* and *baklavas*, a variety of *dolmas, kebabs* and *pilafs*. There was enough food for all the guests. The man who was to perform the circumcision was hired. He advertised himself as *"Fenni Sünnetçi"*, a scientific circumciser. I don't believe he had anything to do with any scientific aspect of circumcision but he claimed to be a "scientist" in what he did. Since the neighbors recommended and attested to his talent, it was decided he must be good. They said his hands were very fast and steady. We did not question his actual credentials as long as he was good and reasonable. The next step was to line up the imam to recite prayers before and during the circumcision. Shopping for my new circumcision outfit in *Konak Çarşı* (shopping area) took days. My mother and I went to buy the white satin embroidered frock to be worn during and after the circumcision along with a white shirt and a white hat with *"MAŞALLAH"* written on it with shiny sequins. The evil-eye charms were hung everywhere, on the walls, on the bed and pinned on my shirt. I remember my mother's taking the entire initiative to have this circumcision done and not delay it any further. I thank God and my mother for that. We were now ready for the big event.

That Sunday afternoon, the house cleaned and nicely decorated with mother's best embroidered linens and doilies, was ready to receive the guests who were bearing gifts. The small living room was packed with about two dozen quests seated on borrowed chairs placed along the wall. The imam whom we call *hoca* was chanting *surrahs* (verses) from the Koran. The ladies, with their heads covered with scarves, were inside the house and because the house was so small, the men were forced to sit outside on the street. All the neighborhood children had gathered, waiting for the arrival of three phaetons, horse and carriages that my parents had hired. There were at least ten kids packed on the first carriage with me sitting next to the driver. I had my white shirt and *Maşallah* hat on. As the carriages started moving towards the *Kordon*, we were all happily singing the songs we knew. The horses were decked with red and green tassels, embroidered saddles, good luck talismans, and they trotted clickety clack on the non-uniform cobblestone streets. The kettledrum and flute players, sitting in one of the phaetons, played melodious tunes for us to sing along. Since there were not many cars on the streets, the carriages moved very smoothly through the traffic along the Kordon. The Izmir Bay looked beautiful and the atmosphere was filled with our cheerful songs. The carriage driver had let me hold the reins to lead the horses. He was a nice man or maybe he just felt sorry for me. As the carriages returned towards the house, the skinny little horses were showing signs of pain trying to pull the crowded carriages. The singing had stopped and when we turned onto our street, the reality sank in. I was the one who was going to be circumcised. My heart started pounding rapidly and all at once fear replaced that happy demeanor. The reading of prayers was finished and everyone was having their refreshment of cool sherbets topped with roasted pinions and rose water and anxiously waiting for my arrival. From there on everything moved at high precision. Upon my arrival, they whisked me upstairs very rapidly and changed me into the white frock. They were moving too fast for me to comprehend what was happening. The atmosphere was very somber and all eyes were on me. I was standing next to the bed that was decorated with new sheets, a colorful quilt fluffed professionally and flower embroidered pillow cases. It must have been arranged earlier for Nihat Abi (Dr.Nihat Önderoğlu) to hold me tight while I was being cut. It is a big honor for the designated person to hold the boy while he is being circumcised and passing into manhood. Well, I did not care about all that. All I wanted was to get it over with. We were kneeling down with Nihat Abi behind me holding my legs wide open tightly with my little shrunken boyhood dangling. *Fenni Sünnetçi* was in front of me with all of his cutting contraptions laid out on a piece of white cloth. He looked ready and anxious. After he checked my "tool" on which he was going to perform his procedure, I was told to look up at the bird flying inside the room.

"*Bak bak kuş uçuyor*"

Who were they kidding? I was too old to believe the bird stories but I was not going to look down either. All I remember saying to the *Sünnetçi* was "Be careful and don't cut too much!"

I was trying to joke as if I was not afraid. Our *Fenni Sünnetçi* was steady and fast as they had said. Everybody was clapping and yelling "*Oldu da bitti maşallah*" (it's all done).

The show was over. The incision was sprinkled with a yellow, powder antibiotic and wrapped with sterile gauze. I was put to bed and everybody flocked around me, telling me how proud they were of me for being so brave. If they only knew how I felt. I fought back the tears that had welled up because I was determined not to cry in front of all those people and I controlled myself. The gifts were then given to me and were piled on both sides of the bed. Nihat Abi gave me my very first wristwatch and I was thrilled to finally have a watch. As guests left my bedroom, I started feeling the excruciating pain on my wound. I was really hurting. The built up tears finally erupted when I was left alone. I did not know when this pain would subside and if it was worth it. I guess a man has to do what he has to do! The guests slowly left and the celebration was over. I spent the next couple of days in bed. When I walked out to see my friends playing in front of the house, I was wearing my white frock, which was very loose, and I was holding it out so it would not rub against my sensitive wound. In a few days the *Sünnetçi* came to change the dressings and within a week I was back to normal again. Oh, what a relief!

Pancar Village (*Pancar Köy*)

> *Orda bir köy var uzakta*
> *O köy bizim köyümüzdür*
> *Gitmesekte, görmesekte*
> *O köy bizim köyümüzdür*

> There is a village in the distance
> That is our village
> Even though we don't go and see it
> It is still our village

Pancar Köy was a village located about 30km from Izmir. It was a typical Turkish village where the villagers would tend to their sheep herds or few cows and grow all kinds of produce varying from wheat to watermelons. A brook ran through the center of the village with a coffeehouse, a school building and a mosque all located around this brook. A little waterfall emptied into a deep pond for the village kids to jump in and cool themselves in the summer heat. I often joined them in the pond to play in these cool waters whenever we were visiting *Pancar Köy*. The village kids, like all the villagers, were very kind and friendly and would rapidly accept a stranger amongst them. Although the villagers had very little, they were very generous and always ready to share what little they did have. No wonder Atatürk had great respect and affection for the Turkish villagers who worked very hard and helped significantly to save our country during the Independence War.

The only single railroad track ran along the village to a nicely built stone railroad station. This was the main connection point to the village. Behind the village was a small hill with wild flowers blanketing the hillside, which decorated the horizon as a backdrop. From the hill one could see a beautiful, fertile and completely flat valley extending to the far distances under a broad blue sky. The winds swept through irrigated lands over the wheat fields moving the plants like a continuous wave. In the valley each villager owned a small parcel of land which they farmed. The farmers consumed part of their produce and the rest was sold. The roads were all dirt, filled with broken stones and there were very few trees around. A couple of very large oak trees next to the brook provided cool shades over the coffee shop for the villagers to sit and enjoy their tea, coffee or water pipe (*nargile*). Everything moved at a slow pace in the village. In the early morning hours, the call to prayers by the *müezzin* from the mosque's minaret would propagate to the far corners of the valley. The days in the village started very early in the mornings. The cows from each house would come out of their stall on their own and follow their usual dirt path and join the other cows into a large herd. A shepherd would then lead the entire herd to the grazing field for feeding. At night, as the sun was setting behind the hill, the cows would return back to the village. I was always amazed how these wonderful animals would leave the herd one by one and find their own corresponding homes by themselves. It was then the milking time.

Some families owned large sheep herds with one hundred or more heads. The shepherd would take these herds for a month at a time to the mountains to graze. His two large *Kangal* shepherd dogs would accompany him for protection. It was the most beautiful sight to watch as the shepherd was leaving the village with his dogs busily running around the herd leading them in one group towards the mountains. There was always a black sheep leading the herd. Little bells hanging from the sheeps' necks ringing sweet tunes could be heard from far distances as they swung in pace with their steps. The shepherd, with a long stick in his hand, and a donkey carrying his monthly supply of food, would slowly follow the herd. After a while the herd would disappear in the horizon with only a white dust cloud rising behind.

In the summertime, it was a ritual for us to go to *Pancar Köy* to visit my mother's relatives. There were a few families in *Pancar Köy* related to my grandmother Pembe. We always visited Sakine Abla and Mehmet Abi and stayed in their modest house. A beautiful grapevine climbing the arbor on a small courtyard in front of Sakine Abla's house added beauty and shade where we all would sit and enjoy the village atmosphere. Mehmet Abi had a large sheep herd, which was a sign of his wealth. He would either take the herd himself to the mountains or sometimes hire a shepherd. They were always happy to have us and were very hospitable. Sakine Abla, like other women of the village was a very hard working and capable lady. Not only did she do the housework and cooking, but she also took care of her vegetable garden, milked the cows everyday and helped in the fields during the harvesting of wheat with her traditional henna painted hands. Whenever we visited them, it was a joyous occasion for us to be together with our extended relatives. There would be plenty of delicious breads, *böreks, kebabs,* and dairy products like yogurt, rice pudding, and cheeses. The dinner came early and lasted a long time. We would all sit on the floor and eat our meals from many dishes placed around a tablecloth. Since we had travelled there from the Alsancak train station on a slow moving steam engine driven train, we would stay overnight. The night came very early to *Pancar Köy* since there was no electricity. Everyone in the village used kerosene lamps like the one we had in our home. After our hearty meal, we all slept on the floor on the mattresses lined up next to each other in one room. Although this might sound very uncomfortable, it was one of the more memorable events in my life I still cherish.

On one of our visits to *Pancar Köy*, one of the village boys was going to be circumcised and we were invited to take part in the festivities. They did not use horse and carriages for the children like we did in the city but the villagers had a different tradition. All the village children would run a kilometer race and the boy to be circumcised would be standing with a ribbon tied between his legs at the end of the road. The winner would cut the ribbon and the prize would be a live rooster. This signified the passing of the boy from childhood to manhood. My family anxiously urged me to take part in the race since I was a fast runner. When about ten of us showed up at the starting line on a scorching summer day, all the village kids were barefoot. I tried to step on the ground without shoes but my feet hurt so much that I gave up that idea. I was amazed how the village kids could sprint so fast with barefeet on the dirt road, which was covered with sharp stones, gravel and thorns from the sun baked dry bushes. I was determined to win this race since a valuable rooster was involved in the outcome. I also did not want to disappoint my father, not because he was interested in my winning, but he had his eyes on that well-fed rooster. Although I started very fast, opening up a distance, the village kids were rapidly closing the gap. I had speed as an advantage, but they had the stamina on their side. In the last two hundred meters it was a very close race but I won with a very short margin. I cut the ribbon and received my rooster. That night, as we were all returning home on the slow moving train, my father had a rare smile on his face, clinching tightly and happily onto tomorrow's dinner. I sat there very proud and satisfied with my accomplishment.

Yes, *Pancar Köy* is my village. I had many sweet, fond and happy childhood memories there. It is now a changed village, with its dirt roads covered with blacktop, electric poles protruding along the side of the roads and apartment buildings have replaced the small single family dwellings. The brook has dried up and the water pond is no longer there. However, the long railroad track still runs through the valley. Our relatives have passed away and their children have moved to the city. At every opportunity I drive to *Pancar Köy* to look around and reminisce. Those sweet memories return with tears in my eyes. Yes, *Pancar Köy* is still my village.

The Democratic Party (*Demokrat Partisi*)

My father continued working hard by making shoes at home, but that barely was enough to put bread on our table. He did not have any alternative and was stuck in this terrible vicious circle of being poor. He believed two things would get him out of this difficult situation: the National Lottery (*Milli Piyango*) which was drawn once a month, or the new Democratic Party (*Demokrat Partisi).*

For years my father had been trying his luck with the lottery. Every month he would consistently buy a ticket hoping for the big win. *Milli piyango* gave the biggest award if all the numbers on the lottery ticket matched exactly to the drawn number. Smaller awards were also given if the last one, two, three or four numbers matched exactly. We would have been happy even with a small award matching the last one or two numbers. The day after the lottery was drawn, early in the morning my father would send me to the Alsancak Train Station to pick up the newspaper and see if any of his numbers matched. Since he could not read, it was my job to do this. There were no matching numbers and of course a big disappointment would follow. All his dreams and plans he had made for the family with his winnings were again postponed. He then heard there was a "lucky" lottery store in *Basmane*, quite a distance from our house and I should go and buy the lucky ticket from there. I obliged and walked all the way to *Basmane* and bought the ticket. Alas, the next month another big disappointment and terrible let down. That taught me a lesson to never rely on the lottery or on similar activities. To this day I do not buy any lottery tickets or indulge in any kind of gambling activities. I believe if you are going to make it, you should make it with hard work.

Whenever we bought a newspaper, either to check the lottery numbers or once in a while just to know what was happening in the country, my father would have me sit next to his workbench and read him the news. Since we did not have electricity we did not have a radio and we could not afford to buy the newspaper all the time. My father wanted to know what was happening with his party. He was a devout "*Demokrat*", believing in his Democratic Party and its leaders Adnan Menderes, Celal Bayar, and Fuat Köprülü. These leaders formed the Democratic Party in 1946 in opposition to Ismet Inönü's Republican Party. In 1945 after the Second World War had ended with the defeat of the Nazis, a new menace of Communism was spreading like a disease over the states in Eastern Europe and was threatening poor countries like Greece and Turkey. The Russians, the eternal enemy of the Turks, were again under Communist control and were making new demands on the Straits, the Bosphorus and the Dardanelles. Inönü resisted any Russian demands and he maintained the size of the military close to half a million men. He committed a lot of the government's resources in supporting the military and thus did not have much left to support badly needed economic programs. Unemployment was high and inflation was out of control. Inönü's party was under constant criticism. Demands on the government were to reduce the strict government controls that existed from pricing to freedom of speech. Inönü's Republican Party, which had just come out of war, was not able to meet the people's expectations. They pushed for increased taxes, stricter controls followed with governmental frauds and an ever increasing inflation. The large population of the country, which was still poor, believed the new Democratic Party would change all of this and bring happiness and prosperity to the country. The Democrats would promise all kinds of new reforms on taxes, education including religious education in elementary schools, economic developments, support for private enterprise, controlling inflation, and many others. By now the Democrats were well organized, addressing the issues of the farmers needs, demands by the working class, employers' arrangements for reduced government controls and intellectuals' requests for full freedoms and making many more loose promises. They were promising all the things that people wanted to hear. They were gathering across-the-board support with an ever-increasing momentum. A lot of people, including my father were religiously devoted to the Democratic Party. When the 1950 elections took place, the Democrats won with an overwhelming landslide and the country celebrated at every corner. For the first time Turkey had experienced a free election and the workings of the democratic system. It was a victory for the Democrats and the Republicans and most importantly for the Turkish nation. The Democrats, with Celal Bayar as President and Adnan Menderes as Prime Minister, started out with great enthusiasm. American aid was helping the country in all sectors and economic prosperity reached everywhere. Even my father felt improvements in his shoe making business. More people were ordering new shoes and that made him feel good. As the economy grew, so did inflation. For most of the people in the country who were still desperately poor, the increased inflation made their difficult circumstances much worse.

I saw Adnan Menderes and his entourage once when my middle school class was taken to the Alsancak Port for the groundbreaking ceremonies of the construction of a large seaport. We were all waving the flags given to us to greet our leaders who took the opportunity to show off to the public what a great project they were initiating. After the ceremonies and speeches, hundreds of sheep were sacrificed with prayers for the new project and for the well being of our leaders. Today, we see how poorly planned the project was with no foresight, since the Alsancak Port is right in the middle of the most crowded section of the city with no proper ground transportation connections available, causing frustrating traffic choked streets.

In the political front, the Democrats were not any better than the Republicans were. Their animosities continued while neither one of them knew how to be a responsible opposition. The Republicans harshly and irresponsibly criticized the Democrats for all their policies causing significant tension between the two. At each opportunity the Democrats would try to suppress the opposition and repress the intellectuals and the press. One incidence I witnessed to my dismay was the changing of my school's name from *Inönü Lisesi* to *Namık Kemal Lisesi*. Unquestionably Namık Kemal was a great man, a nationalist, a poet, a writer and journalist and an intellectual during the latter part of the Ottoman Empire under the autocratic reign of Sultan Abdülhamit. He was one of the patriotic leaders of the Young Turks asking for fundamental, political and social reforms and vehemently published nationalistic articles, plays and poems that were eventually censored by the Sultan. After a long struggle for his country, the Sultan exiled Namık Kemal to Cyprus where he died. Years later while visiting my wife's hometown Magosa in Cyprus, I saw the prison where Namik Kemal was kept and later died. In Middle School I was privileged to be in a play by Namık Kemal called *"Vatan ve Silistre"*. I was very nervous and excited to be playing a major role in the play as a Turkish nationalist. I remember my mother was among the audience, proudly watching me.

The play turned out to be a great success. For as much as Namık Kemal was a great nationalist, Ismet İnönü was a great warrior, statesman and the second leader after Atatürk who saved our country. Changing the school's name was an unnecessary and vindictive act by the Democrats.

We Turks tend to elevate our leaders to the highest levels while they are in power, independent of their performance, and lower them below the ground when they are out of office mostly with a disgrace. This also happened to the leaders of the Democratic Party but their fate was worse. By 1960 the Democrats had already won two more elections but the animosity between the two parties had increased considerably to uncontrollable political turmoil and physical violence. The government was not able to deal with the economic problems, increased inflation, corruption and fraud, and increased violence and demonstrations on the streets. The public, the police or the military no longer accepted the repressive measures of the Democrats on the Republicans and on the intellectuals who were mostly university people, and the press. On May 27, 1960 a military overthrow of the government, led by General Cemal Gürsel took place without any opposition and bloodshed. The Democratic Party was abolished and on September 16, 1961 after lengthy trials, three leaders of the party, Adnan Menderes, Foreign Minister Fatin Rüştü Zorlu, Finance Minister Hasan Polatkan were hanged. Because of his old age, President Celal Bayar received life imprisonment. This was a dark page in the history of Turkish democracy. My father's and a lot of people's hopes and expectations were shattered with the final demise of the Democratic Party.

The Chickens

My father did not have any hobbies. He did not drink, smoke, nor did he gamble or go to the coffeehouses (*kahvehane*). He liked going to the movies to escape from the difficult realities of life into a dream world of make believe. He worked hard whenever he had shoes to repair or sometimes to custom make. He was happy being at his mother's house with his mother at his side; not that he had any other choice. It was difficult for my mother and me to be there. He was not however, too concerned about my mother's feelings. It is not that he did not care, he just did not think about it. Deep feelings and concerned thoughts in our home fell into the luxury category.

One day my father decided to raise chickens in the house. Of course the benefits would be great with fresh eggs every morning and even occasional chicken meat on the table. It would have been a great idea if we had a yard or a garden around our house, but we did not. He solved that problem very readily by installing a long wooden bar under the kitchen table and putting a curtain in front of it. At night the chickens would sleep on the wooden stick with the curtain covered, curtailing the dim light coming from our kerosene lamp. The occasional newspapers we bought were put to good use and spread under the chickens to catch the droppings. In the mornings the newspapers would be replaced with new ones. Every morning the hens and two roosters were let out to the street and since there were few cars outside, the whole neighborhood belonged to our chickens! The roosters would start the day with their loud crowing and wake up all the neighbors. When a hen was ready to lay an egg, it would be rushed into the bottom of the cupboard to her perch. It would contentedly cluck atop her laid egg, informing us of her great deed. Now we had nice fresh eggs to eat and we did not have to pay for them. I could see how macho the roosters were next to the hens. Very often a big rooster would climb on top of a little hen and if not successful he would run after another one. What a life! My father would call his flock and throw them their feed of corn. They would run to the front of the house and peck on the corn. To this day, I don't like eating corn since it reminds me of our chicken feed.

Instead of curtailing it, my father increased his chicken business by going to the Izmir International Fair and buying special exhibition chicken eggs to put under the hen when it was in heat. It took the hen twenty-one days, sitting on eleven eggs, to hatch them. I don't know why eleven eggs, but that's what it was. When my father took the hen out briefly to feed her, it was amazing how she would run back inside and settle herself back on the eggs. Around the twentieth day, we would check the eggs and see small holes being opened by the baby chicks. We would help open the holes a little further and see beautiful little chicks come out. At this point I had a job to perform. I was the designated shepherd for the "chicken herd". This was a very responsible position. Since not all of the eleven eggs would hatch, we would have eight or nine beautiful chicks in front of the house with the mother hen leading them. There were many hungry cats in the neighborhood sprawled out on the tree branches stalking our chickens and waiting for the opportunity to snatch a little chick. I was however there with my long, thick stick to guard the flock. I have to admit though that I did loose one or two chicks to the cats. The cats would gang up, like a team of female lions, attacking their prey. While I was chasing and throwing my stick at one of the cats, another cat would snatch a chick from the flock. Because of my incompetence, I would get a good spanking.

As the chicks grew, my cousin Namık and I had a great idea of racing them. We would take two chicks, one black and one white, and secretly move them away from their mother so that she would not attack us. We would throw some corn to the mother who would call her chicks to feed. We would then release the two chicks that had to run towards their mother and see which one got there first. We decided this would be a good business and invited the neighborhood kids to place bets on our chicken race. We eventually gave up this business since it really was not that great of an idea.

As the chicks grew, my father would slaughter one or two for some festive occasion. When a hen was in heat and we did not need anymore chickens in the house, my father would stick the hen in a bucket of cold water to cool it down. Some of the roosters which were hatched out of the special eggs grew to be big, tall handsome animals. They looked very dominating and protective next to the smaller hens. On the street when workers were walking to the tobacco factories, our roosters would sometimes attack them. The complaints about our roosters brought the police to our house frequently. We were advised to get rid of these animals immediately. After a few complaints and police visits, my father had no choice but to comply. My mother was very happy about this since she no longer had to continuously clean the kitchen after the chickens.

I had never been anywhere far away from Izmir. The farthest I had ever been to was *Pancar Köy*, my village. In the summer of 1950, my mother and father put me on a bus to visit my Aunt Ayşe (father's sister) and Mithat Enişte, who was an Ottoman Bank (*Osmanlı Bankası*) branch manager in Ayvalık. Ayvalık is famous for its olives and olive oil. It is located on the coast of the Aegean Sea, about 250km north of Izmir across from the Greek Island of Lesbos. Many small hills surrounding countless inlets along the coast are covered with the pale silvery green colored olive trees as far as the eye can see. *Çamlık* is a suburban hill of Ayvalık covered with pine trees where many people would spend their weekends. That summer, my uncle Cevat, who was also living in Ayvalık, took us to *Çamlık* to picnic and swim. When he found out I could not swim, he decided he was going to teach me by simply throwing me into the water without any instructions. After rapidly and frantically moving my legs and arms in the water, I found out a slower motion and better rhythm would keep me afloat and moving. As I gained confidence, my motions in the water became smoother and after a few trials, I started swimming. We went to *Çamlık* a few times until I improved my swimming skills. My uncle Cevat, who had only one arm, was an excellent swimmer. He had swum many times to the little *Cunta Island* across from Ayvalik. Today, *Cunta* is known as *Ali Baba* and is connected to the mainland by a bridge and road extension. There are many seafood restaurants along the *Cunta* shore where tourists and locals can sit and enjoy the beauty of the wonderful bay.

4

Namık Kemal High School

Summer Time

At the age of fourteen in May of 1951, I completed my Middle School. This was in the same building as the high school, which was then known as *Namık Kemal Lisesi*. The entire school consisted of one large building with very high ceilings, marble corridors and large windows. The structure was old and left over from pre-Republic days, but it was still elegant. The classrooms, physics and chemistry laboratories were all well equipped. In front of the building was a beautiful flower garden filled mostly with roses. The walkway was lined with pine and palm trees. In back of the building, a big yard was allocated for the soccer field and a basketball court. It was a very pleasant and serene place to go to get an education. No matter how attractive a school building is however, if the teaching staff is not well qualified and committed, one would not get a good education. Throughout my school years at *Namık Kemal Lisesi*, I can honestly say I had some of the best teachers anyone could ask for. Neither my Middle School nor High School was coeducational. It was a general policy in those days not to mix boys and girls students. This was one less distraction.

My Middle School years were not memorable because I did not take school too seriously. I did my homework and thanks to my mother's discipline and persistence I completed Middle School to everyone's satisfaction as an average student.

The family situation at home was still desperate. Father was still making and repairing shoes at home although he would rarely get orders to make new shoes. Most of his work was small repairs with heel and sole replacements and his earnings were minimal. I was now at an age where I understood our difficulties. I helped my father by going to the market in *Çankaya* to buy small amounts of repair materials and still continued straightening bent nails for him to be used again. All this time, my father religiously continued trying his luck in the National Lottery to no avail. The small pension that my grandmother was getting from the government for Grandpa Sadık's military service was a lot of help for our daily existence. My aunts and uncles continued visiting their mother daily and expecting services from my mother. My mother's effort in managing the family and taking care of their mother was never appreciated as if it was expected since we were living there for free. Even my father did not recognize the difficulties my mother was facing. My father was happy being with his mother and seeing his brothers and sisters. We, however, did not have any family privacy.

In the summer of 1951, it was time for me to work and earn some money to help my family. I got my first job at *Tariş* fig factory as an office boy. My job was to fetch tea, coffee, or cold drinks for the office personnel. *Tariş* was a large government owned food-processing institution. Its products were mostly figs, raisins, olives, olive oils and related products. *Tariş* would buy the fresh produce from the farmers at a price set by the government, process and package them. In the factory I watched the workers process the dried figs by hand, shaping them individually and packaging them for the consumer. Since the factory was a walking distance from our home, it was a convenient first job for me. For the first time I learned how a factory operated and I was astonished to see how the workers labored so hard because they were on piecework.

After work at *Tariş*, I would meet my friends and stroll along the seaside *Kordon* to watch the girls. We were now discovering girls and took every opportunity to observe them more closely. The open-air theaters around *Alsancak* were other places to see our neighborhood girls.

It was very disturbing for me to be poor and sometimes even not to have enough money to buy bread. I realized the difficulties my family was going through but I could not do anything about it. I also did not see any immediate solution to our dilemma. By the end of summer I realized that the only way out of this difficult situation would be my getting very serious about my education and doing extremely well in high school. My mother always drilled the importance of education into my head but I did not appreciate it until I realized it on my own and decided to do something about it. That became my life trend, where I looked at a situation, evaluated it, set my goals and came up with a plan and executed it to a final successful completion. That summer of 1951 was a new starting point in my life.

Nermin

At the ripe and impressionable age of fourteen in *Alsancak*, kids would find many activities to occupy themselves. Neighborhood friendship was very important and kids would play together and get to know each other and their families. At that young age, there was always trust and dependency on each other and close bonding. One popular spot for us to play was in front of Nermin's house.

In our neighborhood, Nermin was a beautiful woman living around the corner from us in a very nice private house with a back yard. She was the mistress (kept woman) of a macaroni manufacturer. When the "macaroni man" came to visit her once or twice a week, he came in his 1948 black Buick. This gorgeous vehicle with its sleek lines had a heavy chromium grill and chromium front and back bumpers. It would be parked in front of her house and all the shutters would be closed. After a short admiration of this monstrous but gorgeous car, our minds would wander to the activities inside the house. We were now getting sexually active, at least in our minds, and this was our only relevant experience. We lingered and occupied ourselves in front of the house playing marbles. Sometimes these games would go on for hours until the black Buick had left. Our hope was to get a glimpse of Nermin, who did not appear too much in front of her house. Once in a great while she would come out with a broom to sweep the front steps and walkway. We admired the beautiful full curves of her body that no amount of clothing could hide. When she bent over to sweep we tried to get into a position to see her breasts hanging down but she always had her hand on her chest as if she knew what we were up to.

One sunny afternoon while we were again playing in front of her house, Nermin appeared at her door. She was wearing a beautiful see-through negligee with a shawl over her shoulders. When the sunlight, coming from the back garden, hit her from behind, her legs appeared in full as if they were completely naked. This was the exciting moment we were all waiting for a long time. It was a source of joy, ecstasy and possible relief. Obviously she was getting ready for the macaroni man. She was addressing us when she asked, "Boys, would one of you slaughter this chicken for me?" She was holding a live chicken in one hand and a bread knife in the other. How could anyone at this moment refuse such a request? I anxiously volunteered and grabbed the chicken and the knife from her. I thought this might put me into a favored position in the eyes of this voluptuous female.

My only experience with the slaughter of chickens was when my father was killing them with his very sharp shoemaker's knife. I knew to put one foot on the two wings and the other foot on the two legs of the chicken. With the bread knife in my right hand, I grabbed the head of the chicken with my left hand. I raised my head and my eyes were locked into Nermin's legs that were standing up like two Greek columns. This was now the point of no return, but to accomplish the task at hand. As I thrust the knife into the chicken's throat, I could see it was not cutting. I repeatedly kept sliding and pushing the knife to no avail. This certainly was not the way my father used to slaughter chickens. After a while, with sweat on my body and fear of failure in front of Nermin, somehow the chicken's head was severed from its body. Oh, what a relief! I straightened my back and looked into Nermin's eyes with a great sense of accomplishment. I thought I caught a glimpse of Nermin's smile with an approval. At this point, I stepped aside letting the chicken free. It instantly stood up and started running. I was shocked. This was not supposed to happen. The chicken without a head ran straight into the wall, fell down, got up and continued running until it hit the other wall. I was following the chicken with its head in one hand and the culprit knife in the other. As I tried to catch the chicken, blood splattered all over my pants. I however kept my pursuit. Victory turned into embarrassment in front of Nermin. I now learned the meaning of "running like a chicken without a head". After some time of running and falling, the chicken found her demise. The road was splattered with the chicken's blood. I handed the chicken and the knife to Nermin and in exchange she rewarded me with only 25 *kuruş*. To me that was fine, I would have done it for free for her anyway. When my mother saw my blood stained pants, she got very angry. Later in time I learned that she had gone to Nermin and yelled at her for asking young children to slaughter chickens. She also told her she had no business living in a nice family neighborhood like ours. That gave an end to our activities in front of Nermin's house.

The day after this incident, I used the 25 *kuruş* as admission to the *Yeni Sinema* to see Errol Flynn in "Captain Blood". What a beautiful movie this was. The movie theater was completely packed with people watching the movie standing up in the back and the aisles. Since I had gone early, I had a very good seat. When it was time for me to leave, after watching it twice, I asked people in theaisles if they wanted to buy my seat for 25 *kuruş*. Naturally, I had no problem selling it. I stepped outside the movie theater and spent part of my money on an "egg fight", a game of two opponents trying to crack each other's dyed hard-boiled eggs. The trick was choosing an egg with a pointed hard end and hitting the side of the opponent's egg to win. I was usually successful at cracking my opponent's egg and therefore as my prize got to eat both eggs! The remainder of my money after the egg fight was spent on *"şambalı"*: a sweet dessert made with farina and syrup. I then walked the 2 miles home with a happy contented feeling for a wonderful day.

Errol Flynn

My classes at the high school started, schoolwork was progressing very rapidly and I was now studying very hard. Classes were until late afternoon. After a little bit of play, strolling around or standing at the corner watching the girls, I would go home and start my homework. On weekends our only entertainment was going to the movies. Our neighbor Monsieur Andon was the movie projector operator at *Lale Sinema*. Sometimes his wife would give me his lunch to take to him and get a chance to watch a movie for free. Since I did not have any allowance, this was a very thoughtful way for Madam Ulumya to help me see movies.

During the 1950's all of Errol Flynn's movies were very popular. We would enjoy watching his movies over and over again without getting tired. His role as Robin Hood was something we could relate to. He was taking the wealth from the rich and giving it to the poor. This was so appropriate for our times and circumstances. If only we had someone to do it for us. We also identified ourselves with his swashbuckling moves, flamboyance and great looks. We tried to look and act like him, hoping our luck with girls would improve. He was and still is my favorite actor.

During this time there were also some of the greatest Turkish singers such as Münir Nurettin, Müzeyyen Senar, Safiye Ayla and others on the radio. Since we did not have electricity at home, I could not listen to them. One of our neighbors was a young girl with a beautiful voice who often stopped by our house while on her way to Baha Bey's grocery store and sang for us. She later became a very famous singer known as Gönül Yazar.

On weekends the big event was going to the *Elhamra Theater* on Saturday afternoons and watching the girls from *Izmir Kız Lisesi* (Girls High School). Konak Square and the *Kemeraltı* shopping area were very lively and crowded during this period with all the students out of school idly roaming around. Streetcars, with their bells ringing and wheels squeaking on the rails, added more excitement to the area. Young students congregated at Konak Square and rushed to the *Elhamra Theater*. At the entrance of the theater, we were like a pack of stampeding elephants, rushing inside to our seats. This was part of the ritual and it was fun. When "Gone With the Wind" came to *Elhamra* it was next to impossible to get in. The most memorable moment in the movie in my mind was when Clark Gable locked his arms around Vivian Leigh and because she could not move from his tight embrace, yielded to his kiss. We all dreamt of kissing like him one day when we found a girlfriend.

There were a series of action movies of James Cagney and Humphrey Bogart at *Yeni* and *Lale Sinemas* that my father and I never missed. My father loved James Cagney's movies because he was his favorite movie star. Father looked very much like him, short and stout with strong arms. He liked going to the movies with me because some of the movies were in English with Turkish subtitles. Since he did not know how to read, he wanted me to read it to him. His right ear could not hear well so I had to sit on his left and lean over closer to his ear and continuously read all the subtitles while I was trying to follow the story. I tried to keep my voice low, but even then obviously this was disturbing the people sitting around us. One day, people sitting in front of us got very annoyed with my reading out loud and turned around and told me to stop. My father told them to turn around and leave us alone. However, when they insisted, the scene turned ugly with my father starting a fistfight. He was easily beating the guys with his powerful boxer swings with me barely helping. We were all asked to leave the theater and therefore could not see the ending of the movie. Because of this, I did not like going to the movies with my father. One day again he asked me to go to *Yeni Sinema* to see Steward Granger in "King Solomon's Mines". Steward Granger was another favorite of mine like Errol Flynn with great looks whom I could relate to. In a later movie I saw Steward Granger in "Scaramouche" as a swashbuckler in a most colorful duel ever with Mel Ferrer. In those days many action movies centered on fencing and it was exciting, breathtaking and a delight for the eyes. But he was still no Errol Flynn! This time I told my father I did not want to go to the movies. I did not dare tell him I had other plans. I had my very first date with a pretty but skinny girl to go to the *Elhamra Theater* to see the same movie. My father therefore, went on his own. The movie at the *Yeni Sinema* was dubbed into Turkish and the one at the *Elhamra* was in English. I told my date I would meet her inside the movie theater and we sat together. By doing this I did not have to pay for her ticket. It is not that I was cheap; I just did not have any money. We advanced to holding hands, which was a thrill by itself. However, there was no kissing like Clark Gable's. After the movie, my date had to get back home immediately since she had told her family that she was going out with her girlfriends. At Konak Square the buses going to Alsancak were completely full; therefore I suggested we take the Basmane bus to Alsancak. We were able to get seats on the bus and we continued to hold hands. Before we knew it the bus was completely filled. As the bus passed through *Çankaya* where the *Yeni Sinema* was located, in all the excitement I forgot my father had gone to see the same movie. When the bus stopped in *Çankaya*, my father boarded our bus and saw me sitting with my date cozily and excitedly holding hands. He gave me his famous fierce look with his dark penetrating eyes and I started shivering from fear. I got up and gave him my seat but he chose not to sit down or to speak to me. My date, realizing the awkwardness of the situation, got off the bus at the next stop to walk home the rest of the way. When we got off at the last stop in Alsancak, my father was walking swiftly in front with me running behind him. I was getting ready in my mind for a very good spanking or all kinds of punishment. When we got home my father still did not talk to me but told my mother that I was at the movies with a girl. My mother yelled and lectured me that I was not ready to go around with girls. Instead she insisted that I should be concentrating on my schoolwork. I was 15 years old and felt that I should be able to associate with girls while I was still doing my schoolwork. It goes without saying I never got to see that girl again.

During this period in Turkey it was very difficult for young boys to socialize with girls. In the Turkish culture dating was not an accepted behavior. Turkish society did not allow free and open friendship between boys and girls and families were under intense social pressure not to let their daughters intermingle with boys. The overall social atmosphere was very restricted and uncomfortable for young people.

My Bicycle

Izmir's penetrating damp and cold winters continued year after year. We were still heating the downstairs of the house with charcoal but there was no heat upstairs where I was studying. After dinner I would take my kerosene lamp and go upstairs to the big room where my grandmother and I slept and start studying under the dim light. The light coming from my lamp was a welcome glow on a cold winter's night. My study desk was a hexagonal table with a single support leg at the middle. I had to be extremely careful with my lamp since the leg attachment was very wobbly and unsafe. The light from the lamp was very faint so I had to pull it very close to my books to be able to see the pages. Many times I would get too close to the lamp while studying and my hair would burn leaving a terrible smell in the room.

I was now enjoying schoolwork and doing very well in all my classes. Schoolwork was easy for me and my best subject was mathematics. Mathematical equations, trigonometry and geometry were very exciting, challenging and fun for me. Because our school was an all boys' school, it was easy to concentrate on schoolwork without getting distracted by girls. I was, however, still looking forward to the Saturday movie matinees. At the beginning of the 1950's the country was still struggling due to difficult economic conditions. Except for a few rich people the population was mostly poor. The times were tough for everyone. People did not have much but there was optimism and hope in everyone's mind for the future. Everyone regarded education very highly. Although there were very few schools in the country, they all had excellent teachers. The educational standards were maintained at the highest possible levels. The teachers were very strict and serious. There was fear, respect and love in our minds and hearts towards our teachers. We knew that our teachers cared for us and tried to do their best to give us a good education. The students also responded in turn with the same fervor and zeal towards their assignments. Everybody was trying to do their best and was competing with each other. Schoolwork was taught properly in school and there was no need for after school and weekend private lessons (*dersane*) which has mushroomed everywhere in present days putting the families into financial difficulties and the students into confusion. In this competitive environment I was doing extremely well. I realized at the very beginning no matter how smart I was I would have to study very hard to succeed. Nothing takes the place of hard work and my hard work started paying off.

Beginning in my freshman year, at the end of each semester I would make the honors list as being one of the best students in the class. Without missing a single semester this continued until I graduated from high school. I was very proud to see my picture hanging in the school's hallway in the honors list every semester as one of the the top students in the class. I realized my hard work and accomplishments would be my passport out of poverty and I just stuck to my schoolwork. Outside of school we formed close bonds with some of our classmates and would hang around together. During this time I made some very good friends. I learned one important thing at the very beginning of my life and that was choosing the right friends who would add positive attributes to my life and not misguide me. I have been very lucky and blessed with having some of the greatest friends one could hope for.

In the wintry and profusely rainy Izmir weather, one day our little house got flooded. As the torrential rains continued, we tried to empty the water with buckets to no avail. Because of wetness the floorboards in the living room got distorted and the outside wall started to buckle inwards. It was not safe for us to be in the house, but we did not have the money to have it repaired. We lived in those dangerous conditions for a while until we asked Abdullah Eniste, my aunt's husband, to build a new wall for us. We figured we could somehow pay him later. He was a nice man with very good skills in bricklaying and carpentry. We obtained the material and my father and I helped as laborers. I helped mix the mortar and carried it upstairs together with bricks before I went to school and after I came back from school. My father helped in between. There is a saying, "where there is a will there is a way". We did accomplish that task.

One nice spring day after the long dreary and rainy winter, when I was again routinely checking my father's lottery ticket in the newspaper, I could not believe my eyes. We had matched the last four numbers in the lottery! This meant we had won 2,500 *Lira*, which was a good sum at that time. We could do a lot of things with that much money. We were just jubilant. After paying a lot of our debts, with the remaining money my parents decided to buy me a bicycle. Most of my friends had bicycles and I was very envious but never asked for it. I was now very happy that I was getting a bicycle also.

We decided on a green, German-made, Yale brand bicycle. Since I already knew how to ride a bicycle, it did not take me too long before I was cruising the streets of Alsancak and *Kordon*. My bicycle made me feel good and important. It gave me the freedom of being able to go anywhere I wanted. I could show off to the girls with my bike and sometimes even give rides to them on the front support beam. Once in a while I used to show off riding on my bicycle with no hands! One day, I decided to go to my grandmother and aunts in *Hatay*, riding my bike on a long distance over the newly built steep road called *Varyant*. In those days there were not too many cars on the roads. My aunts and my grandmother were very happy to see me. At times even my father would use my bike to go and buy his shoemaking materials. In Alsancak I was giving rides to all the neighborhood girls and one day I even took Leman Abla, the blond beauty of our neighborhood, for a ride. This was a thrill for me. I kept my bicycle for a long time and it became my family's main transportation vehicle and my pride and joy.

During all my summer vacations, I continued working at different odd jobs. For me, life by no means was fun and games. The reality of life and being poor was all around us. In those days everybody was poor. The country was poor and the people were struggling to make ends meet from day to day. There were very few wealthy people that we all looked at with envy but accepted our fate as it was and continued our struggle to better ourselves.

After working at the *Tariş* fig factory, I got a job in a coffeehouse. Our family friend Orhan Bey who was also delivering bottled drinking water in Alsancak owned the coffee shop (*Kahvehane*). Every time Orhan Bey came to our house with his truck my father asked my mother to make coffee for them so that they could have their periodic visit and chat. The coffeehouse I worked at was close to *Tariş* and other factories. Most of the factories in that area were brick making shops. The plants were hot and dirty filled with red brick sand and coal. The work at these plants was very heavily labor intensive with no automation. Workers did not spend a lot of time in our coffee shop like the other coffee shops in town that were inundated with idle people who spent their entire day having a cup of coffee or tea while sucking on the waterpipes (*nargile*) and gazing outside with empty stares, or playing backgammon with loud noises generated when chips were hit hard on the game board, especially when their thrown dice gave them double numbers. At noontime all the workers would bring their lunch into our coffee shop and order a cup of tea, relax and eat their lunch while enjoying a conversation with their fellow workers. I could see from their smiling eyes that they were happy with their lives and what they had. I liked being among them and serving them. I felt like a member of the working class. After lunch workers would return hurriedly to their difficult tasks of making bricks. In the afternoons, Izmir's blazing summer heat inside the factory would increase with the heat emanating from the brick furnaces. Workers had no choices but to continue their tasks while enduring the unbearable heat. They all seemed undernourished and tired but happy to have a job. I could relate to them because of their hard work and life struggles. My job in the afternoons was to fill two pails with ice and bottles of gaseuse (*gazoz*) and go to the factories. I would shout,

"Gazoz, buz gibi gazoz"
"Gaseuse, ice cold gaseuse"

Unfortunately this was not true because I had just put the bottles on ice and they were still room temperature. To the workers however this was still cooler than the blazing heat inside the factories.

My next job the following two summers was in a lumber yard which belonged to Eyüp Köknar, a well to do merchant. My job there varied from sales and delivery of lumber to receiving cement bags from ships coming from Yugoslavia. In those days, Turkey recently out of many wars, was trying to build its devastated lands. There were very few cement factories and since they could not meet the needs of the country, cement was being imported from countries like Yugoslavia. Later in time cement factories were built everywhere in the country mostly just outside of the cities including some outside of Izmir in Bornova. Over the years, because of poor city planning and foresight, as the cities grew and expanded, the cement mills became located right inside the new city limits. The fine gray ashes coming out of the cement mill chimneys fell on everything nearby including houses and trees. The entire surrounding area was covered with cement ash and turned into gray cement ash color. Even today this unhealthy situation continues because of the irresponsible authorities not monitoring the outputs of the cement mills continuously. People are still living and working under the dangerous ash clouds emanating from the cement factory chimneys while plant owners are busily maximizing their profits by minimizing the use of filter systems.

Eyüp Köknar was doing very well with his lumber and cement business. I thought he was a very lucky man. One day Eyüp Bey told me luck had nothing to do with success. He said luck was a combination of hard work, preparation and making timely and valuable use of the opportunities that came your way. Eyüp Bey had a black Buick adorned with all the chromium decorations it could have just like the black Buick in front of Nermin's house. Eyüp Bey's car, however, was decorated with emblems from all the European countries he had visited. I would stand admiringly in front of this shiny car looking at the emblems of France, Italy, Deutchland, Holland, and other countries and enviously wonder and wish if one day I could possibly go to these far away countries also.

Science Division (*Fen Şubesi*)

In September 1954, I started my fourth and final year at Namık Kemal High School. That year Adnan Menderes' government irresponsibly decided to reduce the high school education to three years. Thus, juniors and seniors would be graduating from high school together, which was a major concern for many graduates and me. First we unnecessarily spent one extra year in high school and secondly, since the graduating student body would be doubled, admission into the universities would be twice as hard. There were not many universities for the students to apply to and with increased student applicants the admissions to the universities would be highly competitive and difficult. My response to this dilemma was to study twice as hard.

In our senior year we had to make a choice in our study branches to either the Science or Literature Division. The Science Division (*Fen Şubesi*) would be more concentrated with science courses of mathematics, physics and chemistry. Literature Division (*Edebiyat Şubesi*) would be mostly liberal arts and literature courses. Although the Science Division would be much harder, it would prepare the students better for university admission exams, especially for the engineering schools. Without much procrastination I chose the Science Division. In the Science Division all of our teachers were very capable and experienced professionals. Our class was filled with a select group of students, all very bright, hard working and highly motivated. Before we knew it we were well into an accelerated class work.

Our mathematics teacher, Rifat Türkeli, quickly completed the basic mathematics and algebra and began teaching us college level calculus. In other science classes he was covering trigonometry and advanced geometry. Because of the fast pace in his teachings, we had finished our textbook and were solving extra problems from a French book. Without hesitation, I was studying diligently night after night trying to keep up with the rapid pace. In many damp and cold wintry nights, I was upstairs next to my dim kerosene lamp solving calculus or geometry problems. Sometimes the burnt smell of my hair would fill my room. I felt like an athlete training for a marathon race. Since we could not afford to buy extra notebooks with blank sheets, I would use the blank edges of the newspapers to solve my mathematics equations. After I had completely used the side edges of the newspaper to solve my problems, I would throw it away. Every blank inch of the newspaper was a valuable scrap paper.

During mathematics exams I was usually the first one to finish. I would sometimes stay and help my fellow classmates. When Rifat Bey realized this, he had me sit at his desk to take my exam. This made me feel important. Physics and chemistry classes had the same intensity as the mathematics classes. Our favorite class however, was our English class because we all had a crush on our gorgeous teacher Bedia Hanım. In class we would just sit and stare at her beautiful face and gorgeous curvitures. Everything about her, from her lips to her hips was exquisite. Fear of embarrassment in front of her forced us to study the assignments she gave us. Our German language teacher Tolun Bey was her husband. Some of us had signed up for a secondary foreign language. We were so envious of him for having such a beautiful wife. Our Biology teacher Edibe Hanım on the other hand, was very homely looking. She was also our homeroom teacher and she sincerely cared about our well being and our education.

At the end of 1954 during our school's New Year vacation, Edibe Hanım arranged a field trip to Istanbul. Twenty of us signed up for this extraordinary trip to the magical city. Istanbul was a dream city that I had always wanted to visit but never had the occasion or the money to go. I had never traveled anywhere far for any vacation. My family collected enough money for me to sign up for this wonderful trip. I had certainly earned it. We left the Basmane train station early in the morning as a group. In the train we were happily singing songs all the way to Bandırma where we took the boat for an overnight trip through the Sea of Marmara to Istanbul. Early the next morning we were at the Karaköy port. As I looked around me in awe of this magical city, I could see beautiful mosques with soaring minarets reaching into the sky forming a beautiful landscape over the Bosphorous. I had never seen such splendor. We walked up the long and steep roads to Galatasaray High School where Edibe Hanim had arranged for us to stay in the dormitories for free because the students had left for their holiday and the rooms were vacant.

Galatasaray was located at the heart of the Beyoğlu district, the main shopping and entertainment center of Istanbul. At one end of *Istiklal Caddesi,* which was the main street of Beyoğlu, was Taksim Square. This was the center of the city. The other end of *Istiklal Caddesi* was the *Tünel* (tunnel) which was the world's oldest underground subway. It was basically a few hundred meters long, belt driven elevator operating at about a 30-degree slope. It connected the hills of Beyoğlu to the shores of Karaköy. Beyoğlu had 19th century buildings, European Embassies, historical churches and synagogues, stores, restaurants, coffee and pastry shops, theaters, bars and whorehouses. Across the street from Galatasaray High School was the *Çiçek Pasajı,* which was once a flower market but now a lively bar and restaurant center.

The main public transportation system in Istanbul was streetcars with two wagons connected to each other. The noise from the clanging bells of the streetcars sounded like chimes in the city's noisy background. The old fashioned tram moved very slowly through the ancient city streets stopping at every corner for passengers getting on or off. The wagons were always filled beyond the limit with people hanging out of the front and rear doors. The ticket masters in each wagon tried to push their way through the crowd to collect fares.

Edibe Hanim had a concise and full schedule for our cultural visit covering many points of interests with historical values. The program included mostly museums, mosques and a boat tour of the Bosphorus. The main attraction of our tour was the *Sultan Ahmet Square* uniquely situated inside the walls of the old city of Constantinople. The Square gets its name from *Sultan Ahmet I*, who built the Blue Mosque or otherwise known as the *Sultan Ahmet Mosque*. Across the street was Haghia Sophia (*Aya Sofya*), an outstanding Byzantine architecture and the world's most remarkable historical church. In this fascinating historical square besides these two marvels were many other sites: the Basilica Cistern, an underground water cistern which was the main source of drinking water for the old city of Constantinople and the famed Ottoman *Topkapı Palace Museum.*

Sultan Mehmet II built *Topkapı Palace* shortly after his conquest of Constantinople in 1453 as his principal residence. This palace served for four hundred years as the seat of the Ottoman government until 1853 when *Sultan Abdülmecit I* abandoned *Topkapı* and moved to *Dolmabahçe Palace*. Our tour continued from *Sultan Ahmet Square* towards *Beyazıt Square* where Istanbul University was located. On the way to Beyazit we wandered through the *Grand Bazaar*, the oldest operating covered shopping mall in the world. This Bazaar was built over two thousand years ago and is still the most shopped place in Istanbul. There are dozens of streets within it with hundreds of merchants selling anything from souvenirs to oriental carpets. The jewelry storefronts glisten with gold bracelets, necklaces and earrings. At Istanbul University we got the first taste of a university environment and what it would be like to be at a higher educational institution. We spent several days absorbing as much cultural and historical information as we could. After so much culture we were ready to sneak out and experience other sides of Istanbul. We jumped off the streetcar and walked through the back streets of Beyoğlu to experience its nightlife. We observed and participated in the activities that the locals were indulging on in these indiscreet areas. To us these were new and exciting experiences. When our visit came to an end after one week of wonderful sightseeing, we were on our way back to Izmir. I was very happy that I was able to visit Istanbul for the first time and hoped there would be many more visits in the future.

Back in school, the rapid pace of classes and homework started immediately. We were at a high gear. I had again made the honor's list. One day Edibe Hanım came to visit my house with a small leather briefcase in her hand. My father, while attending his shoe repair work, welcomed my teacher into the house. My father and mother did not know what to make of this visit until she presented the small gift to my family and to me as a token of recognition with a note inside which read:

> "In preparation for the future, this briefcase, which will carry the books that will become your closest friends, is presented to our valuable student Özcan Tuncel by the School and the Parent-Teacher Association as a remembrance"
>
> Namık Kemal High School Principal
> Hayri Çakalöz   12/31/1954

I was very much moved and my parents were very proud of me. I could barely hold my emotions because this was not commonly done in public schools. Thanks to my parents, all the neighbors, friends, and relatives heard about this happy incidence.

As the school approached towards the end, my mind was now again occupied with a concern for the future. All I knew was that I was going to take the university entrance exams. We did not, however, have the money for me to attend the university. I thought that maybe I should join the military so they would pay for my education. I just did not know what the future would bring.

On weekends I would get together with my friend Erdem Tunçsiper, who lived in Basmane, and we listened to his Nat King Cole records. Erdem always dreamt about America. Although there were a lot of American NATO personnel in Izmir, we did not know much about America. At that adolescent age, we just admired anything and everything that was American. In those days there was no way for kids like us to be able to go to America. We therefore continued dreaming about it while we listened to Nat King Cole's words:

> "They try to tell us we're too young
> Too young to really fall in love . . ."

Such beautiful words about love and what a voice! Our dreams carried us to a romantic dream world, maybe in America.

Back in school the harsh realities brought us down to the real world. As the summer was approaching, school was coming to an end. The final exams signaled the end of high school. I successfully passed all my finals and graduated from Namik Kemal High School with Honors. Erdem, however, had failed a few classes and had to take make-up exams at the end of summer to graduate. Half of the class had failed one or more courses that had to be cleared with a make-up exam. In those days there were no graduation ceremonies. In the middle of the summer when the diplomas arrived from the Ministry of Education, we went to the Principal's office and picked them up. The years of being under the family's protective wings were over. I was now on my own, to determine my own future, and to find my own destiny.

Ali Riza Tuncel, 1935   In front of "*Altın Kundura*" shoe store

Fatma Naciye Toku, 1935

The three sisters; Hanife,
Naciye and Ayşe (sitting left)

Wedding of my parents, November 1935

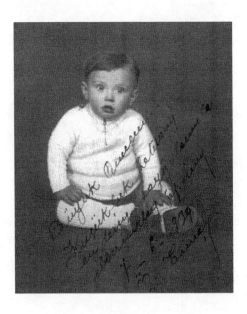

Baby Özcan

Gazi Elementary School with Fazıl Öğretmen, third grade, 1946

Fifth grade student, 1948   Graduation from middle school, 1951

With Namık Kemal High School friends
(Erol Ulucaklı on the left), Feb. 1955

Graduation from Namık Kemal High School, May 1955

My Parents in front of our house at No. 36 Alsancak, 1955

My parents with aunt Ayşe, uncle Mithat and grandmother, 1955

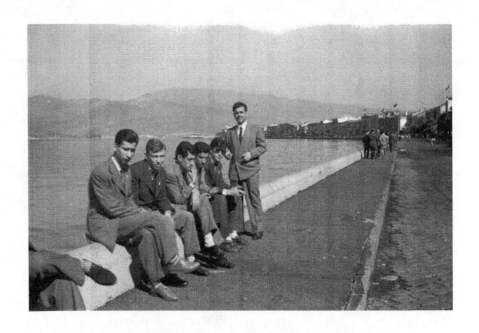

Relaxing with my friends at Izmir Kordon after ITU exams

Leaving Izmir for America with Ihsan Abi and my parents, January 1956

5

Coming to America

Istanbul Technical University (İTÜ)

In the summer of 1955, with the high school education behind me, I was now at a crossroad and I had to choose the best and hopefully the right path for myself. This was the most critical period of my life. In order to succeed I had to study extremely hard to direct myself to a brighter future away from poverty and ignorance. I had no role model or anybody to look up to, to guide me through the choppy waters of life. I had to find my own way. I felt like a sailor in the middle of the ocean without a compass trying to find his way just by looking at the stars. My star was up above when I prayed to Allah to guide me through the ordeal of life. Now a new ordeal was starting: getting ready for the university entrance exams, applying and taking the exams. If I won an acceptance to any university, I still did not know how we would pay for it. I wanted to be a professional, a doctor or an engineer. My mother always wanted me to be a doctor. I did not know much about any of these professions. Except for my schoolwork I was not exposed to the outside world too much. As a family we did not have much contact with higher professions and shoemaking was all we knew. I decided I had better find out what the medical profession entailed. I asked Dr. Nihat Önderoğlu who was then a resident at the Konak Municipal Hospital, to show me the around and explain to me the medical profession. He invited me to the hospital and gave me a tour explaining different functions and activities in all the areas. The last stop on the tour was going into a surgery room and observing a surgery in action. The surgery was about to begin and I was fully dressed for the surgery room with a doctor's gown, gloves, mask, and slippers. The procedure was to remove a cyst a woman had in her abdomen. As I started watching the surgery my attention got distracted to a pretty nurse with a fly swatter in her hand chasing a black fly in the operating room. I did not notice whether she got the fly with a couple of swings or not, but I proceeded to observe the surgery. Looking over the surgeon's shoulder, I saw the first incision through the white flesh which was mostly fat. Blood spurted from the cut and the next thing I remember was hitting my head on the marble floor. I had fainted. The student nurses carried me out of the room and I was mortified. After a while when I felt better I wanted to go back into the surgery room. This time I stood further back to observe the remainder of the surgery. The doctors were in the process of removing the cyst and throwing the pieces into a bucket directly in front of me. I glanced into the bucket to check it out and doing this caused me to faint again. This time the student nurses grabbed me from falling onto the floor and carried me out of the room. When I awoke I realized there was no way I could tolerate the smallest sight of blood. That was the end of my medical profession. Although my mother was very disappointed that I was not going to be a doctor, I crossed off medical schools from my application list.

Since I gave up pursuing a medical profession before it began, my next choice was engineering. One thing that is very important in life is to know what your talents and capabilities are and capitalize on them. I thought I found my calling in mathematics which would fit into engineering very well. My only option in engineering school was Istanbul Technical University (İTÜ) which was the highest ranking institution in Turkey giving a Master's Degree in a five-year education. Roberts College was another excellent private school but we could not afford it, so I dismissed it readily. İTÜ was the only choice and I had to get into it. In those days as young people, our overall goal in life was to get a good education and work for the betterment of our society and environment while living comfortably. The present youth is more oriented towards material achievement with expectations of turning the corner rapidly with minimum effort.

That summer I did not get a job. My family was most supportive and they wanted me to study and get ready for the university entrance exams. Realizing the difficulty of the situation, with very high competition especially for İTÜ, I started studying day and night. I had to be at my best in all the subjects. Mathematics was the highest scoring section and that was my best subject. The scorching summer heat in Izmir made studying much more difficult. I started getting up at 4: 00AM and studying at a very rapid pace under the dim light of my kerosene lamp. Everyday when the heat became unbearable, I walked to *Atatürk Library* in *Gündoğdu* and studied in a much quieter and cooler atmosphere. *Atatürk Library* was a two story marble mansion right at the *Kordon* waterfront. It was the house Atatürk resided in whenever he was in Izmir. It was a beautiful house with very high ceilings and white marble decorations everywhere. After Atatürk had died in 1938, it was turned into a museum with one small area open to the public as the library. Somehow not many people had discovered this wonderful haven and it was empty most of the time. I have learned that Turkish people do not frequent libraries. Over the years the majority of Turks relied on newspapers for their reading habits. Since newspapers are more like tabloid papers with very limited news being reported, people had to buy few papers to make certain they did not miss any of the news. Even then whatever was reported was very superficial without much depth and research into the subject. Instead of reporting scandalous news with overwhelming photographs, newsmen should pursue more responsibly the subjects that need to be addressed in society. The relationships of the news media and the government controls have not been pleasant either. Over the years the governments have used many excuses to curtail the activities of the news media. In the end we the Turkish people have been harmed the most. Day after day, I was at the *Atatürk Library* studying mathematics, physics, chemistry, biology, geology, and many more subjects. After the general studies, I started preparing for the exams in a different manner. This meant I had to anticipate what kind of questions would be asked and I had to be prepared to answer them in proper timing. It was like racing against time. Knowing the type of questions that were asked in previous years, I was feeling more confident that I had a very good chance to win. I had done everything possible to prepare myself for the big challenge that was about to come.

About this time I found out *Sümerbank* had announced that they would send select students to the United Stated and Europe with full scholarships to study metallurgical, textile and industrial engineering. Pre-requisites for *Sümerbank* examinations were that the students should be Science Division graduates from high school without any failing grades. I fitted those requirements readily and applied immediately. Both the *Sümerbank* and İTÜ exams were going to be given at Istanbul Technical University, which meant that I would have to go to Istanbul. That summer there were no extra curricular activities. The entire summer passed with studying. In very few occasions I would stroll with my friends along the *Kordon* and check out the girls. In one of these socializing tours I made a friend with a very nice fellow, Kamuran Akdenizli who was a law student at Istanbul University. I told him about my dilemma of not having a place to stay in Istanbul. He assured me that he would find me a place in Istanbul *Cağaloğlu* Student Dormitories where he was staying. This was a major load off my mind.

Before long I was on my way to Istanbul by train backtracking our New Year's field trip route. In Istanbul, I met Kamuran at *Cağaloğlu* Dormitories. Since the schools had not started yet, there were a lot of empty beds where I could stay for free. The following day I was off to İTÜ to take the *Sümerbank* exams. There were only six hundred select students from the entire country taking this exam and only the first five would be selected for the United States and the next ten for Europe. The exams took the entire day. Mathematics questions were extremely tough. One question was solving simultaneous equations with more variables than the equations given. This meant that variables could not be solved independently and they would have to be solved in relation to each other. This was something taught in college level, not in high school, but luckily I knew the answer and I was sure I had scored very high. When the exam was finished late that afternoon, I felt happy: happy that it was all over and happy that I knew I had done very well. I could not contain my joy. I walked up to Taksim Square and instead of taking the streetcar I decided I was going to walk all the way to *Cağoloğlu*. I passed through Beyoğlu, down the steps to Karaköy, over the Galata Bridge to Eminönü and up the hill to *Cağoloğlu*. It was a very long distance to walk, but it was exhilarating and I did not even notice it. A few days later the İTÜ exams took place. This time the applicants were very large crowds of students filling all the classrooms and hallways to take the exams. After *Sümerbank*'s questions, İTÜ exams seemed much simpler. I handled that very well and I was relieved that it was all over. The next morning I was on my way back to Izmir to wait for the results. We were told it would take about twenty days for İTÜ results to be announced by posting them at the University. That was ridiculous. I could not afford to hang around in Istanbul and wait for the results. I arranged to have Kamuran inform me of the İTÜ examination results by calling our grocer Baha Bey's store since we did not have a telephone in our house. I started waiting for the results very anxiously and nervously.

My father continued repairing shoes at home. Since people were not having new custom shoes made anymore, any work that was coming from the neighborhood was either repair of the shoe heels or soles. He was therefore not making much money. Still, my concern was if I won İTÜ how would I attend the university in Istanbul. The *Sümerbank* results would not be known for sometime and it would be much later than İTÜ's announcement.

One day Baha Bey, the grocer, yelled out for me that I had a phone call from Istanbul. It was the call from Kamuran that I was waiting and praying for. He informed me that I had won the İTÜ exam. I was the 13th in a group of hundreds of students. I ran home crying out of joy and announcing the great news to my family. I shared the news with my friends and with everyone I knew in Alsancak. I also went to my high school and told my principal I had won İTÜ. That year, besides me, my good friend Erol Ulucaklı had also won İTÜ and ten of my high school friends had won various universities. This was a big honor for our high school. The principal, Hayri Çakalöz, informed me that the school had already arranged some financial help for the needy students to attend universities and I was on top of that list. I was so grateful. Eventhough it was a small amount, it would certainly be helpful. Kamuran was going to help me with the dormitory. Things were now working out well for me. My hard work and prayers were answered. What a relief! To celebrate our accomplishment, Erol and I, together with other students from Istanbul, strolled the *Kordon*, visited the Agora and Kadifekale and just enjoyed ourselves. I was beside myself. I immediately secured a "İTÜ-Bee" jacket lapel emblem, which was a highly recognized privilege to wear. I proudly wore it everywhere I went.

Before long I was back in Istanbul starting İTÜ classes. Life in Istanbul was not easy. Every morning I walked down the *Yerebatan Caddesi* to *Sultan Ahmet Square* to the streetcar station. I was now living close to Istanbul's most historic district which we had visited with Edibe Hanim only nine month earlier for the first time. Things happened so fast that I did not have time to comprehend. A few months ago I was a lost child without much direction and full of fears of uncertainties and now I was a student at the most prestigious school in Turkey living in the heart of an overwhelming city of Istanbul. Every morning I rode the streetcar all the way to Taksim Square.The İTÜ campus was just a brief walk from the square. Our classes started very rapidly with a lot of assignments. Our professors were mostly German who had run away from Hitler's persecution and had settled in Turkey. Before we knew it, we were deep into schoolwork. A Saturday night visit as a group to Beyoğlu movie theaters was our only entertainment event. One day my İTÜ-Bee emblem came handy in meeting a beautiful girl on the streetcar. It was "love at first sight". I would meet her every morning on the streetcar and ride together until she got off at Galatasaray where she was a student in a Girl's Art Institute. One night I received a telegram from Izmir informing me that I had won *Sümerbank*'s exam to go to America. I had forgotten all about it. I did not know how to feel. This meant I would have to leave a life and friends that I had established in Istanbul and get ready to go to America. I was very confused. I did not have much time to respond and I was told to go to Izmir to start preparations. The next morning on the streetcar I told my new found girlfriend that I was going to America. My love affair came to an abrupt end before it began. Our little happy interlude was finished and I was again on my way back to Izmir starting a new adventure.

Sümerbank

It was with great sadness that I was leaving İTÜ and Istanbul. I had made a little life for myself attending the most prestigious school in Turkey and living in a dormitory near the most extraordinary historical sites of the Byzantine and Ottoman Empires. It was not an easy life however since I managed on a bare minimum of money and traveled with streetcars long distances to go to school. I had few but very close friends who were very supportive and I even had a girlfriend. On the other hand, in 1955 being able to go to America and getting an education there with full scholarship was unheard of. It was an opportunity that could not be turned down. I felt I was blessed and Allah was looking after me. All at once these wonderful things were happening to me and my hard work was paying off. I did not have much time to procrastinate. In the middle of December 1955, with conflicting emotions, I left İTÜ. Again I was on the train towards the Basmane Station in Izmir. I could not sleep on the train because I was filled with excitement and joy thinking about the New World that was ahead of me.

In Izmir there was a lot of paper work waiting for me to be completed and to be taken to *Sümerbank* headquarters in Ankara. That evening, my father, my mother and I sat next to the dim light of our old kerosene lamp. The young man's joy and excitement now turned into a somber reality. I was going to leave my poor family and not see them for a long time. My paternal grandmother looked very old and frail. Realizing the significance of the moment, I asked me parents if they approved of my going to America. Their answer was simply, "Son we cannot tell you to go or not to go. If we

say don't go and things don't work out well here, then you might blame
us for the rest of your life. If we say go, than we are willing to accept the
consequences and the pain of missing you. It is your decision." That did
not help me much. It put the burden back on my shoulders. Now I had
to make an important decision on my own with lifetime consequences. I
was only 18 years old and I was not prepared for all these complications.
I decided to do some research and went to a *Sümerbank* textile mill in
Kahramanlar. There I met some engineers and asked them how satisfied
they were working for *Sümerbank*. Their answer was not very positive. It
seemed like they were all disgruntled and unhappy workers. That was no
help either. My next step was to consult with my high school principal
Hayri Çakalöz who was very encouraging. He felt that, in this period in
Turkey when no one was able to travel outside of the country, being able to
go to America for education with a full scholarship was a great opportunity
not to pass up. Once again I was grateful to him for his guidance and told
him I would go to America. I then relinquished the scholarship that my
high school had given to me for İTÜ so that another needy student would
benefit. I reasoned to myself that except for my immediate family I did
not have much I was leaving behind. Besides it was only for six years. I
thought to myself, somehow America would give me the opportunity to
pull out of this poverty. I had a lot to gain and not much to lose.

The decision was made. I was now going to America. I was again on the
train from the Basmane Station this time travelling to Ankara to meet with
Sümerbank's management. This was my first visit to Ankara, the nation's
capital. It was a very cold and wintry place, covered with snow. This was
not the kind of weather a kid from Izmir was used to. Little did I know
that the weather in America would be worse. *Sümerbank*'s headquarters
was located in *Ulus Square* where Atatürk's statue adorned the central
square. Meeting with *Sümerbank*'s bosses was very professional. For the
first time the top five students who had won the scholarships; Ali Üstünol
Ernas, Güneş Ecer, Özcan Tuncel, Kaya Özkal, Sevim Aras in that order
were brought together. This was the elite group of students in the entire
country. We would be starting this adventure together as lifetime friends.
Sümerbank told us that we needed to sign a 52,000 TL "promissory-note"
with two guarantors as co-signers. This scholarship required us to work for
Sümerbank of 12 years in exchange for six years of education. Although
the value of a scholarship seems small in today's numbers, at that time it
was a very significant amount of money. The first three students in this
group were selected to study metallurgical engineering and the remaining

two were to study textile engineering. Both of these professions were much needed for the upcoming Turkish industry. The metallurgists would work in *Sümerbank's* Ereğli Steel Mill near Zonguldak on the shores of the Black Sea and the textile engineers would be assigned to the various mills of *Sümerbank*. Working in Ereğli for 12 years and leaving my beautiful city of Izmir did not appeal to me too much. But there was no other choice. We left *Sümerbank's* headquarters with a final instruction that everyone should shave his moustache, not that I had one. They suggested that the Turkish trademark, the moustache, was not looked upon very favorably in America.

That night the five of us went to a movie at *Ulus Square* to see an American war movie, "The Battle City" with Aldo Ray. We were now beginning to feel much closer to America. We felt like we were on our way being Americanized. The next morning we visited our first Grand National Assembly Building where Atatürk had declared the Turkish Republic on 29 October 1923 as a secular, democratic and civil country. I could visualize Atatürk standing on that small and simple podium giving speeches to the first Assembly of the new Turkish Republic. We all remembered, in another speech the great Atatürk had assigned to the Turkish youth the future responsibility of our nation when he delivered on October 1927 the following words:

"Turkish Youth, your first duty is forever to preserve and defend the Turkish Independence and the Turkish Republic. This is the very foundation of your existence and your future.

. . .

Youth of Turkey's future, even in such circumstances, it is your duty to save the Turkish independence and Republic. You will find the strength you need in your noble blood".

We were very much moved and excited to be in such an important place in our history. The five of us felt in our hearts that we were ready and willing to take on this responsibility. We grew up with strong beliefs to Atatürk's Doctrine and would always follow his steps. That morning as I walked outside in Ankara, I would stop and look back on my footprints left in the snow. I thought these footsteps were the beginning of my journey to America, hopefully for a brighter future.

Back in Izmir, I was now getting ready for my journey. Family members came to see me and wish me good luck. My uncle Cevat, the one with one arm, that evening also came to see me off. After some small talks he turned to me and said,

"Now listen Özcan, I have only one advice for you."

I thought to myself, I already knew what he was going to say; he probably would say,

"Don't marry an American girl."

In those days marrying any non-Muslim was not well accepted. I was however surprised when he continued,

"Don't be a Communist".

I did not know where he got the notion that by going to America I would become a Communist. In any case, I assured him that I would not be a Communist.

During all this excitement, I ran into a major obstacle that could prevent my going to America. I could not find two guarantors to sign my 52,000 TL "promissory note". I was frantic and scared. There was nobody in my entire family financially qualified as co-signers. Panic stricken I approached people outside of the family. My first thought was again my high school Principal Hayri Çakalöz who kindly accepted to be a guarantor. The manager in the lumber shop where I had worked became my second guarantor. These two people had faith in me and were signing their future retirement income to guarantee my education. I was forever in debt for their kindness. The preparations for the trip were completed when my parents had a tailor-made dark navy blue, striped, narrow lapelled, double-breasted suit for me. I looked like a member of the Mafia, but still very good in the new suit.

This time I was leaving Izmir by ship. My parents, my good friend Erdem Tunçsiper and some family members with İhsan Abi, my aunt Hanife's husband, holding baby Asuman in his arms, were at *Gümrük Pier* to see me off. After emotional good-byes, the ship left the pier very slowly. Waving our good-byes, the tears continued for a long time until we could no longer see each other. We did not know when we would see each other again but we knew that it would not be soon. We all felt this burden of separation in our hearts but did not talk about it. Tears dropped quietly, reflecting the unspoken words that were in our minds and in our hearts.

Naples and Rome

The next morning my ship arrived in Istanbul's *Karaköy Pier*. I had one small leather suitcase with a buttoned cloth cover to protect it from getting damaged. With the suitcase in my hand I walked up the street where the Sümerbank branch office was located where I joined my other four traveling companions. There we were given our travel vouchers and detailed specific instructions along with one hundred dollars spending allowance per person for the entire trip.

The next morning, on January 20, 1956 we boarded the *S/S İskenderun* to begin our long journey to America. This was my birthday (according to my mother) and I was just turning 19 years old. Güneş Ecer and I had one final picture taken in front of the ship's entrance and we were off towards Greece. The ship sailed through the Sea of Marmara and passed the *Dardanelles* and was now in Greek waters of the Aegean Sea. As it passed the Greek Islands in the midst of the Aegean I could not help but think how my mother as a child was forced by the Greeks to leave her home in Salonica and had passed these islands. As my mother was sailing towards her new home some 30 years ago, little did I know that I was sailing through the same waters towards my new home in America. The next morning our ship had arrived at the Greek port of Piraeus. Together with some other passengers we arranged a tour to go to Athens to visit the Acropolis. This beautiful site located on top of the hill had some wonderful remnants from the ancient Greek civilization. Although we were impressed with the magnificence of these sites, we realized how privileged we were to have many similar if not better sites in Turkey located in *Ephesus*, in Istanbul, in *Bergamum* and in many other Anatolian locations. When we came back to Piraeus, five of us strolled along the shore of the pier close to the ship. Some locals who approached us demanded to know what we were doing there. They recognized from the Turkish flag emblems we had on our jacket lapels that we were Turks. Although we did not understand what they were saying, their yelling turned into more physical actions. This was right after the 1955 demonstrations and riots in Istanbul against the Greeks when the Turkish-Greek antagonism once again had reached a new high. As the local crowd got larger we realized it would be best for us to go to our ship as fast as we could run. That was the most unpleasant experience I had with the Greeks. Their inner animosity, fervent dislike and deep hatred towards the Turks were clearly demonstrated. I was happy to leave Greece.

Our ship sailed towards Italy. The ship's crew told us that if we could get up very early in the morning we could see Stromboli, Europe's only active volcano. The next morning before sun up, we all anxiously watched the lava flow along the side of the mountain into the sea. As the lava touched the sea, steam was generated. The island of Stromboli under the full moon looked romantic, exciting but still very dangerous. We could not understand how fishermen could still live in a small town on the other side of this volcanic island. As the new day started, our ship entered the Italian port city of Naples (*Napoli*). Naples was the last stop with our Turkish ship. Here we would disembark and later take a larger American ship for New York. We had however five days in between for sightseeing in Italy. This was unbelievable. One month ago in Istanbul, as a poor student, I was living with a bare minimum and now here I was in Italy gallivanting around with $100 in my pocket. When we disembarked our ship *S/S İskenderun* five of us called a taxi and asked the driver to take us to a hotel. The taxi driver tied our luggages on top and we all squeezed in. The taxi left the square where our ship was docked and speeded along the shore and turned on to a main street in Naples. The taxi driver continued into much narrower streets where washed laundry was hanging on ropes tied between apartment buildings. It took the taxi driver quite some time before departing the narrow streets and leaving us in front of a hotel on a main street. This was actually quite a sight seeing tour of Naples. The taxi driver demanded $10 which was a lot of money but when we divided it into five it was reasonable. Since my English was the best in the group, I explained to the hotel clerk that we wanted only one room for the five of us. After a lot of resistance from the clerk, I was able to convince him to secure one room. We packed into the room like sardines. We were not here to sleep but to discover. We stepped outside the hotel and decided to walk towards the square on our left. When we arrived at the square we saw our ship *S/S İskenderun* was docked at the pier. We could have walked to our hotel. The taxi driver had really taken us for a ride! During our walk through the streets of Naples we were surprised to see many posters of the Italian Communist Party decorated with hammer and sickle. The Communist Party in Italy was legal and well accepted. In Turkey however Communist menace was secretly active and was not allowed. My uncle Cevat must have known something that I did not know when he cautioned me about Communism. At the beginning of 1956, Italy was still poor and had not recovered from the devastation of the Second World War. This could be seen on the streets, in the people's homes and on people's appearances. Be as it may, we were here to have fun.

For our dinner, we went to a pizza parlor. For the first time we were being introduced to pizza. After our taxi experience we were more careful when ordering our pizza. I had learned from our Italian neighbors in Alsancak to say, "*Uno pizza de Lire cento*": One pizza for hundred Lire. All of us repeated the same statement. We loved eating pizza, who wouldn't? That evening all five of us walked into a nightclub. The club was completely empty except for a few American sailors sitting at one table. The room was filled with romantic music, dim lights and many beautiful working girls. Before we knew it, five gorgeous ladies with long evening gowns came to our table. They were very nice and friendly. Each one of them sat on our laps. Ali Üstünol however did not want any of this. In fact, he had not even taken his coat off. He insisted that the girl on his lap should leave. To save the situation from embarrassment, I pointed the girl to move to my other leg that was unoccupied. I now had two gorgeous girls on my lap. What a life! Of course this all came with a price tag I did not think about when the girls ordered champagne which cost $5 each. I had never tasted champagne before, so when I took a sip from my lady friend's glass it tasted like colored water. I guess it came with the territory. The girls wanted to dance but I did not know how to. My two lady friends pulled me up and started dancing around me to a very nice music beat, "Hey Mambo, Mambo Italiano, Hey Mambo . . ." I was entranced with the beat and started moving around. I was having so much fun. We left the club with our hearts overflowing with joy and walked through the dark, narrow and cold streets of Naples toward our "sardine can" hotel room.

The next morning it was time for us to get some culture. We were off to Rome. At the Rome Central Train Station, Güneş bought a camera to document all the wonderful experiences we were having. Again we got a "sardine can" hotel room for all five of us. We were now ready to discover Rome by walking and by streetcars. Rome was absolutely beautiful. We visited every corner of the Vatican, which was established as an independent state in 1929. We strolled through St. Peter's Square, along the Vatican Gardens and went into the Basilica of St. Peter and climbed to the top of the Cupola that was designed by Michelangelo. The names we read and the pictures we saw in our history books were right in front of our eyes; Michelangelo's *Pieta*, Statue of Moses, Bernini's many works including Holy Water Fountain, Raphael's works, and the Sistine Chapel where Michelangelo labored for seven years (1536-1543) lying on his back painting the ceiling. We continued our walk through the Roman Forum that dates back to the times of Caesar and Augustus and to the Colosseum, which was used for Gladiators' fights and we ended up at the Piazza Venezia near the marvelous Monument of Victor Emmanuel II. Our walk took us to the monumental Trevi Fountain and we rested on the Spanish Steps and of course in every opportunity we tried to make contact with the beautiful Italian girls. To me every Italian girl looked like gorgeous Silvana Mangano whom I had admired in the movie *Riso Amaro* (Bitter Rice). I remembered her in this 1948 movie working in the rice fields with her skirt lifted and shirt top wide open giving her tempting glances to Vittorio Gassman. What a beauty! By the time we left Rome, we got to know every corner of the city very well. That was a well worth visit.

Back in Naples we got ready for the next leg of our journey. One evening in a restaurant we ordered spaghetti. We did not know what it was. It looked just like the macaroni my mother always made but it was much longer. They had not broken it into small pieces like my mother used to do so I started cutting them into small pieces until the waiter stopped me with a scream. He took the knife away from me and gave me a spoon instead. He showed me how to roll the spaghetti with the fork against the spoon and eat it properly like the Italians did. They say, "When in Rome do like the Romans do." I was grateful for that lesson and obviously I still remember to do it properly now. In the early 1950's Turkey was not open to the outside world and our exposure to other cultures was very limited. Except for our textbook knowledge we really did not know much about anything. Every little thing we saw and did was an eye opening experience.

S/S Independence

The S/S Independence and S/S Constitution were the two transatlantic sister ships that carried passengers between Europe and America in the 1950's. Except for S/S America, they were the most advanced and beautiful ships at the time. These ships continuously carried immigrants from Europe to America. America for a long time was considered and looked upon as "the land of opportunity" and was thought as a place where "her streets were paved with gold". The early immigrants to America during the periods of 1820's to 1860's were Germans, Irish and English. After the 1880's, immigrants from Southeastern Europe, mostly Italy, Greece, Poland, Russia, Portugal and Spain were more dominant.Very few people from Turkey in the earlier periods had emigrated to America. Those who did were the country's minorities such as the Sephardic Jews, Greeks and Armenians. Although they did bring some of the Turkish culture to the New World, they were not necessarily representing Turkey. In time they emphasized more of their own ethnic background and less of the Turkish nationality. In the 1940's and 1950's medical doctors, in order to complete their internships and residencies, or scholarship students like us were coming to America. America at that point had reached the pinnacle in technology, economy and culture in the world and select groups of people were traveling there to get an education or follow their fortunes. Here we were, our nation's brightest five, traveling to America to get our share of education. We were not immigrants nor were we running away from any despotic government, persecutions or poverty. Our country was poor but with expectations for a brighter future. Our mission was to represent our country because we were very proud of being Turkish and we had a lot to teach American's about our culture while we were getting our education.

Our ship the S/S Independence had three classes of passengers: the First Class for the rich, the Cabin Class, filled with mostly American middle class people, and the Third class crowded with immigrants. We were in the Cabin Class with four of us assigned to one room with bunk beds. The surroundings were very pleasant and the service was excellent. The American passengers in the Cabin Class were very friendly and it was our first introduction to the Americans. Our ship left Naples and after a brief stop at Nice, France, it continued in the deep blue waters of the Mediterranean towards the straits of Gibraltar. I could not help but think during the reign of *Sultan Süleyman the Magnificent* how *Barbaros Hayrettin Pasha* had turned these waters of the Mediterranean into a Turkish Sea.

Our Cabin Class had a lot of entertainment arranged for the passengers. The musical chair game was my favorite. We watched many movies shown in the ship while we were struggling to understand what was being said with our limited English. In one of the movies we saw, "Scheherazade", the words of a beautiful song reflected how I was feeling:

> "Take my hand
> I'm a stranger in paradise
> All lost in a wonderland
> A stranger in paradise".

One evening we ventured to the ship's bar where we were invited to join some American passengers. When we were asked what we wanted to drink, since we never had alcoholic beverages before, we did not know what to order. I noticed a Coca-Cola sign on the wall. I had heard of this drink, but we did not know what it was. We therefore decided to order the Cola, thinking it was an alcoholic beverage. After a couple of drinks we went back to our room. The ship was now in rough waters of the Atlantic Ocean and the rolling of the boat was not helping our stomachs. We thought we were getting drunk with the Cola. Crossing the Atlantic in the middle of the winter was not a pleasant experience. We were all terribly seasick and could not join the other passengers to enjoy those wonderful meals. Once I stood outside on the deck of the ship and I could see how huge the waves were rocking our boat. It seemed like with each wave our ship's nose, at one time was touching the stars than diving to the bottom of the sea. The ship continued its course fighting January gales and towering seas.

After we finished all the activities in our Cabin Class we decided to venture to the Third Class. Although the passengers could travel to a lower class they were not allowed to go to upper class areas. Third Class was a lot of fun. The salon was filled with people and everybody was singing, dancing and really enjoying themselves. People here did not seem as well off and sophisticated as the ones in the Cabin Class, but they seemed like they were much happier. They were always laughing and intermingling with their fellow passengers. There was an atmosphere of joy and happiness in the air. There were also many more young people that we could relate to. At every opportunity we ventured to the Third Class to have fun. After the seventh day of cruising through the rough, wavy and wintry waters of the Atlantic, we were now approaching America. We were told that in the early morning hours our ship would be sailing into the New York harbor.

We were all up and anxiously watching the shores of America from a distance. The early fog and mist had covered the land, but we were happy to see any small land at that point. As our ship slowly sailed into the New York harbor, we could barely see some of the skylines of lower Manhattan. To us any tall building looked like a skyscraper. All of a sudden on our ship's port side, the Statue of Liberty appeared among the mist like an angel holding her arm above us. She was welcoming us to our New World. In her right hand up above was a torch and her left arm was holding a tablet with the inscription July 4, 1776 in Roman numerals, America's Independence Day. At the base of the statue the following excerpt from the famous, "The New Collossus" by Emma Lazarus was inscribed:

> "Give me your tired, your poor,
> Your huddled masses yearning to break free,
> The wretched refuse of your teeming shore.
> Send these, the homeless, tempesttuest to me."

To me the torch Lady Liberty was holding signified power of light over darkness and hope for the future. It reminded me of the dim light coming from my kerosene lamp in the darkest nights that guided me and brought me to my New World.

For decades the immigrants who passed in front of this Fair Lady were sent to Ellis Island. Ellis Island was opened on January 1, 1892 to accept immigrants into the United States. Just before the First World War, the number of immigrants coming into the country had reached to a peak of one million per year who were being processed through Ellis Island. This has been a revered and sacred ground for many immigrants. Over the years while immigrant policies changed, Ellis Island closed its doors on November 12, 1954 and was later turned into a museum. Because of that we did not need to go through Ellis Island. As we passed the Statue of Liberty, we now knew we were in America. Our ship docked in one of the piers near mid-town Manhattan where we could now see the mighty Empire State Building. When we stepped on the shore it seemed like the entire Manhattan Island was rocking. A Turkish graduate student, by the name of Nevzat greeted us. He was sent to meet us by the Turkish Educational Attaché to take us to our homes in Queens. This time we rented two taxis and were off to a good start.

6

New York, New York

Queens College

Queens College was located in Queens, Long Island, one of the five Boroughs of New York City. The Turkish Educational Attaché had pre-arranged for us to start taking English lessons at Queens College. Teaching English to foreign students was a very lucrative business for many colleges and universities in the area. In Flushing I first settled into an attic room of a house that belonged to an Italian family, together with another Turkish student. The school was located on Kissena Boulevard, a walking distance from the house. We were very happy to meet many Americans who were regular students at the college and we were especially happy to see that the college was co-educational and we could meet some girls. In this very friendly and diversified group, the first business of the classroom was our names that our teacher tried to learn and pronounce. When it came to my name, Özcan, the teacher had difficulty pronouncing it. I tried to explain to him that "c" was pronounced like "j" in Turkish and "can" would sound like "john". He then decided to give me the nickname of John. From that moment on I was known as John Tuncel and I carried that name throughout my entire professional career. Americans, more than any other nation, tend to be very informal and use nicknames more extensively and most of the time they address one another with the first name without any titles. I had started in the Intermediate English class and we were making rapid progress with the language and intermingling with the other students. The school however had a lot of Turkish students and we were improving our Turkish more than our English since we were speaking mostly Turkish outside of the classroom. In order to fully experience America, at times we used to stroll to the corner drugstore to get some soda pops. We would watch American teenagers with saddle shoes, dungarees, and poodle skirts listening to their new idol Elvis Presley singing some new rock-n-roll music. We had never heard of this music before but we enjoyed the exciting beat of "You ain't nothing but a hound dog . . ."

Our first venture into New York City from Flushing was by subway when we visited the Turkish Educational Attaché office on the 79th floor of the Empire State Building. To us the building was like a city within a city, very large and a testament to American ingenuity. In 1945, a US B-25 bomber hit the 79th floor of the Empire State Building causing some damage and death. The rumor was that the Turkish Educational Attaché had rented the 79th floor cheap since no one else wanted that floor. We were happy that they were there, giving us the opportunity periodically to visit the building. The Educational Attaché was in charge of our affairs in the United States and they were also distributing us our monthly allowances of $141 that covered everything except the tuition which was paid directly to the school. This meager amount just met the bare necessities of food, room rental and books. It would not stretch to include any type of entertainment, not even the movies. By the middle of the month I would run out of money and would have to get part time jobs. I was not afraid of working since I had been working all my life whenever I was not going to school. My first job was in an Italian restaurant as a kitchen helper. I never had any previous kitchen experience and did not care for it either. One of my assignments was grating Parmesan cheese with a hand grater. When the cheese became small, I would start grating my fingers. Instead of trying to grate the small pieces, I decided to eat them. In the restaurant I met a waitress who convinced me to move to a nicer house and live with her family. In her backyard I watched the massive Long Island Expressway being built. I was now with a nice American family with two kids really feeling at home and improving my English much more rapidly. It was, however, tough to get used to American meals. In the restaurants, the two slices of white bread we were served was never enough. We Turks like to eat a lot of bread with our meals. We are also very picky about the taste of our bread. When the hot Turkish bread comes out of the brick ovens it is one of the tastiest. In fact, when I bought a rye bread with caraway seeds in it by mistake from a local grocer, I had to remove the seeds individually one by one to be able to eat the bread.

Schoolwork was coming along very nicely except for the fact that I was always running out of money. Every month I had to resort to another part time job again. My next job was being an usher in Lowe's Theater in downtown Flushing. Wearing an usher's uniform, I would show people to their seats and also make sure kids did not put their feet on the seats. When the movie "High Society" was being shown, I would watch it over and over again admiring the beauty of Grace Kelly, listening to the music of Bing Crosby, Frank Sinatra and Louis Armstrong. Mostly young couples who were more involved in kissing than watching the movie took the back seats in the movie theatre. I thought to myself that we could never do this in Turkey. Watching movies continuously while working was a great way to improve my English. My next job was at a Nedick's store in Manhattan near the Chrysler Building on Lexington Avenue. Nedick's were chain stores scattered everywhere in Manhattan specializing in famous hot dogs and orange drinks. This was way before McDonalds and Burger Kings were ever heard of. This job was also a great way of improving my language when the locals were using terms like "Gimme a hot dog". It gave me an opportunity to learn the colloquial language that I could not learn in school and fellow students.

As soon as I had enough money to make it to the end of the month I would quit until the next time. My next job the following month was at the Horn and Hardat Cafeteria on Broadway near Times Square as a busboy. The cafeteria was self-service with sandwiches stacked in rotating displays and customers could get their choices by inserting coins into the corresponding slots. Once I even got a job as a dishwasher that lasted only one day. I hated washing dishes even to this day. I sent some of the extra money I had saved to my parents because I knew it would be a lot of help for them. I was happy to learn that with that money the first thing they did was bringing electricity to our house. One day I had a brilliant idea when I noticed balls in the window of a sporting goods store in Flushing. After purchasing them, with the sales people's assistance in the store, we took the air out of several basketballs and soccer balls and packed them in a box. I sent the box to my high school athletics department, since I knew there was a need for balls to play with. The letter I received from my high school principal was very nice, telling me how much they appreciated my remembrance of the school.

At Queens College, after the Intermediate Class, I completed the Advanced Class. By September I had to decide what to do next. Ali Üstünol decided to start Carnegie Institute of Technology in Pittsburgh. Güneş went after a girl to Michigan. Sevim decided to leave *Sümerbank* and go to live with some relatives he had in New Jersey. We were envious that he could break loose from *Sümerbank* so soon. If only we could do that ourselves. Instead of starting Lehigh University, where I was assigned to go, I decided to stay in New York a little longer and continue the language school at Columbia University's English Language Center. I had a little bit of adventurous spirit and New York City is the place to be when you are young and want to experience life. There were a lot of exciting things to do and many places to discover. There were a lot of other Turkish students in New York that I was friends with also. We had the freedom and the opportunity to expand our horizon more in New York than anywhere else. We frequented the movie theaters on 42nd Street and danced at 14th Street dance halls, if you call what we did dancing. We were just having so much fun. We did not think that we would have this opportunity ever again once we started college and after we returned back to Turkey. In September, I started commuting from Flushing to Manhattan taking English classes at Columbia University.

Columbia University

Columbia University was located on Broadway near 116th Street in upper Manhattan. Besides being one of the best universities in the country, its English Language School (ELS) for foreign students was very highly regarded. The majority of the students at ELS were from Latin America with some Asian students and very few Turkish students. By now, with a Queens College schooling and extensive practicing at my rental home and at my many part time jobs, my English was very good. In fact, it was much better than most of the other students in the school. I was assigned to Advanced Level at ELS. I was well liked and popular among the International students and it was natural for me to seek the Presidency of the ELS Student Council. With the encouragement of the other students, I accepted the challenge. I prepared speeches and delivered them in English. I was sure to win. My opponent, however, was from Latin America and gave his speech in Spanish. Since the majority of the students were Spanish speaking, he won. Dirty politics! That was the end of my political career.

The commute between Flushing and upper Manhattan on the subways was going well and I felt like a real New Yorker. This was not much different than my commute to İTÜ on the streetcars in Istanbul. One Saturday morning I received a phone call from the Arthur Murray Dance Studios. The voice on the phone sounded very sexy:

— Mr. Tuncel
— Yes
— This is the Arthur Murray Dance Studio. You have been selected by our studio to get a free dance lesson if you can answer the following question correctly.
— OK
— Name three US Presidents who have been in the Military.

I did not know anything about US history. In Turkey we spent most of our history lessons memorizing the details of the treaties Ottomans had made, especially when they were rapidly losing their Empire. But I knew the father of the United States, George Washington fought the English to gain Independence and Eisenhower who was the current President, was the Commander of the Allied Forces during the Second World War. I rapidly mumbled:

— George Washington
— You are right
— Eisenhower
— You are right

She said,

— There is one more.

Now I was stuck. I did not know any other American President, let alone one in the military. But everyone knew about Abraham Lincoln and I had heard of the name. So I said

— Lincoln
— You are right!

I later learned, as I studied American history in depth, that Abraham Lincoln, who was one of the greatest American presidents during the Civil War, was never in the military. Be as it may, it was a great relief! Now I could go and get my free dance lesson. I was given the address of the studio in Flushing. Late in the afternoon I dressed up with my dark navy blue "Mafia" suit and tie, and went for my free lesson at the Arthur Murray

Dance Studio. All the girls were lined up waiting for their customers and I had a choice of picking any girl I wanted to dance with. This was just like the nightclub in Naples. The girls were all very pretty, thin, tall and shapely. I picked the prettiest one. This was so exciting. I put my arms tightly around her just like we did on the 14th Street dance halls. She told me that was not the proper way of holding a dancing partner. When the music began we moved to the right and than to the left. On each move I stepped on her foot. She observed,

— You don't know how to dance, do you?
— No. That is why I am here to get my free dance lesson.
— Oh, OK. Come here to the desk and we can sign you up for extensive lessons. For three weeks it's only $49.99. You will be an excellent dancer after those lessons.

I never figured out why Americans used .99 instead of rounding it off. In either case, I could not afford that type of money for dance lessons. So I departed the studio without signing up and no free dance lesson either.

During the Thanksgiving holiday of 1956, one of the Turkish students was going to Raleigh, North Carolina to check out the school that he was going to attend. He asked Barlas Sümer and me to go with him. It was an interesting yet a scary situation we were in. We were young teenagers without any supervision or parental guidance. We could do anything we wanted without asking permission from anyone. We could easily do the wrong things. Nobody was watching over us except for our sound judgment and Allah. Luckily however we did not have any temptations for any wrong doings. We readily agreed and left New York City by bus from Port Authority Terminal. We took our seats in the very back of the bus until we were told to move towards the front since that area was reserved for Negroes. Although there were no signs to that effect, it was understood by everyone. We thought the whole thing was very odd but did not dare to argue. As the bus rolled further into the South, we noticed everything was separated with signs for the whites and for the Negroes; the restaurants, rest rooms, water coolers, schools, neighborhoods, etc . . . . We then understood the real meaning of segregation in America. But it was difficult for us to accept it. In Turkey, we grew up with the belief that everyone was the same and equal and even our Muslim religion had taught us that we were all brothers and sisters. We were disappointed because here was America, where we knew it was the most advanced country in the world and the land of opportunity and freedom, but its people were not all equal.

On New Years Eve my friends and I decided to go to Times Square to watch the ball drop and bring in the New Year of 1957. It has been a tradition in New York City to celebrate the entrance of the New Year at Times Square with thousands of people partying. The entire square was filled with jubilant but maddening crowds. We were so squeezed against each other that it was difficult to breathe. It was nothing but chaos. As the clock approached midnight, the ball slowly came down and everyone started to scream. So we screamed as well. That was it and not much to it. We welcomed the New Year in. It was a different experience, but I do not think I would repeat it again.

It was a memorable year in New York City. We enjoyed ourselves and we got to know the city very well. We did it all. But now it was time to move on. On my last visit to the Turkish Educational Attaché, I found out Lehigh University would not accept freshman students in the middle of the school year. That was very disappointing to hear. The Turkish Educational Attaché inadvertently decided that I should go to the University of Kentucky for one semester than transfer to Lehigh since they had already accepted me. I reluctantly agreed to the plan and prepared to leave New York. In January of 1957 I was again at the Port Authority Bus Terminal going to Lexington, Kentucky. This time I was all alone going to a place where I did not know anyone. I was scared; scared of the unknown in a foreign land. It was not like going to Istanbul where I had friends and I knew people. But it was something that I had to do to get a good education. As the bus sped along the New Jersey shores, I could see the astonishing New York skyline. I thought to myself I will miss New York and the friends I left behind. Isn't that the case whenever you leave the ones you love behind? I felt lonely and homesick. I closed my eyes, and started thinking of my mother and father and realized how much I missed them.

7

University of Kentucky

The Greyhound bus took me to my first stop, Louisville, Kentucky where I stayed overnight. The next day about noontime I arrived in Lexington. After the taxi took me to the University of Kentucky, I walked to the Admissions building with one luggage in my hand. Since all the pre-registration was done I was taken to the dormitory where I would stay. There I met a Turkish student, Mümin Köksoy who was also sent on a scholarship by MTA (*Maden Teknik Arama*), Mineral Technology Research Administration of Turkey, to become a geologist. He was a lot of help for me to become acclimated to the University's environment. The school was spread out on a very large and beautiful campus. I was assigned to a dormitory room with bunk beds. I got used to the school and dormitory environment easily. But somehow I could not enjoy the hillbilly music that most of the students were listening to all day long in their rooms. The country music was blaring at every corner. When classes started I realized that the schoolwork was too simple for me. Mathematics classes especially were considerably below my level. I just could not think of wasting my time in a mathematics class that was the level of my second year high school. I discussed the matter with my teacher and after some evaluation I was assigned to a sophomore calculus class. Even this was barely the level of my high school mathematics class. One day as we advanced into mathematical integration problems, I noticed our teacher was having difficulty solving a tricky mathematical equation. I raised my hand and went to the board and showed the entire class the right approach to solve the problem. My teacher acknowledged and thanked me for my help and I was quite pleased with myself. I could have easily taught this simple class. Schoolwork was too easy and continued without any problems.

The Lexington area was known as the Blue Grass Country. Early in the morning when the sun was rising, the sunlight hitting the grass covered with dew made it look blue. The rolling hills of the Blue Grass Country were home to many horse farms. The white fences stretching for miles separated the farms and kept the horses free to run in their premises. Horses running through these beautiful farms added such beauty to the breathtaking surroundings. The big event in the State was the horse race called the Kentucky Derby held in Louisville with participants coming from all over the world.

The school had a pleasant and comfortable atmosphere. The students were very friendly and they were especially anxious to help foreign students to learn about American ways and culture. I was very happy to be here, a part of this Southern environment. I was once invited to go to a drive-in movie on a double date. I had never been in a drive-in movie before. It certainly did not resemble our open-air theaters in Alsancak. Here we watched the movies in the car. I was pleased with the invitation and excited to learn another American way of life. When we arrived at the drive-in movie, after the speaker was installed on the driver's window, the movie began. My driver host and his girl friend not long after the movie started abruptly began some indiscreet activities in the front seat. This was unexpected, unpleasant and an uncomfortable experience. My new date and I were left in the back seat to watch the complete movie. I continued dating different Southern belles. One of my memorable and enjoyable dates was when my friend Mümin and our dates went to a school dance. We spent most of the time sitting and chatting since we did not know how to dance. The University of Kentucky was co-educational with beautiful Southern girls attending the school. It was not difficult to find dates. The University was also famous for its basketball team known as the Wild Cats. The school trained some excellent athletes for the NBA. One of the main activities in the campus for the students was to go to the home games. Schoolwork was not difficult and I had no problem completing the semester while I was enjoying myself. Communication with my family continued through weekly letters. My friend Erdem Tunçsiper read and wrote the letters for my parents. With each letter Erdem reminded me to help him find a way to come to the United States.

From time to time I had to get jobs for additional spending money. Most of the time, I would find jobs through the school. People living in the surrounding neighborhoods always needed yard work to be done. Taking care of the yards was an easy way of making spending money. Once, the homeowner asked me if I knew how to trim shrubs. I had never done any yard work before much less trim a shrub. I took on the challenge of trimming the bushes just like I had volunteered to slaughter the chicken for Nermin. Anything for a cause! The results in both cases were very disappointing. The trimmed shrubs turned out to be very noticeably crooked. Understandably, I was not called back for another job.

When the semester ended, I decided to stay in the dormitory and get a full time, well paying job. I found one outside of town in a cattle and pig slaughterhouse and meat packing plant. It was a very large plant, which processed a few hundred animals a day. Work started at 5 AM with the slaughter of the animals in two separate areas. The cattle were hit with a sledgehammer on the forehead first and then were killed after they fell down. The pigs however were much noisier when they were grabbed by a hind leg and pulled up with a chain belt. A man on the other end of the conveyor would slash the screaming animal's throat. The process would then continue in both instances on conveyor belts. The meat was then cut and sorted out properly for shipment. My job at this plant was to make high quality, high priced hamburgers with all the left over meats. Throughout the summer of 1957, I spent the long hot days in a cool freezer room grinding the meat and forming them into hamburgers in a press and packaging them.

It was difficult to commute to work by bus. At the first opportunity, with my saved earnings I bought a used 1952 Dodge. My beautiful black car, with a chromium grill and fenders, looked just like the "macaroni man's" car parked in front of Nermin's house. However, I could not drive my car since I did not know how to drive. The students in school showed me how to drive and shift gears. I started practicing on my own in the school's parking lot. At each start the car would stall whenever I tried to change gears. I could never get the coordination of the gas and clutch pedals right. After repeated starts the battery died. We got the battery charged and I continued my frustrating trials. Eventually I mastered the car on my own and got my driver's license.

That summer I met a Turkish doctor, Nevzat Türkmen at a nearby hospital in Frankfort, Kentucky. Mümin and I visited him several times. Since there were not too many Turkish people in the area we were always happy to meet each other. Once, with a group of visiting Turkish agricultural engineers, we also visited Mammoth Cave, a famous tourist center in

Kentucky. This was the largest cave in the United States with a lake inside. It was used as the ammunition depot during the Civil War.

Summer was almost over and by September I had to report to Lehigh University. This time I could not miss the date. It was time to leave Kentucky. I loaded up my few belongings in my car and started my journey again. By the time I got to Charlestown, West Virginia it was late and getting dark. I slept in the car and the next morning I continued driving over the Appalachian Mountains. I felt happy and secure in my car. After my bicycle this was my very first vehicle that I owned with my own earnings. I had a certain bonding towards my car. As I drove on the steep and curved roads of the mighty Appalachian Mountains, I enjoyed the breathtaking scenery at every turn. As my car rolled down the hills, I continued driving to Washington DC where I stayed another night with a Turkish friend. Early in the morning I left Washington for New York City. I was very anxious and excited to see my friends again. On the New Jersey Turnpike when I saw the Empire State Building from a distance, I was beside myself. I was very happy to be in New York again. In New York City I took the new Long Island Expressway to Queens and got out at the Flushing exit to go to my friend's house. Since I had been cruising along at a rather high speed, I did not think of slowing down on the side streets because my mind was still occupied with seeing my friends. At an intersection I crashed on the side of another car which had just pulled in front of me from the side street. The car flipped to its side with a man trapped inside. I noticed gasoline on the ground and instantly climbed on top of the car and tried to open the door I had hit. After afew frantic minutes I got the door opened and the man pulled himself out. The fire trucks and tow trucks arrived not long after. Luckily I had insurance. Both cars got towed away and I picked up my luggage and started walking the remaining two blocks to my friend's house. The joy and excitement of my visit was now gone since I had to deal with the car problem. I had no money to pay for the repairs of my own car because the insurance only covered the other car and I only had two weeks before I had to report to Lehigh. My only option was to get a job and pay for the repairs. I quickly found a job in a manufacturing plant making eyeglasses. My coworkers were mostly Spanish speaking Latin Americans. It would have been nice if I had learned a little bit of Spanish at Columbia from my fellow students. Every morning I greeted the ladies with: *Buenos dias bonito muchachos*!

After I paid for the car repairs, I decided to sell it to my friend Barlas Sümer. Barlas did not know how to drive. He asked me to drive him with the car to Lowell, Massachusetts where he was going to start Lowell Institute of Technology to study Textile Engineering. I hurriedly, but more carefully, drove Barlas to Lowell and returned by bus to New York City to pick up my belongings. It was sad for me to sell my first car but it was luckily the right decision. Little did I know that Lehigh did not allow freshman students to have cars. After an adventurous summer, I was now ready to go to Lehigh University.

8

Lehigh University

Freshman Year

Lehigh University is a private educational institution located in Bethlehem, Pennsylvania about 90 miles west of New York City and 60 miles north of Philadelphia in the center of Lehigh Valley. Its many beautiful, stone, ivy covered buildings on the campus were scattered on South Mountain above the city of Bethlehem overlooking the Lehigh River and the Bethlehem Steel factories. Although the school offered degrees in Arts and Sciences and Business Administration, the main specialization and the school's reputation was in engineering education and engineering research. During the late 1950's and early 1960's when I was at Lehigh, its close affiliation with Bethlehem Steel broadened the educational training into industrial activities. At that period, US Steel and Bethlehem Steel, which were the remnants of Andrew Carnegie's Carnegie Steel Company, were the two major steel industries in the United States. Bethlehem Steel predominantly specialized in structural steels such as I-beams that were being used in the booming skyscraper constructions in New York City and elsewhere in the United States. There were no outside competitors in the steel industry at that time. The work at Bethlehem Steel continued around the clock. At night when the blast furnaces were continuously melting steel, the flames coming out of the chimneys would brighten Bethlehem's night sky as if it was daytime.

The town of Bethlehem was lively, dynamic and rich. Not only was it a university town bustling with students, but it was also home to professors, scholars and Bethlehem Steel executives. Like many other cities, blue-collar workers lived in one section of the town while the more affluent lived in more expensive neighborhoods. The neighboring town of Allentown was larger than Bethlehem with more activities and large shopping centers. The wealth of Bethlehem had spread to Allentown.

Lehigh University was founded in 1865 by Asa Packer, an industrialist and philanthropist, whose goal was to give a good education to the area's young men to prepare them for the technical leadership positions in industrial fields. Compared to the older and larger institutions, Lehigh was a uniquely small university with a very big reputation in its fields of education and research. Because of its manageable small size, students at Lehigh could get individual attentions and guidance from its distinguished faculty. The campus was very beautiful with stone, stucco and brick buildings among the majestic trees lined up on the slope of old South Mountain. The slopes, however, were on a very steep hillside making it very difficult even for the young men to go up and down every day. Each ivy-covered building was more beautiful than the other. The school had a real Ivy League atmosphere. When I was on the boat S/S Independence, I first found out that Lehigh's undergraduate school was all male students. I was very disappointed because there would be no girls for me to flirt with or date. Looking on the positive side however, I consoled myself by thinking that this way I could concentrate on my studies better just like I did at Namık Kemal High School.

Lehigh's affiliation with Bethlehem Steel raised its reputation in two engineering departments into national or even international levels. These were the Metallurgical Engineering and Civil Engineering Departments. In the Metallurgy Department, Professor Robert Stout, Dean of the Graduate School, Professor Joseph Libsch, head of the Department of Metallurgical Engineering, Professor George Conard, Director of Magnetic Materials Laboratory and many others were renowned in their fields with their teachings, research and extensive publications. Students in this department could get the best education in metallurgy while experiencing practical training at Bethlehem Steel. It was now very obvious to me why *Sümerbank* had chosen Lehigh for my metallurgical education. Similarly, the Civil Engineering Department benefited doing structural research and testing on large components manufactured by Bethlehem Steel. Fritz Engineering Laboratory was the headquarters for the Department of Civil Engineering. Mechanical Engineering and Chemical Engineering Departments were also very reputable.

Lehigh encouraged and with industry's support, financed ongoing research among its faculty whereby they published many papers and books. The school's environment was very conducive to studying and at last I felt like I belonged at this place. Being among so many well-known experts made me think how lucky and privileged I was to be here and be able to get one of the best technical educations anyone could possibly obtain. I realized it was up to me to make the best of this opportunity and in my heart I knew I was committed to do so.

As freshmen students we were assigned to the Freshmen Dormitory, the Clintic-Marshall Hall. The building consisted of three floors with all double rooms on each floor. The building was rather new and each room was comfortably furnished with two beds and two desks across from each other. It was far better than anything I had seen until now. The dormitories were on top of the hill and during the day we tried to minimize our exhausting climb. Once we trotted down from our dormitory we attended our classes until they were all finished and then we climbed the hill back to our rooms.

In September 1957 when I reported to Lehigh, I could feel in the overall atmosphere that this school, unlike the University of Kentucky, was going to be tough and competitive. I now found my match and I was ready for the challenge. In the first day of orientation for all freshmen, we were gathered in a very large auditorium. After a few welcoming and introductory remarks, the school officials reminded us the seriousness of our studies. The Admission Officer told us, "Look to your right and then look to your left. One of you will not be here next year." That was scary because I certainly did not want to be the one eliminated. I was determined not to be that one. Besides, *Sümerbank* required a high-grade average in order for our scholarship to continue. At the end of each semester our report cards were forwarded to the Turkish Educational Attaché in New York City for review.

The dining hall was at the University Center just below our dormitories. It was a short hike to the Center where we ate all our meals. For dinner we were required to wear a jacket and a tie. There was a formal atmosphere with the dining room tables covered with white linen tablecloths and all the students in jacket and tie attire. I bought my first blazer with a Lehigh emblem embroidered on the top pocket. I now looked like a real ivy-league student. The very first dinner served at the Center was a nice roast beef sliced to any size we wanted. This was just exquisite. A few days later however, when a pork roast was served, I told the kitchen staff that since I was a Muslim I could not eat pork and the vegetables would suffice. They felt very bad and took down my name and assured me that the next time they were serving pork they would prepare a special meal for me. A week later when everyone was being served a small slice of ham, my special meal turned out to be half a chicken. When the other students saw this special treat, they anxiously asked me how I got it. Before long, half of the student body claimed to be either Muslims or Jews just to get the special meal.

Freshman classes included introductory physics, chemistry and calculus. I had no problem with any of these classes. Here calculus was more advanced than the calculus I had at the University of Kentucky at the sophomore level. Even though I was a foreign student, I was in the same English literature class as the American students. Lehigh at that time did not have too many foreign students and those foreign students who were there were mostly graduate students. Although it was tough for me at the beginning, the English lessons introduced me to some excellent western literature. I mostly enjoyed Thomas Hardy's classic novel "Tess of the D'Urbervilles" which he wrote in 1891. To me his description of the rolling hills of the English countryside, which went on for pages, was extraordinary. I later read all of Thomas Hardy's books. Stephen Vincent Benet's book "John Brown's Body" taught me the horrors of the American Civil War of which I knew nothing about. I was learning many new and enjoyable things at school and I was very happy. I looked like a typical engineering student with piles of books covered with Lehigh book covers under one arm and a big slide rule casing hanging from my belt on the other side. We used our slide rules for all our numerical calculations including logarithmic and trigonometric numbers in lieu of using tables. I got to be very good with my slide rule, flipping it back and forth while doing my calculations. Computers were just starting at that time but we did not have them. The only single computer the school had was in the Mathematics Department.

When Christmas came, Bethlehem was decorated with beautiful lights everywhere. A gigantic cross was lit on top of the hill shining over the city. The city had embarked into the Christmas spirit. The City of Bethlehem was very proud of sharing the same name with the Sister City in the Holy Land. The people of Bethlehem tried to reflect that spirit in all their activities. Bethlehem was rich in historic traditions with picturesque houses, gardens and churches. In 1740 Moravians had settled in Bethlehem adding new diversity to the town's traditions and history. On Christmas Eve of 1957 Professor and Mrs. Eppes invited a few foreign students to their home. Professor Eppes was in the Mechanical Engineering Department and he was also our Foreign Student Advisor. After dinner the evening continued with attendance to the Moravian Church's midnight candlelight service. That evening I learned more about the meaning of Christmas and appreciated how Christian Americans profoundly believed in their religion.

When Gerald Leeman, our Physical Education instructor found out I was Turkish, he was elated. In 1948 at the London Olympics he had wrestled against Nasuh Akar in BantamWeight class (125 ¾ lbs.) and had lost. That year the Turkish Wrestling Team became world champions with four gold medals and two silver medals. Everybody in Turkey was very proud with our team's accomplishment and each wrestler had become a national hero. The names of the gold medal winners Nasuh Akar, Gazanfer Bilge, Celal Atik, Yaşar Doğu and silver medalists Halit Belamir and Adil Candemir became household names. Their pictures were everywhere and wrestling became the main national sport. Even I had tried to learn a little bit of wrestling in one of the clubs in Alsancak. Although Gerald Leeman was a silver medalist in the Olympics, he had a lot of admiration for the Turkish Wrestling Team and its members. He wanted to correspond with Nasuh Akar and asked me if I could help to locate him. I wrote several letters to Ankara and eventually found his address. I discovered with dismay that Nasuh Akar, our Olympic Gold Medalist was in Konya working as a head porter (*hammal*). How soon we had forgotten our heroes. With me as translator, Gerald Leeman and Nasuh Akar had some very pleasant correspondence going on for a while. When Leeman found out I had some wrestling training in Turkey, he decided that all Turks were good wrestlers and put me in Lehigh's freshman wrestling team. I did not last too long! I was physically weak, skinny and no match to well-fed, jacked American kids. At least that got me out of compulsory early morning swimming classes in the middle of winter and I was happy about that.

Besides me, Professor Fazil Erdoğan and Leon Bahar were the other two Turks at Lehigh. Professor Erdoğan had graduated from Istanbul Technical University in 1948 and had received his Ph.D. from Lehigh in 1955. Both Professor Erdoğan and Leon Bahar were in the Mechanical Engineering Department. Leon Bahar was a graduate of Roberts College in Istanbul and was working towards his Ph.D in Mechanical Engineering and Applied Mechanics. We rarely got to see Professor Erdoğan who was always busy with his teaching duties and research work. Leon Bahar and

I would often get together to talk in Turkish and reminisce about the old days in Turkey. This was my only chance to speak in Turkish since there were not too many Turkish people in the area we could socialize with. It was a very lonely situation. Since schoolwork kept us very busy, we would not get too nostalgic and low in our spirits because of our yearnings for our families and homeland. Homesickness however, always stayed with us. Remembering our old memories we had with our families and friends transformed in our minds as wonderful experiences we wanted to repeat. We knew one day we would again be with our loved ones and we were looking forward to that moment.

The Turning Point

In my sophomore year at Lehigh I moved to another dormitory, Taylor Hall. This was a very pleasant building with a center court. My roommate was Alfred Myers, one of the nicest, considerate and clean-cut individuals I have ever met in my life. He also came from a very modest family background. He could afford Lehigh only by being in the Army ROTC (Reserve Officers Training Corps) program. This program was designed not only to give some military training but also to develop individual character and attributes essential to an officer. Alfred was very proud of wearing his uniform whenever the occasion required and he looked very good in it. During my second Christmas holiday at Lehigh, Alfred invited me to his home in Western Pennsylvania, just south of Pittsburgh. His family lived on a farm and they were very hospitable and made me feel at home. I enjoyed driving their old tractor around the farm and eating home cooked meals. I spent a very pleasant Christmas holiday with the Myers family and forgot my loneliness at least for a few days during this festive occasion.

Schoolwork was getting hard and I was now taking profession related courses in metallurgy, chemistry and mechanics. My favorite classes, however, were mathematics and mechanics, which involved a lot of mathematical calculations. Metallurgy classes dealt with the understanding of the basis of the metals. We had to study the structural properties and processing of the metals and alloys. This required a lot of laboratory evaluation and observation of the true structure of the metals with photomicrography. We had to prepare specimens with metallographic polishing. In the metallurgy laboratory we labored for days by cutting and mounting the specimens, polishing and etching them to a defect free perfection. No matter how meticulously I polished, there was always a scratch on the surface of the specimen. That meant back to the grinding stone! To me this was very boring and I did not have my heart in it. In Advanced Physical Metallurgy classes, studying alloy equilibrium diagrams, to me seemed very dull and I was not enjoying these classes at all. Furthermore, the Metallurgy Department required a lot of chemistry courses. In my sophomore chemistry class we were studying the qualitative and quantitative evaluation of chemical compounds. One day in the laboratory I was using a pipette, which was a calibrated glass tube open on both ends. It was used to transfer volumes of liquid from the bottle into the test tube. In this case I was trying to transfer HCl, Hydrochloric Acid, to my test tube. I tried to suck a little bit of the acid with a small pipette but I did not see the top line of the liquid and I sucked a bit more. This time it was a very large amount, which came into my mouth. The acid burned the inside of my mouth instantly. I rinsed it with water right away but the burns inside of my mouth were very extensive. I was rushed to the school's dispensary where I had to stay for three days. I could not close my mouth nor could I eat anything. I was on a liquid diet being fed by tubes.

In my hospital bed I started thinking about my future and the direction I was going. I was not happy with the profession *Sümerbank* had chosen for me. This profession would be something I had to live with the rest of my life. I was unhappy and not at ease with myself. I felt I should do something about it. I therefore decided to change my major from metallurgical engineering to mechanical engineering. I had thought about it very thoroughly and extensively. Obviously *Sümerbank* would not accept my switching my major and there could be repercussions, such as stopping my scholarship, pulling me back to Turkey and demanding pay-back. I had nobody to depend on except myself. It was a very scary situation. No matter what the outcome would be I decided to switch majors. This was the turning point in my professional career and I felt a great relief. A lot of times it is not difficult to implement a plan or a program. What is most difficult is to make the decision and to stick to it. I did not immediately inform *Sümerbank* because my plan was to finish my undergraduate studies and then let them know. If they wanted pay-back then I would reimburse them by working somewhere.

In the second semester at the beginning of 1959 I was now a mechanical engineering student. The classes I was taking were heavily concentrated in mathematics, mechanics and structural engineering courses. I loved them and I was doing very well. In the Applied Mechanics classes our instructors, Professor Ferdinand Beer, a Frenchman, was also the head of the Applied Mechanics Department and Professor Deneuwelli, a German, were well known and highly experienced. I was taking thermodynamics class from my friend Professor Eppes. All in all, my schoolwork was now harmonious and enjoyable.

All my classes were in Packard Hall. The building was a five-story sandstone structure beautifully located at the entrance to the university. James Packard, who was a Lehigh University graduate, designer and founder of Packard Motor Car Company, donated it. The entrance to the building was decorated in a beautiful Italian style with the hallways covered in colorful marble. There were classrooms as well as Electrical and Mechanical Engineering laboratories in this building.

I did not have much of a social life because I did not have much money nor did I have a car. At Lehigh, to have a date with a girl from the neighboring colleges or just to get around, one needed to have a car. The popular girl's school for Lehigh students was the Cedar Crest College located on the outskirts of Allentown. Since I did not have a car, I could not indulge in any of those activities thus leaving me more time for my studies. On one occasion, one of my friends in my dormitory offered me his car to take his sister at Cedar Crest College on a date. I was very happy and excited at this opportunity. The car was a 1950 Ford, which was very popular at that time. It had a front grill that was streamlined like a torpedo. I was all dressed up and looking forward with great anticipation meeting my blind date. I drove through downtown Allentown to the end of Hamilton Boulevard to Cedar Crest College. When I met my date, it was a real big let down! She was not much to look at and she was quite fat. That is why it was a blind date, because nobody was taking her out. I took her to a movie in downtown Allentown and in a gentlemanly manner immediately returned her to her school afterward. At least I enjoyed driving the Ford.

Most of the time on weekends, I would go to the movies in Bethlehem alone. I walked down the hill and crossed over the Lehigh River on the rusted, iron bridge to Broad Street where the town's only two movie theaters were located. When I was on the bridge, I would stop and look at the Bethlehem Steel Plant with blast furnaces going at full rage with flames gushing out of the top. The plant was completely lit and looked very busy. The country was expanding continuously with new constructions everywhere. Bethlehem Steel, even with a three-shift operation, could hardly meet the demand. Bethlehem was a boomtown. At night when I was returning from the movies, I could feel the strong cold winds over the

Lehigh River trying to blow me away while the blast furnaces were still going strong. Back on campus, as I passed Packard Hall, I would see one little window on the third floor to be the only one lit in the whole dark building. My Turkish friend, Professor Fazil Erdoğan was still in his office laboring on a new research project in Fracture Mechanics.

I finished the school year successfully without many incidences. I was now on my way to becoming a mechanical engineer.

Junior Year

In the summer of 1959 I was feeling pretty good. I had my life directed the way I wanted by choosing mechanical engineering as my ultimate career. My schoolwork was coming along very well and I also had a very good summer job in the Fritz Engineering Laboratory. Fritz Laboratory, part of the Civil Engineering Department, was performing tests on very large structural components. The laboratory had the world's largest universal hydraulic testing machine, capable of applying a 5,000,000-lb. load to tension or compression members. This equipment was housed inside a seven-story building. The facility was used for research and development purposes in conjunction with Bethlehem Steel to test their products. My job was setting up tests on the tensile machine. On one occasion we were testing individual steel wire ropes manufactured for large suspension bridges. The steel rope was made of individual strands rolled into a large sturdy load-carrying component. The test basically involved establishing the maximum load carrying capability of the steel rope. Both ends of the rope were secured with very powerful vises of the test machine. Before the test started the entire building was evacuated. We started applying the load gradually with hydraulic power supplies going at full speed. The load was increased at 100,000-lb increments. Near 1,000,000-lbs we could hear from the strained noise it was generating, the component was reaching its limit. We could feel the building rattling with the large force applied by the tensile machine. The load was now being increased very slowly with loud squeaking noises coming from the straining of the steel wire rope. Not long after that the wire rope abruptly snapped and broke with a huge loud bang. Individual wire pieces, making up the steel rope, were flying and penetrating into the concrete wall like arrows. It was a major task to remove these pieces from the wall. This was my first job getting involved with technical projects and I was thoroughly enjoying it and was happy to have such an opportunity.

Whenever I had the time, I went to New York City to be with my friends. By this time my high school friend Değer Tunç was in New York attending Columbia University. I had helped Erdem Tunçsiper to come to the United States by finding someone to write an Affidavit of Support for him. Erdem was living with Değer in an apartment in Manhattan near Columbia University. Another friend, Hüseyin Aktuğ, from my Namık Kemal High School was also in New York. Visiting them periodically in New York City made me feel great and made me forget being homesick. With Erdem's coming to the States, my father and mother had lost their helper in reading and writing my letters. They would use whomever they could find for our communications with letters. It had been almost four years since I talked with my parents and heard their voices. Since they did not have a telephone, I could not call them. I continuously wrote to them and sent them money as often as I could. In the evenings, alone in my room, when the lonely moments occupied my thoughts, I realized how much I had missed them.

Back at Lehigh, in September of 1959 a new school year had started. I was taking many mechanical engineering classes with mechanical design and mechanical engineering laboratories. In a machine design course, "Operation of Mechanisms", our professor made us buy some cheap but famous Japanese "tin toys" and told us to take them apart. It was very interesting and impressive to see the technical details of complex mechanisms the Japanese had built into these "tin toys". All the design principles we were learning in our mechanism class were already incorporated into these cheap Japanese products. They were making full use of the existing technology while copying the new ones. The Japanese were just starting to build their industry from the ashes of WWII. At that time Japanese products had the reputation of being cheap and not very good. They were however gradually and diligently expanding their country to become a leading industrial nation and technological powerhouse in later years. It was a very impressive success story.

Although Lehigh emphasized technical training for its engineering students to the fullest, additional courses in liberal arts were required for all to broaden their vision and enrich their personal lives. In one of my liberal arts classes, I studied the philosophy of contemporary civilization and read a book by George Santayana, entitled "The Life of Reason". This Spanish born, Harvard University instructor's philosophical approach to the relationship of the mind and life was very difficult for me to understand. I struggled through this course. I then decided to learn more about

Christianity since I was living among them. I signed up for a course on religion. On the first day, the teacher gave us a brief quiz, asking questions such as naming the first four books of the Old Testament. I did not know any of the answers. Most of the students in the class were Catholics and they could answer all the questions. They were only taking the course to get a good grade to raise their average. I went to the teacher all perplexed and explained that I was a Muslim and I was taking this course to learn about Christianity. He assured me that the first test was to see how much everyone knew and that he would evaluate the individuals with the progress they made. I spent the following evenings reading the Bible while everybody else was suffering through the Advanced Mathematics homework problems. I got a better understanding and appreciation of all three major religions, Christianity, Judaism, and Islam and about how similar they all were. I was also enjoying the broader education I was getting at Lehigh besides heavy engineering subjects. I finished my religion class with a paper entitled "Religion In Modern Life" and got a B for the class.

My scholarship from *Sümerbank* continued coming but I knew I would have to pay it back one day. I was living with the fear of them finding out about my major change and the money could be cut at any time. But I believed in the philosophy "nothing ventured, nothing gained", so I ventured forward.

The Cosmopolitan Club was an association for the international students at Lehigh. In my junior year I got elected to be the President of the Cosmopolitan Club. After my Columbia University fiasco of loosing the election, this felt good. That same year my Turkish friend Professor Erdoğan became the Foreign Student Advisor. Our club was very active holding meetings and bringing the foreign student body together with the Americans for mutual understanding and appreciation of each other's cultures. Most of the time I was able to find guest speakers; mostly professors from various departments to speak at our meetings. That year I was in charge, as the President of the Club, to arrange the Christmas gathering for the international students with American guests. I arranged our party to be held at the home of a Bethlehem Steel executive. The family was very generous in opening their home for us. I persuaded Professor Erdoğan, who was always busy with his research work, to come this time since he was the Foreign Student Advisor. I must have made a good convincing argument because he did come. The host family had a lovely daughter, Barbara, who had taken charge of the activities in her home. She was very tall, attractive and a friendly young lady.

Our Christmas party was very successful and everybody enjoyed themselves. It must have been Professor Erdoğan's lucky day since he had the opportunity to meet Barbara at our party. Not long after that, they got married. I was pleased that I had something to do with that happy development. Leon Bahar and I were among the honored guests at their lovely wedding in Bethlehem.

Research Assistant at Lehigh

During my senior year at Lehigh I moved to a one-bedroom apartment on the first floor of a building on Fourth Street in town. Across from my apartment in the building was a lawyer's office. One of the lawyers was Nick Carboliadis, a Greek-American. Nick and I became very good friends. I bought a used car, a yellow 1955 Chevrolet BelAir. It was a beautifully designed car that later in time became a well-known classic. My car was always parked in the back of my apartment, which made me feel important. I was now getting accustomed to American way of life. Only one block from my building was a very popular nightclub known as the Mexican Club. Since there was not much social life in Bethlehem, this club was well attended by the locals. Entrance to the club was by membership only and Lehigh students were not allowed to join. They felt the students would over run the club. The Mexican friends I had made at the Cosmopolitan Club at Lehigh secured a free membership for me at this Mexican Club. The place was always packed and it became a place I enjoyed going to frequently. There were a lot of Latin girls who could dance to any type of music. When they asked me to dance, I told them I did not know how to. They took this as a challenge and decided to teach me all the Latin dances like the Cha-Cha-Cha, Samba, Rumba, Fox Trot, Tango and Merengue. All winter long I labored on these dances with the same girls at the club. In the evenings alone in my room I would practice these steps until I perfected them. By the end of the winter I was getting quite good and comfortable on the dance floor. My Mexican Club experience during my Lehigh days taught me how to dance and I enjoyed dancing at every opportunity the rest of my life. My favorite dance however was still the slow dance!

In my senior year in one of the advanced mathematics classes I met a Turkish girl, Sumru Alp who was a new graduate student. In our math exams she would tell me she was going to get an A but ended up getting lower grades than I. When I asked her what had happened she explained that she always aimed for the highest grade and hoped to get close to it. From her I learned to always aim for the top.

During this time, I met a Cedar Crest College student from Allentown whose name was Elaine Sherman. She was a very nice girl and we became good friends. Since I now had a car, I had mobility and I could go to Allentown very easily. Her parents were divorced. Elaine and her two sisters were living in a small apartment on Walnut Street together with their mother. Her father had remarried and was living with his new wife and three additional children in a house outside of Allentown on a small hill. He raised chickens in his small yard just like my father was raising them at home in Turkey. I helped Elaine's father build a machine, which I called the "Chicken Plucker" which was a big rotating cylinder with corrugated rubber fingers protruding out of the cylinder. The rotating rubber fingers would pluck the chicken's feathers when they hit the chicken. It needed some adjustments on the rotating speed of the cylinder before the design was fully operational. I was already acting like a mechanical engineer.

I spent a lot of time at the University's library. It was a very impressive building with Gothic style architecture all covered with ivy. I liked going to the library and being among the students and the books. The library was nice and quiet and I could get a lot of studying done. I could concentrate better here just like I did when I was getting ready for my entrance exams at the *Atatürk Library* in Izmir. By the time the summer of 1960 came, since I had switched majors, I was short of a few courses to graduate. I had to continue taking courses for one more semester.

That summer I got a job as a Research Assistant with Professor Erdoğan who was just promoted to the position of Associate Professorship. His research work on Fracture Mechanics was continuing and he was publishing many papers on his research dealing with a new concept of "crack tip stress intensity factors". With his work on Fracture Mechanics, Professor Erdoğan became internationally known and distinguished expert who brought a lot of fame and research funding from industry and government to Lehigh University. While he was continuing his analytical work together with Professor George Sih, I was hired as a research assistant to do experimental work to verify their analysis. At this time I was still an undergraduate student. Although it was unusual for an undergraduate student to get a research assistantship, I felt very privileged working together with well-known professors on the forefront of technology.

At the end of 1960 I completed my school work requirements and received my Bachelor of Science degree in Mechanical Engineering from

Lehigh University. I stayed at Lehigh to continue towards my Master's degree besides; I already had a research assistantship. It seemed like schoolwork would move very smoothly from here on.

Graduate Student at Lehigh

In the early 1960's universities emphasized research and publications. The concept of "publish or perish" was well known and readily accepted among the university staff. Each school had one or more research institute specializing on various subjects. The university staff members would get proper recognition and awards by the amount of money they brought to the school and the number of papers they published. This created a lot of anxiety and competitive environment among the professors. Professor Erdoğan started the Fracture Mechanics Research Institute at Lehigh University with financial support from the Boeing Aircraft Company. Boeing was interested in fully understanding the stress distribution on the aircraft's outer shell especially on locations with the riveted joints. These rivet holes were susceptible to stress concentrations and to possible crack initiation and propagation. The subject of Fracture Mechanics later gained importance in ship building when large super tankers and dry-load ships would split into two in the middle of the ocean caused by crack propagation from the rivet holes. The US Navy also supported projects on Fracture Mechanics at Lehigh. The three Turks, Professor Erdoğan, Leon Bahar and I were the original members of this Institute. Leon was working towards his Ph.D. and I was a new graduate from Lehigh working towards my Master's degree. I was now financially in a good position getting a salary as a Research Assistant and still receiving scholarship money from *Sümerbank*. I was putting the scholarship money aside to pay *Sümerbank* back in the near future.

By the time I started Graduate School at Lehigh, I had already completed most of the advance courses during my senior year. What were left behind were rather difficult and specialized subjects. Most of our studies included works by Timoshenko and Sokolnikof on the Theory of Elasticity and Plasticity and Dynamics of Rigid Bodies. These were of Russian origin, analytical works with heavy emphasis on mathematics. Work by Mushkelishvili was the basis of the analytical studies on Fracture Mechanics. It was ironic because we had finished the English based books and were now studying Russian works. I noticed a parallelism between this and my high school mathematics class when our teacher Rifat Türkeli was using French mathematics books after we had finished the Turkish ones. "History repeats itself," they say. I found this to be true many times during my lifetime. Russian works were mostly analytical with very advanced and complicated mathematics. My professors Fazil Erdoğan and George Sih were very good in analytical studies. My research work, however, concentrated on the experimental verification of their analysis. I was designing and building test set ups to run tests to evaluate the behavior of cracks under different types of loading. I was full of energy and enthusiasm and I liked what I was doing. I was fast at everything I did. One day Professor Erdoğan said about me" I cannot keep up with that guy's activities". Before long I finished my first research project in August 1961 and submitted it as my Master's Thesis one year prior to my graduation. In 1962 it was published as an ASME (American Society of Mechanical Engineers) paper entitled "An Experimental Investigation of the Crack Tip Stress Intensity Factors in Plates under Cylindrical Bending". The following abstract of the ASME paper briefly explains the contents of the research work I did as a young engineer.

"This experimental study was undertaken to investigate the validity of the theory based on the crack tip stress intensity factors to explain the fracture of thin cracked plates subjected to static bending moments. Plexiglas sheets were used as specimens and the loading was pure cylindrical bending. The results indicate that there is in fact a critical value of the stress intensity factor at which the crack starts growing. It was found that, while in static tensile tests the crack growth was unstable, in case of bending, the external load (here, the bending moment) which starts the crack growing is not sufficient for the complete fracture of the plate if it is maintained constant. That is, when the critical value of the stress intensity factor is reached, the crack starts growing on the tensile side of the plate whereupon the crack tip takes a triangular shape and the system again becomes stable. In order to make the crack grow further, a considerable increase in the load is required."

In spite of some difficulties I felt I had come a long way from my Namık Kemal High School days. I was pleased with myself that at the age of 24 I was doing some advance research work and publishing technical papers. In the following period my research work continued to verify more advance concepts of evaluating crack tip behavior under combined loading especially under pure shear loading. I designed and built a new test set up to apply pure torsional load on a big Aluminum cylinder. My initial work on this test rig was subjecting the test cylinder with a crack only to static loading. The crack tip was subjected to various types of loading with good results being obtained from my test rig. The test set up was working very well. After I graduated and left Lehigh, a Ph.D. candidate took over my research and completed his thesis on this torsional rig by extending his work to dynamic loading. I was pleased that my test rig was put to good use even after I had graduated.

Some of the mathematical techniques we learned in graduate school, called "Relaxation Methods", which involved numerical solutions of harmonic and biharmonic equations, later became extinct with the advent of computers. During the time I was in school however, computers were not used much. We resorted to solving engineering problems to analytical techniques mostly as "boundary value" problems. My favorite subject however was "Optimization Problems in Mathematics" where I learned that optimization techniques could be applied to everything we do in everyday life. By the time I graduated in May of 1962, we three Turks had made an excellent reputation at Lehigh. This paved and opened the opportunities for many Turkish students that followed us for decades.

Life on a personal level was somewhat dismal, with full of loneliness and resignation. My schoolwork however kept me extremely busy from feeling sorry for myself. It had been six years since I had seen my mother and father, or heard their voices on the telephone. They seemed like they were doing fine based on the periodic letters I received from them, which was written by others on their behalf. It was not the same as if they had written them themselves. Even if they had problems and concerns they would not write to me and have me worried. My father and mother now spent all their time missing and anxiously waiting for their son whom they had not seen for six years to return which would not happen for some time. They did not have much to do except wait for the mailman to deliver a letter from me. When none came, my mother would walk to the Main Post Office at *Gümrük* and ask if there was a letter from her son in America. When the answer was negative, she would walk back disappointed and sad with tears in her eyes hoping the letter would come the next day. As a student I could not do much for them except send them some money periodically to make their life a little easier. I always wished to be with them but because of schoolwork and striving to succeed I could not spare time for them and not even for myself. The loneliness and missing them usually got worse when our *Bayrams*, religious holidays came around. Oh, how much I yearned to be with them and be able to kiss their hands! I did not have much contact with any other Turkish people since there were very few of them around, but we always seeked them everywhere.

I was still living in my Fourth Street apartment and occasionally getting together with Leon Bahar for coffee at the corner coffee shop. I sometimes ventured to the Mexican Club to meet the girls and dance. I enjoyed dancing and was getting better with time, not like my days in the Naples night club or at the Arthur Murray Dance Studio. I was now 25 years old and graduating from Lehigh with a Master's Degree. I was popular with girls and they thought I was a "good catch". Most of the girls I met were interested in getting married but I was not ready for that. I was still seeing Elaine who was also waiting with marriage in mind. I thought it was time for me to leave Bethlehem and do what we as students always said "to get out there and learn life".

In reality, at this point in my life, I was supposed to return back to Turkey and start my 12-year stint with *Sümerbank*. First of all I had kept from *Sümerbank* that I did not become a Metallurgical Engineer but instead a Mechanical Engineer; secondly, all along I was planning to leave *Sümerbank* and pay them back; and thirdly, in the future I wanted to get a Ph.D. These thoughts directed me towards looking for a job. With the opportunities there were in the United States, there was no reason for me to rush back to Turkey. I did not think too far beyond that. I signed up for interviews with the companies that came recruiting at the school. After the initial school interviews with seven companies that I signed up with, I received invitations from all of them to go to their plants for interviews and plant visits. All the plant visits were very pleasant. Everyone I met was very cordial and professional. These plant visits for me were real eye openers. I realized for as much as I knew the basics of engineering from the text books I did not really know much about the actual machinery the industry was designing and building. It was a scary and humiliating experience. After the plant visits and interviews all seven companies, which included Ford Motors Company, Allis Chalmers, SKF Bearing Industries, General Electric Company and Sperry Gyroscopes, offered me jobs with slightly varying salaries. With all the offers coming in, I was confused and did not know what to do. I simply could not make a decision. I found myself in the same situation as I was when I had just graduated from high school and I could not decide whether to stay at Istanbul Technical University or go to America with *Sümerbank*'s scholarship. At that time I had gone to see my high school principal to help guide me with my decision. Again, history repeats itself. I went to see Professor Owczarek, my Fluid Mechanics professor, who had just come to Lehigh from General Electric Company. After reviewing all the offers I had very thoroughly and discussing them with me one by one, Professor Owczarek recommended that I accept General Electric's offer. Based on his experience at GE, he assured me that I would have a lot of opportunities to learn much more at General Electric while I was working. I would be working with some of the best engineers and scientists in the country.

Although GE was not the highest paying company, it offered better opportunities and brighter prospects for the future. Finally, after much procrastination on my decision I decided to accept General Electric's offer and join the Company's Large Steam Turbine-Generator Department in Schenectady, New York. Oh, what a relief! It is amazing how wonderful it feels after one makes a big decision.

I attended the graduation ceremonies at Lehigh and received my Master's Degree in Mechanical Engineering in May 1962 on a Sunday. That afternoon I packed my few belongings and my textbooks into my 1955 Chevy and bid farewell to Lehigh University and to Bethlehem. I thought my student days were over, at least for the time being. As I drove to Schenectady, I was nervous and scared, wondering about the future. That Sunday night I checked into a hotel and the next morning I reported to work at GE. Without any break I was now starting to work at General Electric that would continue for the next forty years. At the time I did not imagine that I was going to work for one company for such a long time, nor was it planned that way. It was what we called in our religious belief, my "kısmet" (fate), or "alın yazısı" (written on my forehead). I really believed that. It seemed like all my life I had been either studying or working without any break. Very little time was allocated to myself to play, travel or even just to relax and enjoy myself. Luckily, I liked studying and working and that became a good substitute. I, however, did not enjoy my childhood and youth much because I was too busy.

Five Turkish students America bound in front of Acropolis, January 21, 1956

On the streets of Rome, January 1956

Queens College students sightseeing around Manhattan

At a dance at the University of Kentucky with Mümin Köksoy, February 1957

Lehigh University student, 1958

Lehigh University graduation, 1960

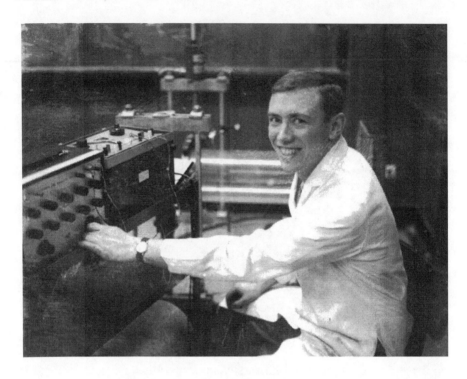

Research Assistant at Lehigh University, 1962

With my parents at the 1964 World's Fair in New York

9

General Electric Company

Schenectady, New York

Schenectady is located in upstate New York about 180 miles north of New York City and 240 miles south of Montreal, Canada. Schenectady was founded in 1661 by Dutch pioneers under the leadership of Arendt Van Curler. It lies on the shores of the Mohawk River at the eastern side of the scenic and mountainous Mohawk Valley. The Dutch influence in Schenectady was visible in much of the architecture of the historic Stockade District near Front Street and lower Union Street that included homes built in the 1700-1850 period. Van Curler's name was given to a hotel, a restaurant and to a square in the beautiful Stockade area. Early American history can be seen and felt at every corner of this historical district. In the neighboring cities, the Dutch influence can further be seen where some cities are named; Amsterdam and Rotterdam. Originally this area and the surrounding mountains and forests were home to the Mohawk Indians. In the Stockade area an exquisite bust of a Mohawk Indian adorns the square reminding visitors of the early inhabitants of this territory. Further up along Union Street, the Union College campus is spread out in the middle of the city. Union College, which opened in 1795, has a beautifully designed campus and a great reputation as a small educational institution. The engineering school at Union College has always been supported by General Electric Company and by its well known engineers. Union College also presented a good opportunity for General Electric employees, especially engineers to further advance their education while working. General Electric always encouraged its employees in their endeavors for their educational advancements and paid for their tuition with a tuition reimbursement program without any obligation, quite contrary to my scholarship from *Sümerbank*.

In the early 1960's, General Electric Company in Schenectady was at its peak employing over 40,000 people working in its many departments. GE in Schenectady had a long history and it would not be surprising to find many third generation Schenectadians who were all employed by General Electric. Located at one end of Erie Boulevard, GE had installed a very large GENERAL ELECTRIC sign on one of its main tall buildings illuminated by hundreds of GE bulbs. This logo dominated the entire General Electric plant and made quite an impression when lit at night. On the other end of Erie Boulevard, ALCO, a locomotive company was located. ALCO (American Locomotive Company) was the second largest manufacturing plant and employer in Schenectady and was well known for its diesel locomotives. ALCO had a great reputation for the quality of its products and engineering know-how. With the two industrial giants located on either end of Erie Boulevard, Schenectady was well known as a high technology manufacturing city.

Next to the historical area of Schenectady was the downtown shopping area, lively with its many small shops and eateries lined up along State Street. Proctor's Theater, centrally located on State Street, was a 1926 vaudeville house with many Broadway shows, dance and music events happening periodically. Downtown was a desired location where GE employees took their walks along Erie Boulevard during their lunch break to enjoy the shops or one of the many eating establishments. The German restaurant, Nicholaus, at the corner of Erie Boulevard and State Street, was a well-known and popular site for its German knockwurst, sauerkraut and beer.

Another scenic place in Schenectady was the Rose Garden in Central Park with beautiful flower gardens to be enjoyed in the spring and summer. The small pond in the center of the park was home to some of the most beautiful swans I had ever seen. I enjoyed watching them glide on the surface of the water, especially the rare black swans. There were also ducks and geese in this beautiful pond. The geese however were easily agitated and would sometimes attack people around the park.

The Mohawk River starts at the magnificent Adirondack National Preserve and the Adirondack Mountains and runs from west to east until it joins the Hudson River near Troy, New York. The Mohawk River separated Schenectady from Scotia, which were connected with a long bulky concrete bridge. In the summertime many of us GE employees ventured to the Scotia side of the Mohawk River shores to enjoy barbecued large hamburgers at the local fast food restaurant, Jumping Jacks. Unfortunately, we could see the increased pollution of the river with dead fish and dead birds floating on the surface of this big and once beautiful river. Years later GE was found guilty of polluting this river with PCB and after years of appeals, GE agreed to pay for the cleanup of the river.

One can take a short drive about 30 miles north of Schenectady to visit Saratoga Springs well known for its Revolutionary War history. The Saratoga National Historical Park is 3200 acres of vast battlefield park with Saratoga Victory Monument highlighting the area. The park commemorates the battles of Saratoga, fought on September 19 and October 7, 1777 in which General Horatio Gates' American forces defeated General John Burgoyne's British forces. The most critical battle in North America came early in the war when Gen. Burgoyne, marching south from Montreal was defeated and surrendered on October 7, 1777 to the American forces near Schuylerville (Old Saratoga) preventing the British control of the Hudson Valley. The victory at Saratoga over the British is considered the turning point of the Revolutionary War. Besides being an important historical site, Saratoga Springs is reknown for its thoroughbred races and reputed hot water mineral spring spas. At the beginning of the 1900's it was the summer destination of the "rich and famous" New Yorkers. Even now in August the thoroughbred races at the Saratoga racecourse bring large crowds of spectators to this very famous site. In the middle of this lovely city is Skidmore College, an excellent private women's educational institution.

Further north of Saratoga is a summer resort village located at the southern edge of the 32-mile long Lake George, known with the same name. Lake George is the gateway to the vast and majestic Adirondack Mountains, forest preserves, lakes and rivers. The Adirondack region encompasses about two thirds of upstate New York State. Outdoor enthusiasts and nature lovers frequent this spectacular natural beauty. At the southern edge of the Adirondacks, the Sacandaga Reservoir is a huge man-made lake connected with a dam to the Hudson River. The water in this reservoir is said to be used to maintain proper water level on the Hudson near New York City.

Just south of Schenectady, the state capitol of Albany is only 15 miles away. In 1962 when I arrived to this area, the downtown section of Albany was run down and dilapidated. Although the renewal construction had just started, it was completed years later with the personal efforts and commitments of Governor Nelson Rockefeller changing the downtown area into a modern government office, cultural and convention centers. The eleven building skyscraper complex named Governor Nelson A. Rockefeller Empire State Plaza not only rejuvenated the downtown area but it could be seen from miles away outside the city as an impressive landmark.

To the east of Schenectady, the old industrial city of Troy is located on the shores of the Hudson River. Because of the waterpower, during the 19th century it became an important mill town. Troy's Rensselear Polytechnic Institute is one of the nation's foremost technological institutions of higher learning and one of the oldest engineering schools in the country. Russell Sage College in Troy is another well-known women's private school for higher education.

The tri-city area of Schenectady, Albany and Troy was a very dynamic, exciting, industrial, educational and governmental area. Being located along the Hudson-Mohawk River Valley and near the Adirondacks, the tri-city enjoyed comfortable, rich and reputable tradition and benefited from its rich heritage.

From May 1962 until December 1978, to me Schenectady was a special, unique area and most importantly it was my home, giving me a new sense of belonging and a feeling of security. During the next 16-year period I enjoyed being in Schenectady and the tri-city area and benefited from all kinds of wonderful opportunities the community offered. Here I started my profession and my family with three wonderful children. For me it was a period of personal and professional growth with many accomplishments that gave a positive and fulfilling direction to our lives. I was very happy to be in Schenectady attending my work at General Electric while I was raising my family.

Early Years at General Electric

In his small laboratory in New Jersey, Thomas Edison had experimented on everything varying from electric bulbs to telephones. He held more patents than anyone else in the United States. He was a pragmatist, an engineer, a scientist and a genius. In 1879 Thomas Edison demonstrated the incandescent electric light and in 1882 he built the first electric lighting station on Pearl Street in New York City. At the same time, in 1885 Elihu Thomson was experimenting with alternating current. Edison's incandescent lamp, though not the first electric light, was the first to be conveniently small and it could be turned on and off at will. The central power station, which he devised on Pearl Street, used a dynamo or generator, was a fairly efficient machine but it had to be driven by means of a steam piston engine that was very cumbersome. In 1901 Charles G. Curtis successfully developed the first steam turbine generator in practical form in the United States. The early developments of the electric lamp, central power station and the steam turbine-generator, three main ingredients, brought to the country electric power which became one of the cornerstones of our civilization and the main business of the General Electric Company.

It is said that one day when Thomas Edison was traveling to Buffalo, New York by train he noticed an empty row of old brick buildings in a small town and he inquired about them. Not long after that Edison bought the building complex and in 1886 transferred his Edison Machine Works from New York City to Schenectady, setting into motion the events that would establish Schenectady, New York as the site where the forerunners of all modern steam turbine-generator were developed. It was a period of rapid growth and expansion in the electrical industry. As the demand for electricity grew, improvements and refinements in the equipment used to generate electricity were needed. In 1892 the leading electrical firms of that time, the Edison Company and Elihu Thomson's Thomson-Houston electrical plant in Lynn, Massachusetts were brought together establishing the General Electric Company under the leadership of Charles Coffin. This consolidation of industrial resources led to great advances in the design and manufacture of electrical equipment under the auspices of the General Electric Company. Parallel to the growth of the electric power consumption in the country, the business of General Electric grew rapidly making the plant in Schenectady a mega-complex industrial center.

When I joined the General Electric Company in Schenectady in 1962, the GE plants were scattered at every corner of the city. The world-reknown General Electric Research Laboratory had moved to a new building complex in Niskayuna, a beautiful suburb of Schenectady. The Research Laboratory specialized in electronics, material sciences and chemistry with very famous Nobel Prize winners, scientists and engineers continuously developing new materials and products. Just like Edison's laboratory, General Electric's first industrial laboratory was born in a barn behind the house of GE's own genius Dr. Charles Proteus Steinmetz in Schenectady in 1900. Under the guidance of Dr. Willis Rodney Whitney, the concept of industrial research and development took root and flourished. Over the years at GE's Research Laboratory new ideas and products evolved varying from the tungsten lamp, x-ray tubes, silicones, and diamonds and to the new fields of meteorology and high energy physics. The General Engineering Laboratory in downtown Schenectady however, concentrated more in mechanical and electrical engineering topics. I had heard of the names of some of the famous people working in this laboratory when I was a student at Lehigh. These two laboratories were later consolidated into one as the General Electric Research and Development Center (R&DC) continuing innovations even to this date in a wide range of research targets. Next to the Research Laboratory in Niskayuna was Knoll's Atomic Power Laboratory. In this facility General Electric developed nuclear reactors for the US Navy to be used in submarines and aircraft carriers. The most significant innovation since World War II has been the spectacular nuclear-powered submarines and super carriers. General Electric's propulsion turbines and reduction gear units also furnished these vessels.

The Large Motor Department, Gas Turbine Department and Large Steam Turbine-Generator (LSTG) Department were three other major departments in GE's main plant in downtown Schenectady. The Large Motor Department manufactured the largest possible DC motors, mostly for steel-mill drive systems and other applications. The Gas Turbine business was growing rapidly in industrial applications for process and pipeline services and as peeking-units supplementing additional power next to steam turbines. It was the Steam Turbine-Generator business however that revolutionized the field of power generation.

At the turn of the century, massive reciprocating steam engines produced most power but were unpractical even for small power needs. It all began in 1896 when Charles G. Curtis of New York arrived at the Schenectady office of the newly consolidated General Electric Company's Vice President, E.W.Rice with a new idea of steam turbine that would radically change the drive of dynamos or generators. After technical and financial evaluations, Rice recommended Coffin to support Curtis's idea to develop a more efficient and economical machine to supply power to meet the growing demands. Another GE engineer, William LeRoy Emmet, joined Curtis and in 1900 two small steam turbines of 5,000 kilowatts were jointly designed and built by the Curtis-Emmet team. Successful testing of these turbines opened the way for the first commercial 5,000 kilowatts vertical shaft turbine to be designed and built. Commonwealth Edison Company of Chicago bought the first two of the 5,000 kilowatts turbines and began the successful operation in 1903. The success of these turbines gave further impetus to GE's rapid growth and was the beginning of a brand new business. The steam turbine-generator industry was destined to be one of GE's largest. By 1909 the design and efficiency of GE turbines had so drastically improved that two large sets at 12,500 kilowatts were shipped to replace previous Commonwealth Edison turbines. Over the years and decades that followed, the vertical shaft concept was discontinued. To improve and refine the early designs, thousands of GE men and women devoted their energies to making steam turbines much bigger and more efficient and reliable. The modern turbine evolved through many improvements as the product of GE's impressive new and radical design.

Little did I know when I joined General Electric Company's Large Steam Turbine-Generator (LST-G) Department in 1962 that I would spend the next 25 years of my professional life in the turbine business. I felt very priveleged and honored to follow the footsteps of the industry's giants: Thomas Edison, Charles Curtis, William L.R.Emmet, Charles Coffin, Edwin Rice, Dr. Charles P. Steinmetz, William Campbell and later my friend Charles Elston. In the following years, I was able to make some significant contributions of my own to GE's turbine business. During the period I was associated with LST-G Department, the turbine size grew from 200,000 kilowatts to an impressive 1,300,000 kilowatts (1,300 megawatts) for nuclear power plant applications.

Because of the rapidly increasing power generation business and the big demand for GE's turbine-generators, in 1950 the entire business was moved to a new building: Building 273, which was the world's largest turbine manufacturing facility. It was a big financial commitment for GE but it certainly paid off. When I walked through this building during my interview, I was overwhelmed to see two levels of cranes up above carrying huge turbine and generator rotor forgings, generator stators and turbine casings which were all being manufactured on the floor. For as much as I had an excellent textbook education at Lehigh, I did not know much about turbine-generators. To me they were all rotating machinery. Who would not want to be a part of this most exciting technology and industry? I was just happy and excited to be here. One of the most interesting processes in the turbine-generator business at that time was that everything was being manufactured in GE's Schenectady plant and some other satellite plants. Nothing was "out-sourced" and there were no "farm-outs". GE's own foundries would cast the steel turbine casings. Huge generator stators and rotors were machined, manufactured, assembled and tested in Building 273. Complex turbine blades, which were called "buckets", were all manufactured in the plant using a procedure where 4 to 6 blades were manufactured simultaneously following a master. Buckets were assembled on the turbine wheels and were finally tested. GE's work force was highly experienced and very capable.

Charles Elston, a well-known turbine engineer, headed the LST-G Department and Carl Schabtach managed the Engineering Division. Both of these engineers were graduates of GE's famed Advanced Engineering Program. This department had gathered some of the best engineers and manufacturing personnel in the country. The Materials and Process Laboratory was a special Laboratory established to support the turbine business and General Electric gave special importance to ongoing training of its personnel. Just like in the universities, GE encouraged the publication of technical papers. Some of the well-known names in various technical fields were GE people especially in turbine technology. High level technology was one of the features that had attracted me to GE. Turbine Engineering was divided into different groups in accordance with turbine components: turbine casings, stationary parts, turbine controls, turbine accessories and turbine rotating parts called Bucket and Rotor Engineering. I was hired as a young apprentice engineer to be in the Bucket and Rotor Engineering group.

Bucket and Rotor Engineering

The manager of the Bucket and Rotor (B&R) Engineering Unit, Abdon (Don) Rubio, had interviewed and hired me to his group. Don Rubio was originally from Brooklyn and was a brilliant engineer. He had written most of the bucket vibration calculation computer programs that were being used at the time. He had a very strong engineering team working on the design, development and field service of the turbine buckets and rotors, the most critical components of the turbine.

A steam turbine is simple in principle but its improved efficiency and high reliability, that are of utmost importance, are obtained in the way it is designed and with the extreme accuracy it is built. Steam at very high temperatures of over 1,000 Degrees Fahrenheit and at extremely high pressures of over 3,500 pounds per square inch enters the turbine casing and impacts the first stage buckets. The impact of the steam moves buckets sideways and starts the rotor turning. The steam then rushes through the succeeding sets of nozzles and rows of buckets, called wheels, adding to the spinning of the rotor. The turbine buckets operate in extremely severe conditions of very high temperatures and pressures in the first stages and at supersonic speeds at the tip of last stages. This makes the Bucket and

Rotor Engineer's job very challenging. Since the buckets and the rotors are moving components in addition to static calculations, a precise vibratory evaluation of each row of buckets is one of the basis of the reliability of the turbine.

I started working at General Electric on June 1, 1962. I was assigned to the design group with Team Leaders Joe Ouellette and George Thiessen and worked with Art Wheeler and Earl Barnes. Since I was the only new hiree and also the youngest in the group, these people looked after me and were always ready to help me. I now had to learn all about turbines from these coworkers. My very first assignment was the design of a turbine bucket dovetail that attaches the bucket to the wheels. Before long I mastered the dovetail stress calculations. Designing a steam turbine was a major undertaking with many teams working diligently on each individual turbine design. Each unit was built to order to fill particular power requirements of the customer's power plant. Each design would have periodic design reviews where representatives from different components would present their design and the drafting department would generate a quarter size drawing. After the design calculations were finalized, the drafting department, paying utmost attention to tight clearances among components, would draw the full size drawing. I first attended these design reviews together with a senior engineer. In six months I was presenting my own designs of two 125 MW (megawatts) units for Southern California Edison's El Segundo plant by myself. I was very happy to see all the engineering principles I had learned in school being applied to real life designs and all the mechanical principles being turned into real machines. In this case it was generating electricity for millions of people all over the world. I felt we engineers were doing some useful things for society and for the well being of our fellow men.

I had rented a one-bedroom apartment in downtown Schenectady in the Stockade area on Union Street. It was a beautiful, historical neighborhood with the Edison Club right down the street. After I got acclimated with the town, I needed to make some friends. Across from my apartment was an old church. I met some of the young members of this church who invited me to a weekend camping trip in the Adirondacks. When we arrived at the campground, the first night we slept in sleeping bags. This was my first real camping experience. Except for a wild bear scare, which turned out to be a hoax, it was a pleasant experience to be outdoors. The next morning we picked up our canoes and headed for the lake. We were to paddle from one end of the lake to the other like Mohawk Indians. I had no prior experience paddling and to my luck a very heavy girl was assigned to my canoe who did not like paddling. I had to do all the work and paddle. In the heat of the day paddling with a single paddle was a very torturous work. I was a mile behind when the others arrived on shore. After lunch I had to carry the canoe to another lake. I turned the canoe upside down with my head sticking inside the canoe and I lifted it on my shoulders. My fat friend was no help. Luckily the other lake was much smaller. When I made it back home that evening I decided that outdoor activities were not for me.

I was now settled down into a nice apartment and had a good paying job. I felt like I had just found my new freedom. I started dating all the girls I met who were either secretaries or computer programmers. One day I was going to Saratoga Springs to pick up my date who attended Skidmore College. As I was driving my 1955 Chevy, its hood opened up and hit the windshield while snapping off the hinges. I looked at my rear window and saw the hood flying in the air behind my car. Fortunately there were no cars behind me on the road. I pulled the hood off the road and into a ditch and continued to Skidmore College to meet my date. She was not too happy with the appearance of my car without the hood and the engine showing. I soon sold the Chevy and bought a new 1962 VW Beetle, or the Bug, as it was known.

There were no Turkish people in Schenectady and I felt lonely and homesick. I therefore spent the weekends commuting to New York City to be with my friends Erdem Tunçsiper, Değer Tunç and Hüseyin Aktuğ. It was very nice being with them and speaking Turkish. I constantly communicated with my parents by mail and sent them money at every opportunity. The summer of 1962 passed very rapidly. By continuously dating and traveling to New York City on the weekends, when the end of summer arrived, I had no money saved and felt like I had wasted the entire summer. So much for my new found freedom.

Advanced Engineering Program

By the time September came I was in for a rude awakening. All of a sudden I had a new found freedom and many things I never had before and I was not making good use of them. The entire summer was gone and I was running around idly with no direction. Although I was making good money, at the end of the summer I had no savings. I had a lot of obligations towards my family, myself and a big debt to *Sümerbank*. I realized it was time again to pull myself together and give a new direction to my life.

One of the benefits of being at GE was associating with very high quality engineers and personnel and being able to receive additional training.

General Electric Company always picked some of the best among graduates of the American universities and then chose some select group among them for further training. On top of the training programs list was the highly recognized and acknowledged Advanced Engineering Program (AEP). The Advanced Engineering Program was a gruelling three year engineering training program designed solely for a select group of GE engineers to prepare them for the future and for a leadership position in the Company. All the engineers in this program would receive a solid foundation of scientific knowledge and a disciplined approach to solving problems of the present and developments of the future. Most of the top management and some of the best reputable engineers at GE were AEP graduates. The AEP had a long history with its first graduates in 1926. Each year of the program was identified as the "A Course", "B Course" and "C Course". The classes were held once a week where a select member of the Company or an academia presented a subject and a real life problem was given as the assignment. Within that week the problem had to be solved and be documented in a full report. This intense program not only taught the students how to solve technical problems but also forced the individuals to write paper reports.

When I graduated from Lehigh I had a strong desire to become a good engineer and to have a successful professional career. Although I had passed creditably all my courses in college, I still had to learn the application of these principles to practical problems. I now had a great opportunity to do something good about my career. I thought the Advanced Engineering Program would give me an opportunity of a lifetime to prepare me for the future. It would also save me from idleness and give a better direction to my life. I discussed my desires and plans with my boss Don Rubio who agreed to support me. After many interviews and evaluations of my background and capabilities by the Program Administrators, I was accepted to AEP. This would be at a substantial cost to my LST-G Department whose upper management also agreed to finance me. Contrary to *Sümerbank*'s scholarship, I was pleasantly surprised that GE did not require any compulsory services in exchange. I now had a goal in my life and it was a major commitment by everybody involved, LST-G Department, AEP institution and myself. The Company of course expected us to fulfill our job commitments to the full extent while we were in this program. On the average the program required an additional forty hours of course work, problem solving and documentation.

Our Schenectady A Course 1962-1963 class supervisor was Don Mack with Ray George, Tom Alge, John Anderson, Gil Bulloch, Tom

Urbanowsky, Steve Blanchard, Jim Watson, Al Shartrand and I as the entire class members. We were allowed to work in teams in solving problems but documenting was done individually. This program, thus for the first time, introduced us to the "team work" concept and showed us how to achieve results as a team. I teamed up with Tom Alge and John Anderson. Every night we would get together and work into the late hours laboring on our assignments. Both Tom and John were married with children, which made it more difficult for them with greater sacrifice from their families, than it was for me since I was just a happy bachelor. But even that took a big toll on my social life since I had to neglect my girlfriends who gradually decided to relinquish me. Difficult weeks followed each other but we continued pushing forward week after week meeting our commitments both at work and at our assignments.

At the beginning of 1963 there were unexpected but exciting announcements informing us that GE had made plans with some of the universities that a select group of AEP students would be sent to a Ph.D. program. At the time this announcement was made, we were working extremely hard but after the announcement the competition to be selected to the Ph.D. program increased considerably and we found ourselves working incredibly harder. It was the most difficult and stressful period of my life just like the time when I was studying for the university entrance exams in Izmir. By the time summer arrived I successfully completed the A Course and got selected for the Ph.D. program at the Polytechnic Institute of Brooklyn.

The Polytechnic Institute of Brooklyn

The Polytechnic Institute of Brooklyn, as the name implies, is a higher educational institution located in Brooklyn, New York. The Polytechnic, or Brooklyn Poly as it was also called, had a very long history. It dated back to the American Civil War and when the war was raging in the spring of 1861, the Brooklyn Collegiate and Polytechnic Institute was then seven years old. At the end of the war, Polytechnic adopted the colors blue and gray to symbolize the unification of the nation. Later, at the opening of the 20th century, the Polytechnic Institute became a model school for engineering in all the fields. The Institute trained engineers to meet the country's needs in newly developing fields. During World War II the Polytechnic made significant advances in technology and innovations in the areas of communications systems, electronics and aerodynamics. Opportunities for advanced research at the Polytechnic brought prominent scientists and engineers from Europe mostly from Germany. Among them was Ernst Weber in electronics and microwave research, Herman Mark and Fredrick Enrich in Polymer Science, Isidor Frankruben and Paul Ewold in X-ray crystallography and Nicholas Hoff and Hans J. Reissner in aeronautics. Through these men the Polytechnic became one of the most reputable technical schools in the country educating many bright minds in the greater New York-New Jersey area with its daytime and evening programs. The Polytechnic had also attracted many foreign students creating a very cosmopolitan atmosphere in its Brooklyn campus.

The Brooklyn Polytechnic Institute was the first school to recognize General Electric Company's Advanced Engineering Program and devised a plan to bestow Ph.D. degrees for some of the deserving candidates. Half of our Schenectady A Course class members, including myself, and students from other GE sites were selected for this program. The B Course and C Course students and even graduates of the program also insisted to be a part of the selected group to attend Polytechnic. That summer there were 125 of us at Brooklyn Poly's Farmingdale, Long Island campus where we stayed at the nearby Farmingdale Agricultural School's dormitories. During the six-week summer session we were assigned to take five graduate courses. That many graduate courses in such a short period was unheard of. Again, GE students gave their best efforts. Every night we put in exhaustive long hours of studying and doing our homework. Early in the morning we would wake up to the sounds of the cows from the nearby farm belonging to the agricultural college and rush to lectures all day long. I had one advantage over most of the students and that was I already had a M.S. degree where I was familiar with some of the subjects. At the end of the six weeks more than half of the class was dropped out of the program. It was also obvious the school would give most of the remaining students only a Master's degree. I certainly was not interested getting another Master's degree so I decided I would somehow attend regular classes at the main campus and go for my Ph.D. degree directly with regular students. I survived the arduous summer program and returned back to my work at GE in Schenectady.

Turbine Development Engineer

Back at Bucket and Rotor Engineering, I was working on the design of new dovetails and buckets performing stress and vibration calculations. My manager Don Rubio moved me from the design group to the development group. The development area was more challenging and I had the opportunity to contribute with some new development work. My first assignment was investigating turbine wheel failures under partial arc loading. The pins supporting the turbine wheel, being subjected to cyclic loading due to partial arc steam admission, were experiencing fatigue failures. This was my very first development work where I put a great deal of effort to incorporate all the things I had learned to date in evaluating this failure and coming up with a solution. I reported this analysis in a data folder dated August 1963 entitled "Pin Bushed Wheel Failures under Dynamic Loading". The analytical work I had performed was later accepted and published as a paper in the ASME (American Society of Mechanical Engineers) Transactions; Journal of Applied Mechanics June 1964 entitled "Circular Ring Plates Under Partial Arc Loading". I now had a taste of doing development work and I enjoyed it.

In the development group, I worked with Vic Musick, Russ Chinoy and Dick Nickerson. Dick was a C Course graduate and a wizard with computer programming. He helped me with my computer programs. In those days engineers had to write their own computer programs using IBM Fortran language. I sat next to Russ Chinoy who was a Pakistani from India. Some of his family members were still living in central India in a city called Allahabad. He was not a Moslem or a Hindu but a Zoroastrian. This was the first time I had met someone of that faith. He was married to an American and had three children. We became very good friends. Later, Russ moved on to become a Manager in the Materials and Processes Laboratory.

My second assignment was quite different, dealing with the investigation of turbine bucket erosion due to water droplet impingement. In the later stages of the Low Pressure (LP) Turbines, the expanding steam contains a significant amount of moisture in the form of water droplets. When the tips of the LP turbine buckets, moving at supersonic speeds, impact the water droplets, an extensive amount of erosion occurs. Erosion of the blades reduces the efficiency and reliability of the turbines. I did very extensive research in the literature and did my analysis explaining and formulating how high-strength steel would erode with water droplet impingement. I derived a formula to predict the rate of erosion on steam turbine buckets, which is used even to this date as design criteria. This work became much more useful later in application to nuclear turbines where the steam temperatures are lower and the amount of moisture is much higher causing increased erosion. During my research I ran into the name of Olive Engel at the National Bureau of Standards who had published many papers on the subject and I called her up to inquire about her research. She sounded very knowledgeable and pleasant and informed me that she was coming to Schenectady to visit the Research Laboratory and would meet me to exchange information. I got very excited thinking I was going to meet a lovely young woman. She was as pleasant as she sounded on the telephone but to my dismay she was much older than I had imagined.

My next assignment dealt with the vibration of bowed rotors. I was to verify the results of my analytical calculations with an experimental test. I set up a test rig duplicating the behavior of the bowed rotor and measured the response of the rotor. To do this experimental work I got help from a brilliant engineer named George Fischer in the M&P Lab. It was ironic that George and I would work together the next forty years. This was my first introduction to experimental work at GE and in a short time I had a great opportunity working on a variety of projects. I was being involved in existing designs and doing some development work while I was getting additional education. I was publishing all my development work on internal GE data folders and the list of my reports was growing steadily.

In September 1963 I was back in the second year of the Advanced Engineering Program, the B Course. On November 22 while I was in my office attending my work, we heard the terrible news that President John Kennedy was assassinated. Everybody in our office was filled with grief and sorrow. I left work and went home with terrible despair in my mind and watched the continuation of unbelievably sad events on television. It was a big loss for all of us and for the country.

In the midst of all these happenings, General Electric got my student visa changed and I received the "Green Card", my permanent residency. I had also been communicating with *Sümerbank* and started paying back what I owed them on a monthly basis with a very high interest rate. At the same time I continued helping my family financially.

In the office next to mine was a well-known engineer by the name of Boris Wundt. I had heard of his name and read some of his papers on material creep and rupture when I was at Lehigh working on Fracture Mechanics. I went into his office and introduced myself. Boris was from Warsaw, Poland where the Nazis had killed most of his family members. Although Boris was much older than I, we became very good friends. He later invited me to his home where I met his lovely wife Selma and his two children Susan and Chuck. Over the years our relationship grew and bonded like a family.

I felt I was accomplishing a lot in a short time with some significant goals in mind. I had a very busy but lonely life. My personal relationship with girls was pushed to a second priority and this was obvious when the last girl I was seeing, Diane Kottke, informed me she was leaving Schenectady and moving to Rochester. It seemed like I had no time to spare for myself while most of the young people my age at GE were having a lot of fun spending winter months skiing at the surrounding mountains while I was trying to succeed in my career. I had no choice but to finish what I had started. It was not the question of how smart I was, but the question of perseverance to achieve what I had set out to do.

Father and Mother in the US

The hard work in the B Course continued like the previous year. We were now on our own with no team members. While I was in the B Course, I was asked to lecture in the A Course. This privilege was usually given to the graduates of the Program who had established themselves in their fields. I was rather pleased for the opportunity. I prepared a small book entitled "Static Energy Methods in Engineering Analysis" and lectured from it to the Schenectady A Course class. This was very well received and I was asked to give the same lecture to the A Course students at GE's Locomotive Division in Erie, Pennsylvania. In a short time I was making a good name for myself in the organization. For me this was very important because the environment at GE was extremely competitive and to survive for a long time at GE one had to build competence in his field with a very good reputation. Furthermore, I always felt that as a foreigner to succeed, I had to be better than my American counterparts. There had never been any discrimination inside and outside of GE towards me at any time. I was always treated very well and equally by everyone within GE and even my salary increases were always within the upper 25 percentile levels. I was very happy and content at GE. I was doing real engineering work for which I was trained and was continuously getting additional on-the-job training. In May 1964 I successfully completed the second year of the Advanced Engineering Program and became a B Course graduate.

It had been two years since I graduated from Lehigh and in such a short time a lot of things had happened after my bleak and uncertain days at Lehigh. I was now settled in Schenectady, working on some interesting projects on turbine design and development, finished two years of GE's Advanced Engineering Program and I was going towards my Ph.D. degree at Brooklyn Polytechnic. I had also started paying back what I owed

Sümerbank in Turkey for my scholarship and I was financially supporting my parents.

After the B Course, the next step was to go to Brooklyn Poly for a second summer session, but the thought of another exhausting summer school did not appeal to me. I also did not like the idea of Brooklyn Poly giving a Master's Degree to most of the GE students with very few possibly getting a Ph.D. degree. Since I already had a Master's Degree, I was not interested in getting another one. I was determined to somehow get my Ph.D. degree but I had to come up with another plan that would be agreeable to all the parties involved. I first talked with my manager Don Rubio, who was by now my mentor, and proposed to him that I should attend Brooklyn Poly at the regular winter and spring semesters, and then take my qualifying exams. Instead of GE sending me to two more summer sessions, I suggested they should sponsor me to the two regular semesters that would guarantee my Ph.D. I also felt that the competition with regular students would be much less than with GE students. Engineering Management reviewed my proposal and agreed to send me to Brooklyn Poly as a regular full-time student in September. I then applied to Brooklyn Poly to have me accepted and registered as a Ph.D. candidate at the regular sessions. After reviewing my Lehigh transcripts and GE-Brooklyn Poly course work, the school accepted me as a full time student for its Ph.D. program. This was a big relief and I was going to have my summer free.

It had been exactly eight and a half years since I had seen my mother and father or heard their voices. All these years had passed with a tremendous amount of longing. There was not a moment that I was not thinking of my parents in these far away places. Because of many commitments towards schooling and working, I could not take time for myself and for my family to be together with them, nor could I financially afford it since I was paying a big debt to *Sümerbank*. I was not trying to prove anything to anybody but was just trying to succeed in life. This eight and a half years of separation, sacrifice and longing for my family left terrible feelings and regrets in me that I felt the rest of my life. I later made a point of being with my family at every opportunity as often as I could.

Now that I had the summer free, it was time for me to be together with my parents so I therefore decided to bring them to the United States. I made all the arrangements and sent them the money to come. It was cheaper for them to take the train from Istanbul to Paris and fly from Paris to New York City. Since they could not speak any other language besides Turkish, it was difficult for them to make the trip. Luckily there were Turkish workers on the same train who helped them throughout their journey to Paris. This was their first trip outside of Turkey and they were overwhelmed. They found the trip somewhat adventurous but they seemed like they enjoyed it nonetheless. I was full of anxiety and happiness anticipating their arrival. I went to New York City and stayed with Şakir Bey and my distant cousin Ülkü and her husband Nevzat in Flushing. In the afternoon we all went to the airport to welcome my parents. At the arrival terminal I was at the outdoors balcony where I could see the arriving planes and disembarking passengers. I saw their Air France plane land on the runway and pull in front of the balcony where I was waiting. When the stairs were pushed against the plane's door, I could hardly control my excitement and nervousness. When the passengers started deplaning and I saw my father and mother coming down the steps. I screamed, *"Anne, Anne, Baba, Baba"*. My mother heard me and waved which made me burst into uncontrollable tears. After such a long separation we were finally together again.

The next day we drove in my Volkswagen to Schenectady and got settled in my apartment on Van Vranken Avenue. They were so happy to be with me in my home. During the weekdays when I was working, they would keep themselves busy discovering the neighborhood by walking around and going to the supermarket. My mother was continuously cooking all the dishes I had missed over the years. One day when I was driving home from work, I saw my mother and father sitting by the curb with a huge watermelon next to them. They had gone to the nearby supermarket and could not resist buying the watermellon. They did not realize how heavy it was to carry all the way home. Coming home after work, seeing their happy faces, and eating my mother's delicious cooking kept on reminding me how much I had missed them.

One weekend I decided to take them to Lehigh and show them where I had studied and spent six years of my life. I could tell they had mixed feelings of sadness for my lonely existence yet they were very proud of what I had accomplished so far on my own. I also took them to Niagara Falls where they marveled at the magnificence of the falls. On weekends we frequently went to New York City where I showed them the World Expo, Empire State Building and many other sites. Since most of their time was spent in Schenectady and at the time there were no Turkish people around for them to talk to, they were quite lonely during the day. As the summer came to an end, their departure date was approaching as well. There is a saying in Turkish: *"Sayılı günler çabuk geçer"* (Numbered days go by swiftly). We were again back on the road to New York City for their return. After a lot of hugging, kissing and crying, I put them on the plane and sent them back to Turkey by way of Paris with a promise I would visit them soon.

I had arranged the timing such that after my parents had left at the end of summer, I could start school immediately without loosing any time. From the airport I went directly to Brooklyn Poly and checked into the dormitory.

10

Getting Married

Brooklyn, New York

In September 1964 I started the Fall Semester at the Polytechnic Institute of Brooklyn as a Ph.D. candidate in the Mechanical Engineering Department. I was feeling very good since I had just spent the entire summer together with my parents in the United States. That was a very happy and fulfilling experience for me and I was now ready with renewed energy to take on new challenges. The main campus of the school was located in downtown Brooklyn in a very crowded section of this great metropolis just a few blocks from the famed Brooklyn Bridge. The school was housed in a big but old building at 333 Jay Street in what had once been the quarters for the American Safety Razor Company.

Like Lehigh, Brooklyn Poly was heavily concentrated in technical fields. It serviced students from the greater New York City area both with daytime and evening classes. The school did not have dormitories for graduate students but rather it had rented a few floors of the Bossert Hotel in Brooklyn Heights as residences for the graduate students. Down the road from the hotel was a park overlooking the lower Manhattan skyline with the historic Brooklyn Bridge spanning the East River in view. It was one of the most beautiful locations of the city that I frequented to enjoy the impressive skyline, especially in the evenings when the whole city was illuminated.

I was taking five graduate courses in each semester and doing very well in them. My roommate was a Master's degree student from India. He was from a very wealthy family in Bombay but he was more interested in having fun than studying. New York City has always been a great place for young people to be in and experience. However, it is a very distracting place for those students who are trying to study. I was very happy to be back in New York City again with a lot of exciting things happening all around and away from the isolation and loneliness of my Schenectady life. I was meeting a lot of people and dating many girls. I would often take my dates to a Greek restaurant on 41st Street in Manhattan that served excellent lamb shank with vegetables and roasted potatoes. This food was the same as Turkish cooking and since there were no Turkish restaurants here at the time, I frequented this place a lot. The food was tasty and reasonably priced. One day I decided to splurge on a Turkish-Greek delicacy: lamb's brain. Since the menu was very greasy and difficult to read, I asked the Greek waiter "Do you have any brains?" He somewhat jokingly responded, "If I had any brains would I be working here?" I did however get to eat my lamb's brain.

On one occasion, I was seeing a Jewish girl from Brooklyn named Amy, who was a mathematics major at Brooklyn Poly. One day she invited me to her home for dinner and to meet her parents. This was a different experience for me. When they spoke, presumably in English, I did not understand half of the things they said. It was as if they were from another country speaking a foreign language. It was most interesting how Brooklyn Jews, different than anyboby else in the United States had a completely different dialect and a language of their own.

Keeping my car in the city was very difficult because I had to park it on the street. Every morning I had to move it to a different location because of parking restrictions. My parking tickets were accumulating faster than I could pay for them. For as much as having a car in the city was burdensome, it was also convenient for me to rush to the parties in Manhattan when I got invited at the last minute. With my friend Orhan Erdil we would go to Greenwich Village on dates and periodically I got together with my other friends Erdem, Hüseyin and Değer. At Brooklyn Poly I met a lot of Turkish Ph.D. candidates who were sent there by the Middle East Technical University (METU). METU had just started in Ankara, Turkey and had a shortage of faculty members with higher degrees. The government therefore sent a large group of faculty members to get Ph.D. degrees at Brooklyn Poly. It seemed like a mass-production of Ph.D. candidates. I was really having fun on weekends but during the week I devoted all my time and energy to my schoolwork. The courses I was taking were all advanced level but because of my Lehigh education and GE's Advanced

Engineering Program work, I was well prepared for these challenges. I also had excellent relationships with the faculty members, Professor John Curreri, who was the Department Head, Professor Yi-Yuan Yu who was an authority on stress analysis and vibration of sandwich plates and Professor Bernard Koplik. At this time, Professor Yi-Yuan Yu had agreed to be my Ph.D. thesis advisor.

On some weekends I visited my distant cousin Ülkü and her husband Nevzat in Jamaica, Queens. One day Ülkü had a great idea. She said that there was a large and well-established Turkish community in the area with families that had eligible daughters who were anxious to get married. She would arrange with one or two of these families each weekend for us to go and *see* the eligible girls. I readily agreed to this wonderful idea. This was an old Turkish courting custom, continuing even today, where meeting the girl took place under the tutelage of chaperoned parents. It was a *görücü* or matchmaker system where the boy's side visited the girl's family on a pre-arranged date. We proceeded with this plan. In each visit of ours the girl was well dressed and groomed and walked into the living room where we were sitting and anxiously waiting for her appearance. She usually started by serving us Turkish coffee while trying to afford a smile under the due stress she was being subjected to. She then served us *böreks, baklavas,* cakes, and many wonderful Turkish delicacies I had not had for so long. This was just wonderful! After serving us, the girl found a spot at the corner of the room and sat quietly with her head bowed down, eyes aimlessly pinned to the ground, without saying a word. She did not dare to raise her pretty eyes to meet my gaze. Although I did not want to stare at her in front of her family, I felt I had to evaluate her properly. In fact, in Turkey people usually have strong tendencies to stare, so I thought why should I be any different. After a few glances at the girl, I tried to get her to speak a few words but to no avail. I knew she kept stealing shy glances at me. I could not judge the candidate properly unless I had a better opportunity to be with her alone. That probably would have happened if I really was interested, but I did not feel any spark or excitement in any of these visits. I was also thinking of the next upcoming weekend feast. In the end, no matrimonious results came out of all these visits and *seeing* many lovely girls, but for a bachelor student, the feasts were well worth it.

Every year on October 29, the Turkish Republic's anniversary, the Turkish communities celebrate Republic Day with a Ball at every corner of the United States. The local Turkish-American Associations arrange it in their own cities. The Turkish community in New York City always organized the most lavish entertainment at every Republic's Day with over a thousand people attending. When I told my Indian roommate about the impending Ball, he insisted that we go together. Although initially I had not planned on going, I could not refuse my roommate and took him to the hotel in Manhattan where the Ball was being held. Little did I know that, that evening's encounter would change my life's path.

Meeting Ilkay

As expected, the Ball was very well organized with over a thousand people occupying all the tables and filling the ballroom. The entire room was filled with cigarette smoke and the conversational noise made the live orchestra music barely audible. It seemed like people were happy to be there with their friends and countrymen and they were enjoying themselves. My roommate and I stood around and observed the activities. After a while the organized portion of the program started with the Turkish and American National Anthems and was followed with a few short introductory speeches. During this period I decided to stand on a chair to get a better view of the podium and the people. Just as I was looking around, a beautiful, tall, slender girl with dark hair and a very attractive figure walked in front of me. My eyes inadvertently but intently followed her as she walked away. I felt an electrifying attraction towards her. I had to meet and know her. I immediately asked one of the fellows nearby whom I knew if he knew who she was. He very authoritatively told me he knew her; she was from Cyprus and she was married. My heart sank and I almost believed him since he was also from Cyprus. When this girl passed in front of me again, I watched her sit at a nearby crowded table. Being an engineer with an incessantly curious mind, I decided to seek my own answers.

I went to her table and asked her in English, "Would you like to dance?" She seemed somewhat surprised but pleased and glanced at her father for permission. He nodded approvingly. On the dance floor I made my move and held her very close and tight against my body. We were locked together without any words being exchanged. I knew most of the Cypriots in New York at the time were living in the Bronx. I thought to myself this would be an excellent catch to go around with. She was much better than the ones I had been dating or even going to *see* on weekends. She broke the silence in my tight grip by asking me who I was. After I learned that it was her sister who was married and not she, I told her I was in New

York studying for my Ph.D. When I told her I was from Izmir, she did not believe me. I later learned from her that since I was blond with blue eyes, she thought I was German. Because our conversation was taking place in English, she asked if I spoke Turkish. When I briefly said yes, her eyes lit up and she said, "Why don't you speak to me in Turkish then?" As if I was a conquering hero I continued to speak in Turkish. She immediately stopped dancing, grabbed my hand tightly and pulled me to her table to introduce me to everyone. She said, "Baba, he is Turkish and he's studying for his Ph.D." while still grabbing my hand tightly. I must have met the first two requirements because they immediately and excitedly scrambled to make room for me at their table and her father offered me a drink. I was now being bombarded with all kinds of questions and my answers were pleasingly being approved. When I asked them where they lived, to my dismay I found out they lived in Baltimore and not the Bronx as I had expected. I was disappointed but not discouraged. Since I had been living alone so many years facing many challenges by myself, being discouraged was not in my nature. I anxiously volunteered the fact that I passed through Baltimore often whenever I went to visit my friends in Washington, DC. Ilkay readily, with a happy smile, extended me an invitation, "Next time you are going to Washington, why don't you stop by?" I responded immediately, "I am planning to go there in two weeks." I thus secured a date, although I had no friends in Washington DC. I had not been there since I passed by during my return from the University of Kentucky nor was I really planning to go there.

The following week a pleasant postcard from Ilkay arrived giving me directions to her home in Cockeysville, Maryland which was 20 miles north of Baltimore. I responded immediately informing her that I would be there as was discussed. I spent the next two weeks anxiously getting ready. I invested on a nice navy blue overcoat for myself. I had a nice box of baklava prepared from an Arab bakery on Atlantic Avenue in Brooklyn to present to her parents. My little blue Volkswagen took me to Ilkay's house in no time. The visit extended into a dinner with shish kebab and all kinds of Turkish foods. *The road to a man's heart is through his stomach*, especially when the man is a hungry student. The darkness came early and since I did not make any move to leave, I was asked if I would like to stay overnight. I assured the family that it would be all right if I visited my friends in Washington the next day. After lingering around most of the next day also, I left and returned to Brooklyn by early evening. I quickly sent Ilkay a thank you note and she in return responded with another invitation.

In two weeks I was again on the road with my VW to Cockeysville. I did not miss the opportunity and I spent the next two months going back and forth to be with Ilkay. In each visit I was introduced to their many friends and relatives as Ilkay's boyfriend. I was now at last in a serious relationship with love letters flying in both directions.

On December 31, 1964 Ilkay's parents had a large New Year's Eve party for their friends and family. There was lots of good food, drinks and lively music to dance to. I gave Ilkay a beautiful gold scarab bracelet with precious, multi-colored stones. I had learned that January 1 was also Ilkay's and her father's birthdays. The family seemed somewhat disappointed when they did not see a diamond engagement ring but instead a bracelet. Ilkay and I had talked about marriage and we decided to do it properly according to our Turkish custom. This meant my family members would go to Ilkay's family and ask for her hand in marriage for their son. I unfortunately did not have any close family members in the United States to carry out that duty. I therefore decided to personally ask for her hand in marriage from her parents. It turned out to be a much more difficult task than I realized. In 2005 when my son-in-law Christoffer came to ask for my daughter Muge's hand in marriage, I tried to make it as easy for him as possible since I knew what he was going through. I was extremely nervous and did not really know how to do this. Before I started, Ilkay made it sure her father and I had a drink in our hands. I think she was trying to guarantee the outcome. While Ilkay was watching intently from behind a door to make sure that I did not fumble, I sat across from her father and asked his permission to marry his daughter. He said, "I don't know what to say, let us ask her mother." When her mother was asked, she said, "Why are they asking us while they have already decided to get married anyway? It's all right by us." What a relief. I said, "Thank you!" and when I walked out of the room I was trembling from nervousness. I said to Ilkay, "Let's go to the movies", which was what we did.

Our engagement party was held at Ilkay's house on February 6, 1965 with the same crowd who were at the New Year's party. From my side, Ülkü, Nevzat and his father Sakir Bey were the only people attending. I so wished my father and mother were there to see their only son's engagement. They had just left the United States and financially it was not possible to bring them back since I was still paying a big debt to *Sümerbank*.

Now that I was engaged, I was more focused on completing my schoolwork. After the winter semester, realizing that he was not doing well in school, my Indian roommate's family called him back to India. My new roommate was a Japanese student studying for his Ph.D. in electrical engineering. During the spring semester I put an extra effort on my studies. At one point I had to give my car to Ilkay to keep it in Maryland while I was still in school. I was getting a parking ticket almost daily and my glove compartment was filled with unpaid tickets. At the end of the spring semester I completed all the course requirements for the Ph.D. program. Before returning to GE, I had one more hurdle to overcome and that was the Qualifying Exams. These exams were the final overall exams encompassing all the related subjects in Mechanical Engineering to determine if the candidate was qualified to get a Ph.D. It was a two, full day grueling exam. After I successfully passed them, I returned back to Schenectady. My boss Don Rubio was extremely pleased with the overall results, especially when he saw all my grades were straight A's.

Back in Schenectady

By the summer of 1965 I was back in Schenectady completely immersed in my GE work. I rented a small apartment on upper Union Street making plans for my upcoming marriage. I was very pleased and happy with many things I was able to accomplish in a short time. I completed all my course work at Brooklyn Poly, passed the qualifying exams for my Ph.D. degree, and I was engaged to a beautiful girl whom I loved very much. I had many loose ends, however, that had to be completed. I was still in the Advanced Engineering Program with one more year to finish the C Course. I had to write a Ph.D. dissertation and I still owed a lot of money to *Sümerbank*. I was also planning to get married soon. I always believed that if it was a good idea I should finish the task I started and not leave it half done even if it took a lot of extra effort and time. Since I was very much goal-oriented, these goals were going to be achieved.

Meanwhile, back at work my new assignment involved an important project on the first stage buckets in high-pressure steam turbines. When the supersaturated steam enters into the turbine from the boiler, it impacts the first stage buckets with a devastating force in a very harsh environment. These buckets, operating at temperatures close to one thousand degrees Fahrenheit and over 3500psi pressure, are subjected to steam impacts once every revolution due to partial arc admission of steam. A new dovetail design attaching these bulky buckets to the wheel with axial pins had been experiencing extensive failures. A failure in the first stage of a turbine causes turbine shutdown with enormous financial burdens and loss of thousands of kilowatts of power. I was asked to evaluate both analytically and experimentally the cause of the failures of the axial-entry dovetails and come up with a foolproof new design. My analysis involved using the theories of "finite beams on elastic foundations" and instrumenting the dovetail thoroughly with many strain gages and testing them to understand the load distribution. After very extensive and lengthy study and testing, I found the cause of failure on these types of dovetails and changed the design to a very heavy circumferential dovetail with three pairs of hooks. I am happy to say this design is still operational and in use today. I also came up with a design criterion for the first stage buckets called Partial-Arc Excitation Number (PAEN) which is still used today for all the new designs without any problems. One of the things I learned from this study is that if there is an extensive component failure, small modifications in the design, which I called "Band-Aid fixes", will not solve the problem and significant design changes will have to be made.

My work on the first stage buckets continued to study the vibratory behavior of buckets at full speed under centrifugal forces. I worked with the test personnel from the Materials and Processes Laboratory and designed and built a new test rig. We devised a test wheel with buckets rotating and being excited with a magnet attached to the wheel. Both the excitations of the magnet and collecting the strain gage data were done through the brush rings. At full speed we could change the frequency of the magnet to excite the buckets to identify the resonant frequencies. I was now getting involved with laboratory work, which was much different than analytical work I had been doing and I was enjoying it. Since the "wheel box test" of the first stage buckets was very cumbersome, we had to come up with an alternate way of testing. I had heard the General Electric Company's Electronics Laboratory in Syracuse, New York was experimenting on a new laser technology. In those days laser was completely a new technology, not used extensively. I approached them to see if we could use the Laser-Doppler effect in measuring the first stage bucket vibrations. I devised another test where I had to do unusual and unsafe steps; namely gold plating the side of the bucket for the laser light to reflect, and keeping the top of the turbine wheel casing open for the laser light to reach. Since we could measure the motion of the bucket only in the direction along the laser light, we could not get all the mode shapes and this procedure did not pan out to a success. We, however, tried the laser technique for vibration measurements many years before it became popular in all sorts of other applications. By now I was the first-stage bucket expert in the department, and most importantly, my management was very supportive of my endeavors.

In September 1965, I started the C Course, which was the third year of the Advanced Engineering Program. As we were progressing in this course, I started exploring subjects for my Ph.D. thesis. If I could find a subject that could be used for work application, the thesis could be a work project as well. My extensive research and my discussions with Professor Yi-Yuan Yu led me to a project involving disk vibrations which could be applicable to turbine wheel vibrations. I started doing some preliminary work on that subject. At that moment however, besides my job, most of my efforts were concentrated on the C Course. I was also making wedding plans to take place at the end of the C Course. Periodically, I commuted to Baltimore to see Ilkay and to finalize our wedding preparations. Once again, I had a lot of things going on all at once. I would say "my plate was more than full: it was overflowing!" The very few years I was away from my family, all by myself in this far away land, taught me to be self-reliant and self-sufficient. I was determined to accomplish all these tasks successfully. Life for an immigrant has always been an ongoing struggle to survive, to prove himself and to succeed.

At every opportunity I visited the Wundt family. They always welcomed me to their home and were always caring and concerned about me. Their son Chuck was an excellent wrestler in high school with many State Championships and medals to his name. With my past interest in wrestling, we always had something in common to talk about. Unfortunately, later in life, this young man's life was ruined when his wrestling coach got him hooked on enhancing and hallucinogenic drugs. Besides being a well-known engineer, Boris Wundt was very knowledgeable in every subject varying from classical music to fine wines. Selma had been taking real estate courses to become a broker. She had just gotten her real estate license and was working at Preisman Realty. As my wedding day was approaching, one day we had a brain storming session about what to do for housing after I got married. We decided I should buy a two family house because by renting out one unit, I could live in the other practically free. Selma took it upon herself to find me the proper house. After a couple months of searching, we found a nice, well-maintained two family house at 1039 Gillespie Street in Schenectady. I was Selma's first customer and this was my very first house. I made the arrangements to have the closing done together with my new bride right after I came back from my honeymoon.

At the end of April I successfully completed the C Course and was a graduate of General Electric Company's Advanced Engineering Program. I was now ready to go and get married.

Marrying Ilkay

After the wedding plans were finalized, I traveled to Baltimore. On May 6, 1966 we went to the Baltimore City Hall and had a civil ceremony, with only the immediate family present. The next day was the big event with a religious ceremony at the Islamic Center in Washington, D.C. The Islamic Center, which was the only mosque at the time in the entire northeastern United States, was a gift to the United States by all the Muslim nations. In those days there were not too many Moslems in this country, and those Muslims who were here, had small *mescids,* or prayer halls. I had asked my professor from Lehigh University, Prof. Erdoğan to be my best man at this ceremony. A lot of my friends from General Electric traveled to Washington D.C. to attend my wedding. Professor Yi-Yuan Yu was also among the attending guests. It was unfortunate and very sad however that nobody from my family could be at my wedding.

After the religious ceremony everyone went on to the beautiful reception site in Baltimore. The reception was very enjoyable with entertainment, live orchestra music, open bar and delicious food. The next day, Ilkay and I were on a plane to the Bahamas for our honeymoon. We flew to Nassau and checked into the Montague Beach Hotel, at the edge of the city. This was the most beautiful place I had ever been to. I had never had any vacation in my life nor had I traveled anywhere extensively. I therefore enjoyed our stay at Nassau very much. We returned to Schenectady at the end of our honeymoon as a married couple and met with the closing attorneys to sign the papers for our new home.

Except for the very basics, we did not have any furniture in our new home. With the wedding gift money we had in our hands, we first purchased a Castro convertible sofa bed. This would have to do until we had our bedroom furniture. We went shopping and ordered a nice bedroom set, dining room table and chairs, and a few armchairs and end tables for the living room. It felt good for me to have my own home. I always remembered with dismay all the difficulties and idiosyncrasies we had to put up with at my grandmother's house where my parents and I lived. Ilkay right away took charge of our household and finances. My first duty in our two family house was to increase the rent from $75 to $90 a month for our upstairs tenants. Their rent was much lower than the market value and besides, they were tenants at will. Ilkay urged me to go upstairs and talk with them. As a first time landlord I was rather nervous but I was able to convince the tenants readily.

Ilkay and I decided to redecorate our unit to our own taste. The existing wallpapers on the walls were old fashioned so we decided to replace them. Neither one of us had any experience in doing this sort of work, nor any type of house repairs. In attempting to remove the wallpapers we found out there were three layers on top of each other. They were not strippable as they are today but had to be scraped off layer by layer. This was very discouraging. A simple job turned into a grueling major project. I was advised to rent a steamer to remove all the layered papers. On the hottest day of August, with the steamer going full blast, I forced my way inch by inch removing all the wallpapers. I then learned a lifetime lesson: even the simplest appearing project is not as simple as it seems. In fact, I found out that nothing in life is simple; it requires hard work and perseverance. At the time I had a lot of initiative, youthful energy and enthusiasm. I continued doing a lot of repair work around the house such as upgrading the garage, rebuilding two porches with concrete blocks, some plumbing jobs and putting in a blacktop driveway. With Ilkay attending to the flower gardens, our house started looking beautiful. Before long, Ilkay got a job at St. Claire's Hospital Billing Department. We had a good summer getting settled and putting our house in order. This was a good start.

When September came, I received surprising news from Brooklyn Poly that my advisor Prof. Yi-Yuan Yu was leaving the school and was joining General Electric's newly established Aerospace Division at Valley Forge, Pennsylvania. This was very disappointing news for me since I had done so much work on my dissertation and now I had to find another advisor with a new dissertation topic. After a lot of effort, I found another new topic dealing with turbine blade vibrations with Prof. Bernard Koplik as my new advisor. I was also very lucky to get Dr. Hans Buechner as my GE advisor. Dr. Buechner was a world-reknowned German mathematician who had left Germany during Hitler's time and had joined General Electric Company. At GE his job involved working only on special projects. When I explained my situation to him, he gladly accepted to be my Company Advisor. Although Dr. Buechner was much older than I, we became very good friends and our friendship lasted many years. We spent a lot of wonderful times together hiking through the woods collecting wild mushrooms. Being a very learned scholar, Dr. Bueckner would identify each wild mushroom we found with his reference book to be sure that they were not poisonous. We would then enjoy eating them with our wives.

Meanwhile, Ilkay, who had graduated from Baltimore Junior College with a two year Liberal Arts degree, decided to complete a four-year school. She registered and started attending Russell Sage College in Troy, New York on a part time basis in the evenings. By the time 1967 arrived, both Ilkay and I were involved in our schoolwork.

At my work at GE I started working on turbine bucket vibrations. I was writing computer programs to calculate bucket frequencies with the old technique of "lump parameters approach". At the same time, together with Dr. Buechner, we were looking for a new approach to solving very large mathematical Eigenvalue problems representing bucket vibrations in a unique way. All this was much before the present day's Finite Elements techniques and powerful computers were available. One of the most critical engineering challenges in turbine design was to understand the vibratory behavior of turbine rotors and turbine buckets. After much design work and related development studies, I was now specializing more on turbine bucket vibrations testing together with the Materials and Processes Laboratory team. Everyone in the Department regarded me very highly since I was a key individual contributor on turbine bucket vibrations. The environment at GE was, and has always been, very competitive. At that time technical competence and technical contributions were the main qualifications for success that followed with corresponding salary and position level increases. My management in both respects treated me very well.

My boss Don Rubio knew about my debt to *Sümerbank* and my efforts in trying to pay it back. There must have been many behind the door meetings and discussions by GE Administration when I was called to the Engineering Manager Carl Schabtach's office and was told that GE would help me pay the remainder of my debt to *Sümerbank* in full. I could pay GE in installments without any interest. This had never been done before at GE nor would it ever happen again in the later years. In those days GE always looked after its key contributors and helped out in every possible way. Thus, I closed the final chapter with *Sümerbank* in 1967, paying them back in full what they had spent for my scholarship plus a hefty interest. I was very much moved and extremely grateful to General Electric's management for their thoughtfulness and generosity.

By April 1967 I completed my dissertation work using the *Method of Diakoptics*, which was cutting a large mathematical network, so called Eigenvalue problems, into small pieces and solving the small pieces individually and then tying them together as a whole for the final solution. At that time computers could not handle solutions of large network problems. Dr. Buechner had come up with the *Method of Diakoptics* and I extended it to the solutions of large network of turbine bucket vibration problems. The title of my dissertation was *"An Application of Diakoptics in the Determination of Turbine Bucket Frequencies by the Use of Perturbations"*. This work was later published as an ASME paper under the same title in 1968.

I submitted my dissertation to Brooklyn Poly for evaluatios and it was readily accepted. I was then invited to the school to defend my dissertation in front of a large faculty staff. The defense of my dissertation took about two hours and I was then asked to step outside the room and wait. The ten-minute wait seemed like ten days. When Prof. Koplik stepped out of the examination room, he approached me to shake my hand and he said, "Congratulations Dr. Tuncel." In my excitement I almost passed out!

Ilkay was anxiously waiting outside the school, just like the day I had asked for her hand in marriage from her father. I informed her I had passed and again said, "Let's go to the movies." We went to Radio City Music Hall to see the nice floorshow and a new movie. After all these years of hard work I had accomplished what I had set out to do: I completed the Advanced Engineering Program, I received my Ph.D. degree from Brooklyn Poly, I paid my debt to *Sümerbank* and above all I was happily married and not alone. All of a sudden I had a funny feeling of emptiness. All this time for so many years I was always busy studying with an important goal in mind, a major task in front of me and now all of a sudden everything came to a final end. Instead of feeling happy I felt very low. I wondered what I was going to do with all my free time now.

Union College

Our house on Gillespie Street was located only half a block from Union College. Although Union College was a very reputable but small engineering school, it offered Master's Degree programs to graduate students in some key engineering fields. Most of the students who attended the Graduate School were GE engineers trying to better themselves. This was a great and convenient opportunity for them. I was recommended by a friend to Professor Gardner Ketchum, the Head of the Mechanical Engineering Department at Union College to teach a graduate course on Mechanical Vibrations, as an Adjunct Professor. I had just completed my graduate-school work and everything was very fresh in my mind. Adjunct professorship was a part time additional job while I was working full time at General Electric. Professor Ketchum offered me the job and wrote to me explaining the role of the adjunct faculty. The letter stated, "The Mechanical Engineering Department is greatly strengthened by the adjunct faculty we have been able to draw into the program, because they are extraordinarily competent and because they share interests of our regular faculty in the students and the program."

I felt it would be a great opportunity for me to better myself and I took on the challenge with great enthusiasm and interest. I wanted to do a good job teaching the Mechanical Vibrations course while getting some valuable experience in teaching, in self-confidence and in making presentations to an audience. I also felt I could make additional contributions different than the regular faculty by utilizing examples from real-life engineering applications based on my GE experiences. To my amazement, my classroom was filled with twenty-five master's students, which was a very large size class for a small engineering school. I realized teaching any subject would be much more difficult than being a student on the receiving end. Since I was teaching this course for the first time, it required a lot more preparation and I put extra effort to get ready for each lecture. In fact, at the beginning I practiced lecturing in front of Ilkay to get her opinion. I was extremely nervous the first day I was in the classroom. After personal introductions and preliminary comments, I started lecturing. As soon as I started writing equations on the blackboard while talking, I was relaxed and at ease. I filled the board with equations from the left top corner to the bottom right corner in no time. After erasing the board, I continued writing until the class was over. The lectures were going very smoothly and from my discussions with the students, they were learning and enjoying the class very much. By the time the final exams came, we had covered a lot of materials. The students did very well in the finals and I was very pleased with the overall outcome. At the end of the semester a survey was performed evaluating each teacher's performance. The feedback on my teaching was extremely positive and complimentary. Based on this, I was asked to teach another graduate course for the spring semester. I accepted the offer again and decided to teach a course entitled "Stress Analysis", mostly dealing with theories of machine design calculations. I knew I had to spend a lot of time again preparing for this course. I took this challenge on the same way as I had done with the previous course on Mechanical Vibrations. During this time Ilkay continued working and taking courses in the evenings at Russell Sage College.

During the mid 1960's and later, the power generation business in the United States and overseas was growing very rapidly. Large power plants were being erected everywhere. To meet the ever-increasing demand, turbine generator sizes grew correspondingly from 150MW (megawatts) to 500-600MW units. Orders were pouring into our department for new units. The factory in our massive Building 273 was operating 24/7, on a three-shift basis with rotor forgings filling every open space on the floor. Even with the extraordinary manufacturing capability we had at General Electric, our management realized they could not possibly deliver all these orders on time. They resorted to establishing "Manufacturing Associates" (MA) with Hitachi and Toshiba of Japan to share the excessive work. This decision in work sharing opened up a new era for GE which years later would end up haunting us. We gave the Japanese the task of manufacturing, assembling and testing of the low-pressure turbine rotors. As part of the work-sharing arrangement, GE also promised to share certain critical technologies with the Japanese. In the 1960's the Japanese were trying to advance themselves from cheap gadget production to high tech manufacturing. With significant American contributions, Japan transformed itself from a burnt-out shell of a country in 1945 to the world's second largest economy in the early 1990's. Japan benefited from the lessons on manufacturing techniques from many of America's leading production experts; access to US patents at bargain basement royalty rates; favored-nation admission to the US market for its products; subsidies in the form of massive assembly sub-contracts from American corporations, and many other give aways. I was asked to work with the Japanese engineers from Hitachi and Toshiba and teach them how to calculate turbine bucket frequencies and turbine-generator rotor critical speeds. All that advanced turbine technology we developed over the years was transferred to the Japanese on a golden platter in a very short time. We also transferred technology to the Japanese by giving them our corresponding computer programs. Because of this MA arrangement, Japan became one of our biggest customers in buying numerous large turbine-generators for their new power plants. Later in time, however, they became our biggest competitor.

One day my boss Don Rubio announced at an office meeting that he was leaving our unit because he was promoted to GE's Mechanical Drive Systems Department in Fitchburg, Massachusetts. I was shocked and very disappointed because for the past few years he had been my friend and my mentor. I felt that he was such a competent individual that nobody could possibly take his place and would be a devastating blow to our department.

Before long I learned a good lifetime lesson, that no one was indispensable at GE. The Bucket and Rotor Engineering was divided into two groups with Vic Musick as Manager of the Design Unit and George Fischer as the Manager of the Development Unit. I was then promoted to a Senior Engineer position in charge of the Bucket Development team. With the new orders continuously coming in we were being challenged to develop new and larger last stage buckets for the low-pressure turbines and to further develop and improve the efficiencies of the turbines and generators. It was one of the most exciting periods of the turbine-generator business and I found myself right in the middle of all these activities.

The news from my family in Turkey however was not good. My paternal grandmother, my aunt Melek and her husband had all died within a one-month period. I was very saddened by not being able to see them ever again. Now that my grandmother was gone, my father's brothers and sisters demanded that my parents either move out of the house so it could be sold or else pay their equal shares. I suggested to my parents that they should buy a newer house and forget about this dilapidated structure. My father however was adamant that he would not leave his mother's house. This meant I had to send them money immediately to pay off my uncles and aunts. Once they had the house appraised, I paid each one their due share. Although I paid all the siblings, my deceased uncle Malik's Italian wife had moved back to Italy and could not be located. My parents therefore could not get a title to the house in their name. At least for the time being, everybody who was involved in this transaction seemed very happy. The old house needed endless repairs so I continued sending them money to take care of all the necessities. By the time the repairs were completed the house looked very nice. It was not long after that Dr. Nihat Önderoğlu called me one day informing me that my father had had a stroke. I was reassured that my mother was taking very good care of him and I should not worry, Over a short period he gradually recovered but with signs of slight paralysis still remaining. I was now more then ever very concerned about my father's health.

In Schenectady we met a Turkish engineer, Teoman Uzkan and his family. The Turkish Navy had sent him to the United States and he had received his Ph.D. from Stanford University in California. He was working at General Electric's Corporate Research and Development Center. His assignment was for a very short time and he had to return back to the Turkish Navy. We became good friends in the short time he was there and when it was time for him to go back, I volunteered to help him move out of his apartment by helping him build crates to ship his belongings to Turkey. When he was unable to sell his car, he left it for me to sell for him. Our fate was such that we would be together as close friends for many years to come.

It seemed like I had never-ending problems. For as much as I was working very hard and accomplishing many tasks, I still had a problem that was hanging over my head like the sword of Damocles. In Turkey, military service was a compulsory national duty that every young man was expected to serve. If I did not perform my military duty I could never go back to Turkey to see my family and the land where I was born and grew up. I did not want that to happen. Ilkay and I reviewed our situation and decided we should go to Turkey to complete my two-year military service and at the same time have an enjoyable, extended visit with my family. There is a Turkish proverb that suited to our situation exactly: *Evdeki hesap çarşıya uymaz*, "What you calculate at home does not match the market". By the time I paid *Sümerbank*, bought a house in Schenectady and another one in Turkey for my parents, we did not have much money left. Although the adventure of going to the Turkish military service would cause an extreme hardship on us, it had to be done and we decided to do it.

I was leaving a very satisfying career at GE with a much brighter future behind and starting a new unknown adventure just to serve in the Turkish military. I discussed my perplexing situation with the GE management and presented them my plans. Their first reaction was, "Are they paying you more money?" I assured them that I was not going to get much of anything and in fact we would have to manage financially with whatever money we had saved. Once again GE came to my rescue. It seemed like they were always watching over me. GE management decided to grant me a Leave of Absence for two years in order for me to go to Turkey to serve in the Turkish military. My job would be waiting for me upon my return. Today in Turkey the same military service for people who are in my situation is only for twenty-five days plus a payment of about $10,000.

During the next remaining few months, we started our preparations. The plan was that Ilkay would stay with her family in Baltimore for six months while I got started in the military school and then she would follow me to Turkey. Boris and Selma Wundt again extended a helping hand to us and stored some of our belongings in their house. Selma gladly took on the responsibility of looking after my two-family house that was then fully rented. All my GE colleagues gave Ilkay and me a wonderful farewell dinner and we were sent off with the hope of returning in two years. On July 17, 1968 I started my leave of absence from General Electric.

11

The Turkish Navy

Returning to Izmir

In the short time since I graduated from my high school, *Namık Kemal Lisesi*, I had experienced so many wonderful things in America that I had never dreamed about. It was with considerable disdain however that I was now leaving everything I had worked for behind and returning to Turkey to serve my military duty. I was giving up bright job opportunities and a lucrative income for an unknown situation with no income. But the decision was made and we were going to do it as best as we could. We had nobody to depend on but ourselves. Preparations for our adventurous trip took no time. I made two large crates to store our bedroom furniture, dining room set, a new gas stove and a window air conditioner for Dr. Nihat Önderoğlu, which I shipped directly to Izmir. Since we had little money, everything we did was very carefully calculated. Ilkay was going to remain behind with her family in Baltimore and find a temporary job until she could join me.

In those days airfares to Turkey were very expensive so I bought a one way ticket to Munich, Germany and planned to complete the rest of the trip by train. After my good-byes, at the beginning of August 1968 I flew to Munich and stayed overnight in a hotel near *Hauptbahnhoff*, the main railway station. The next day I was on the Orient Express from Munich to Istanbul. My small compartment in the train was filled with six people, all Turkish. Four of the passengers were Turkish guest workers; one was a military officer and I. Like today, there was a large Turkish population in Germany then and most had come from rural Anatolia being challenged not just to meld into a Christian culture but into a highly industrial one. Germans in reality however had not welcomed them. When the first group of Turks arrived in the early 1960's, they were considered *Gastarbeiters* or guest workers, expected to return to their homeland. These guest workers played an important role in the German economic miracle. In time however, they made Germany their permanent home while trying to fit into German society. Although more recently most Turkish immigrants have assimilated, many continue to live a life apart.

The Turkish workers on the train had so much luggage and packages of food that we could not fit them into our compartment. Thinking that I could buy food on the train, I had only brought one sandwich and a drink with me. Before long I found out there was no food service on the train. I was hoping the workers would share some of their food with me. In the early evening as the train rolled through the magnificent Swiss Alps, loneliness and anxiety took over my happy demeanor. Before falling asleep on my pullout berth, I wrote a letter to Ilkay. Meanwhile the Orient Express was speeding through the mighty Alps. In the middle of the night loud noises and banging sounds awakened all of us. It was the Yugoslavian border police checking on our passports. They were treating passengers, especially the poor workers, very rudely and looking for handouts. We were now in the unpleasant territory of Tito's Communist country.

The workers in my compartment were friendly, pleasant and warm-hearted individuals, sharing their meager foods with me in the usual Turkish hospitality. At each stop I would go out and buy some food and drinks and share them with my traveling companions. They all seemed very happy and excited going to their families with some little money they had saved doing menial labors in Germany. I learned from these people that they were given some of the worst jobs that the Germans would not consider doing themselves. They labored in the worst places and lived in deplorable conditions so that they could save some money for their families left behind in their villages. After all that hard work and labor these workers had devotedly given to the Germans, it was unfortunate that the Germans did not accept them more readily and help them to assimilate into their society. As our train was now rushing through the Balkans there were many small incidences we observed and experienced on our Orient Express train but nothing to match Agatha Christie's stories.

The next night at the border of Communist Bulgaria, the same rude treatment of all the passengers by the Bulgarian police repeated as if the Bulgarians were trying to outdo their Yugoslavian Communist counterparts.

As the train rolled towards Turkey I started getting anxious and excited. I was returning to my country that I loved so much after twelve years of absence. At the Turkish border I was surprised and disillusioned to see our treatment by the border police was no better than the previous Communist police. Furthermore, all the outside doors and windows of the train were locked until we got to Istanbul. To my amazement I learned this was to prevent the workers from throwing out packages at pre-arranged locations to avoid strict Turkish customs and pay heavy duties on them in Istanbul. The train pulled into *Sirkeci* station in Istanbul and I checked into a nearby hotel. After twelve years since I was at Istanbul Technical University, Istanbul had changed immensely. The city had expanded with bigger new apartment buildings erected at every corner. It was much more crowded and seemed more dynamic. I felt like a lost child in my own country. I also realized since I had not spoken Turkish much in the past few years, it was not as good as the local people and I had forgotten quite a bit. Since I was blond with blue eyes and spoke Turkish with an accent, I was always mistaken for an American.

I met my friend Teoman the next day at the Turkish Naval Academy at *Heybeliada* where he was teaching. He introduced me to the Commander of the Academy and they both promised they would try to help get me assigned to the Turkish Navy. In Turkey, like many other poor third world countries, you can advance not on the basis of your merits but by whom you know in important positions. I certainly did not know too many people in Turkey, let alone in important positions. That evening I was on a bus travelling to my home in Izmir with my heart throbbing all the way. I was nervous because of the changes I was going to see and excited that I was going to unite with my parents again. When I arrived at my home in Alsancak, my parents hugged and kissed me with affection and my father said, "*oğlum benim*" my son, while trying to squeeze me with his arms. However, he had no strength in them anymore. They were no longer those strong arms of an ex-boxer, a shoemaker and the father I had left behind some twelve years ago. My father looked much older than his age and he seemed very frail. His hair was thinning and grayer than I remembered four years ago when he was in America. He also used to be taller. The stroke had left its mark, where he was dragging his left foot slightly. Otherwise he was fine. I was so happy to be with them and they felt more at ease and secure with my presence there. It was so sad and unfortunate that I had to stay away for so long because of necessities and other priorities. It saddened me very much and I vowed to myself not to stay away from my family that long ever again.

Our newly remodeled house looked very nice. It felt good to be home after a twelve year absence. This house contained many childhood memories for me, some good and some bad. Everytime we refer to the past we say, "the good old days". But unfortunately they were not all good. I think the human brain somehow remembers only the good old days, eradicating the bad ones. Our street did not seem as wide as I had remembered. Everything I looked at in my neighborhood was carved in my mind as being bigger than it actually was. Now in reality they were all much smaller, older and mostly worn out. At the end, how things had changed. I of course had also changed. Nothing was the same anymore. The old neighborhood was gone and so were the neighbors. A lot of older people had died, including my grandmother, aunts and uncles. Down the street my old little house where I grew up as a baby was torn down taking with it the little memories I had in it. I walked to the *Kordon,* admiring Izmir Bay which I had dreamt about so many years when I was in America. Even that was not the same. I could not walk along the *Kordon* because of the deplorable stench coming from the bubbling sewer outlets pouring into the Bay. Being an engineer, my curious mind took me to observe the outlets of the sewer lines right under the sidewalk. I could not believe seeing the stinking sewage gushing into the beautiful Bay. This was the same Bay we swam in when we were young children. The beautiful villas along the shore with flower gardens were replaced with multi-unit concrete apartment buildings with no character and no aesthetics. During my absence the city had grown at least ten times its former size. People had swarmed in from remote eastern villages like locusts, settling into *gece kondus*, squatters houses, which sprouted in many shanty towns overnight. Antique little houses had given way to haphazardly constructed, half-finished concrete jungle homes, painting the city gray. While walking around my neighborhood I did not recognize any of the faces. I barely knew anyone in Alsancak any more. This was no longer the "beautiful Izmir" I once knew and yearned for all those years when I was in America. All of a sudden I felt lonely and despondent and started thinking of Ilkay and how much I had already missed her.

I immediately took charge of my parents' affairs. I attended all their needs from house repairs to financial problems. My father had not been able to work for many years because there was no work and later because of the stroke he had. I made sure they did not worry about money or any other thing.

I found out my two crates had arrived from America. I now had to face the ordeal which I dreaded: getting my personal property out of the Turkish

Customs. From what I had heard, dealing with the Turkish government officers in any government organization was bad and the Custom's office was one of the worst. When I appeared in front of the thickly moustached Custom's officer, he was sternly sitting behind his desk with an everpresent cigarette between his nicotine colored fingers. A half full *çay* cup adorned the top of his otherwise empty desktop. His desk drawer was half open, displaying money inside, signaling for more to be added. In other words he was ready for a bribe. I knew this was a well known and readily accepted way of doing business at the Custom's Office. I also knew that some money equivalent to about one hundred dollars would have remedied my situation but I refused to yield to corrupt afflictions of the Customs officers. I emphatically and persistently explained to him that I was not a rich businessman sneaking in goods to sell on the black market, but rather I was here to serve my country. He did not budge one bit. His drawer was still open and his imbecile demeanor had not changed. I think he would have sympathized with my case and let me have my personal effects but that would have been against his own acquired and accustomed immoral habit of taking bribes. At this point I reluctantly had to yield against my principle and threw in some money into his desk drawer. He hurriedly signed my papers for me to get my crates out and I bolted out of there. I recently found out from a friend that even today the most sought-after job in the Turkish Government is to be a Custom's Officer.

Turkish Military Service

Turks have always prided themselves with their mighty military. With the total personnel of more than 1,000,000 strong, Turkey's armed forces are the second largest in NATO. Turkish forces fought alongside the Americans in Korea under the United Nations Command and have always supported the vital interests of NATO and the U.N. For years the Southeastern Command of NATO headquarters was located in Izmir. Some 10,000 US military personnel and their dependents were stationed all around Turkey, including a major airbase in Incirlik near Adana. With a common border with the former Communist Soviet Union and control of the straits leading from the Black Sea to the Mediterranean, Turkey has been a vital guardian of the South Eastern flank of NATO. The Turkish military, since the beginning of the Republic, has kept the Nazis and the Communists out of the country and has maintained a stability within the country. With strong, reliable and well disciplined personnel, the Turkish military has been steadfast in protecting the country from the enemy both inside and outside. The Turkish military has also been the guardian of Atatürk's Doctrines of a free and democratic country. One of Atatürk's many capabilities was his foresight. In 1927 in his speech addressing the Turkish youth, Atatürk had said, "There may be malevolent people at home and abroad, who will wish to deprive you from defending the Turkish independence and the Turkish Republic." Recognizing the troubles that could come from many directions in a difficult part of the world where Turkey is located, the Turkish military has been very alert and attentive to its duties.

The Turkish military never had enough resources to maintain and modernize its equipment. Although the Turkish people and the Turkish government have always been very supportive of their armed forces, the Government's budget had been strained with a large percentage of the resources going to the military. Over the years assistance from the United States and other NATO allies have been helpful in upgrading Turkish military capabilities. In order to meet the needs for additional professional services, the military resorts to recruiting professional people as Reserve Officers. Since prospective job opportunities would usually require completed military service, young men would apply and join the military as Reserve Officers right after college. This would also give them an opportunity to get some practical training in their trade.

In the late 1960's when I applied for the military service, which was compulsory for every young man, it was for a grueling two year period. Those young men who did not have a four year college education were drafted as soldiers. Being a soldier in the Turkish military was not an easy or pleasant job. Some families, therefore, would send their sons to the universities just so they could avoid being soldiers. Most of the draftees were sent into the Army with very few chosen for the Navy and the Air Force. I wanted very much to be in the Navy where the environment and locations were much more pleasant.

I travelled to Ankara to get my diplomas from Lehigh and Brooklyn Polytechnic approved by the Department of Higher Education. Although it was Sümerbank, a government organization that had sent me to the United States, my diplomas still had to be approved by the Ministry of Education in order for me to be accepted as a Reserve Officer by the Ministry of Defense. I was now learning how things were done in Turkey. After my experience in the Custom's Office, I found out that the other Turkish government organizations were also immersed in extensive bureacracy, paperwork and sometimes influence and bribery.

I faced another significant and scary problem. In order to become an Officer or Reserve Officer in the Turkish Military one could not be married to a foreign citizen. I was a US Permanent Resident but although Ilkay was a Cypriot Turk, she was a US citizen. This meant that I could not be a Reserve Officer but instead I would be a soldier. This was an outdated rule and it was later changed. With all my educational credentials I was not willing to be a soldier. Since my marriage in Baltimore was not registered in Izmir, I applied to the military service as a bachelor. When I appeared in front of the Recruiting officer in Alsancak's Military Recruiting Office, he asked me about my educational credentials. I told him I had a Doctorate in Mechanical Engineering. After evaluating my file he emphatically argued that my Doctorate was in Philosophy not in Engineering! I do not think I convinced him with my explanation of what a Ph.D., Doctor of Philosophy in Mechanical Engineering was, but he reluctantly forwarded my file to the next crucial step of individual interviews. The interviewing team seemed much more pleasant and knowledgeable. They were very interested in my educational background, in my extensive experience in turbo-machinery at General Electric and in my teachings at Union College. I knew that the Turkish Navy had many ships using General Electric gas turbines and I was hoping and praying that with my relevant know-how I would be selected into the Navy. At this point of the selection process most of the highly influential people would use all their connections in the Government to get their sons into the Navy. In my case I was relying only on my technical merits and presonal knowledge. It was after a week of agonizing wait that I found out I was selected to be a Reserve Officer in the Turkish Navy. I guess sometimes reason prevails with some help from Allah. I was just happy and relieved. Within a month after I left the United States I was able to get into the Turkish Navy. Although I did not get to see my parents that much, I assured them there would be many opportunities for us to be together. After I said my goodbyes to them, I left and reported to duty at the Turkish Navy's Reserve Officer School in Gölcük.

Reserve Officer School

My service in the Turkish Navy started on October 1, 1968. A total of 120 candidates were supposed to be at the Reserve Officer School in Gölcük. At the beginning only about 100 of us were present. The remaining twenty trickled in as late as one month after the school had started. These were the children of the influential families. Most of the candidates in school were the graduates of the Merchant Marine Academy in Istanbul and they would be assigned to ship duties after graduation.

Gölcük was the main Turkish Navy Base located at the end of a long narrow bay called Izmit Bay. The main fleet of the Navy was located at the Gölcük Base which was 80km east of Istanbul. A Navy shipyard was also located within the base where they were maintaining the Navy's fleet. The shipyard had very capable personnel and engineers and one of their specialty was overhauling the old, World War II vintage diesel powered submarines given to the Turkish Navy by the United States Navy.

The Reserve Officer School was located inside the base next to many naval facilities, administrative buildings and the fleet headquarters. When we arrived at the school, we were gathered to listen to a welcoming but not so inspiring speech by the school's commander, Hikmet Bingöl. Immediately, those who had indulged in fashionable long hair were sent to the barber for a military style short haircut. I did not have that problem since my hair has always been short. We were assigned to large sleeping quarters with bunkbeds accomodating 30-40 people in each room. We were going to be in this school for the next six months with the last three months allocated for practical training. After the six months, we would graduate and be assigned to different locations. I was hoping I would be assigned to the Turkish Naval Academy in *Heybeliada*, one of the beautiful Princess Islands on the Marmara Sea near Istanbul where my friend Teoman was teaching.

Soon after our arrival the training started. For the first few weeks we spent the days marching around the school and the base. We were periodically given *çay* (tea) breaks and continued marching again. After a while we were trusted to march with the long, heavy and antiquated M-1 rifles which were handouts from the USmilitary. In between we were told to sit on the grass and clean the rifles for hours until they were completely spotless and passed inspection. After that came more marching! The weather was cold and damp and there was no heat in any of the buildings where we were staying. There was no running hot water either. After going without a shower for one week, because of many complaints from us, the school's commander yielded into sending us to the base *hamam* (Turkish bath). At last we were going to take a bath. With our towels and soaps tucked under our arms, we again started marching. This time however,we were happily singing military songs in step with our faster than usual pace. When we arrived at the *hamam* to our dismay we found out it was closed due to broken pipes. After a second week of marching without any shower, we were allowed to go out of the base for the first time and take a bath in a public *hamam* in Gölcük.

I was in school only two weeks when the school commander informed me that I had a visitor. I couldn't imagine who that might be. It was my father! After twelve years of separation, since I was not home for long, he had missed me and wanted to see me again. He arrived in Gölcük by bus a night before and spent the night in the sailors barracks. The next morning he was brought to my school. The Commander, who found out about my circumstance, gave me permission to spend the day with my father in Gölcük. We walked out of the base slowly with my father dragging his left foot and we had lunch together. That was a quality time I had with him which I still remember. He seemed like he had a lot of yearning for me. In the afternoon I put him back on the bus and sent him back to Izmir. It saddened me to see him this way, like a broken down human being from a giant I remembered from my childhood. But he was happy to see me and be with his one and only child. He was thrilled to be on a military base which reminded him of his father's military days and he was proud that his son was now in the military.

I found out all the candidates were very friendly and considerate people. We had plenty of time to meet and get to know each other and I became good friends with most of them. In 1968 there were not too many people who came from America, so they were rather interested in me. They were always kidding me about my Turkish since I spoke it with an American accent and had forgotten some of the words and terminologies. I started a concerted effort to improve my Turkish, not only the accent but also the vocabulary. Besides myself there were two other Ph.D.'s in the group: Talha Dinibütün from Istanbul Technical University and Öner Arıcı from Brown University. Talha and I became very good friends. In addition to marching, there were some useless classroom instructions as well. We had a lot of idle time on our hands because there was not much to do but sit in the cafeteria, read newspapers while sipping *çay*, and smoke if you desired all day long. I did not see anybody reading any books however. The school did not have a library either. During all this idle time some of the students would clear up some tables and play "table top *futbol*" with coins. Two competing players, each with a coin representing his team, would try to score goals with a smaller size coin ball. The coins moved around with their nails. Sometimes after dinner Talha and I would start our table top *futbol* and play for a while. I thought to myself what a waste of the country's resources this was: two Ph.D.'s playing this silly game. I don't think anybody thought about it or cared. Recently, after being the Dean of the Engineering School at Istanbul Technical University, Talha became the President of Doğuş University in Kadıköy, Istanbul.

The candidates from the Merchant Marines Academy, after their military service, would join the commercial vessels and sail all over the world. In my discussions with them I found out their English was extremely poor. They showed a lot of interest in learning English since they would need it in their foreign travels. They asked me if I could teach them English. I thought to myself it would be much better than playing table top *futbol* so I agreed to do it. After dinner every night I held English classes in one of the classrooms. Although we did not have any books, I gave them lessons on the board and then continued conversational English. In the classroom they were forbidden to speak Turkish and were forced to speak English only. It seemed like everybody was having a lot of fun learning. This went on for a couple of months until we were assigned to our professional training groups.

Although my friend Teoman was teaching at *Heybeliada*, his house was just outside the base in Gölcük on *Yüzbaşılar Mahallesi*. The neighborhood was beautifully stretched along the Izmit Bay with single family homes among beautiful flower gardens. It was nice to have Teoman and his wife Semra with their two children so close after being together in Schenectady. I spent a lot of time in their home especially on weekends.

One day I was summoned by the Commander of the Gölcük Base, Admiral Bülent Ulusu, who later became Prime Minister of Turkey. He said, "Son, I hear you speak English very well. We need you to translate Navy training films given to us by the Americans." I naturally agreed but said, "Sir, I will be happy to translate the films but I will need help with the Turkish terminologies." He said it was not a problem and he would assign a few officers to help me. In a dark room we started watching the American training movies and periodically stopped to translate them into Turkish. Before long I found out all the technical Navy terms in English were the same in Turkish. After a while I did not need help from the officers. Admiral Ulusu was so happy with the results that when I asked him for a pass to go to Izmir to see my family, he was more than generous. Soon the three months of schooling was coming to an end and my next assignment was at the Naval Shipyards' Engineering Department.

Gölcük Shipyard

The second phase of our training continued as field assignments. All the Merchant Marine Academy graduates were sent to different locations for ship duties. Most of the engineers were assigned to engineering duties in the Gölcük Shipyard. I was in the Design Engineering group working together with the Navy's engineering staff. The candidates with connections at the highest levels of the Government found their assignments mostly in Istanbul close to their families. The Shipyard was extremely busy with the new construction of small torpedo boats and the overhaul of two submarines. I never figured out what these antiquated, diesel engine propulsion submarines would ever be used for. But at least they looked good for the Navy. In the Design Engineering office we did not do any new design work like the ones I used to do at General Electric. All the design work was already done in Germany for the ships that the Turkish Navy had bought and we were building a couple of additional ones based on the German design. My job was to translate the German blueprints, operational and maintenance handbooks from English to Turkish. The job was not much of a challenge but it was something that kept me occupied.

There was another big activity going on at the shipyard where the very first large commercial ship, *S/S Sadık Altıncan* was being built. Everybody was very excited about this project. Towards the end of our assignments the ship was ready to be launched. A big celebration was prepared and everybody in the shipyard including the Navy officers gathered to watch this festive affair. Prime Minister Süleyman Demirel, waving his famous hat in his hand, arrived with a very large group to bless the launching of the ship. That was the highlight of my three-month assignment at the Gölcük Shipyard.

During our practical training we had much more freedom to go around especially on weekends. On a few weekends I rushed to Izmir by bus to see my family. Not wanting to waste my precious time travelling, I would board the early evening bus and be home the next morning twelve hours later when my parents arose. Although it was a long trip, it was worth it for me. My parents were always happy to see me with my father giving me bear hugs with a robust embrace and saying, "*oğlum benim*" (my son). At other times, since I did not have any other family close by, I spent a lot of time with Teoman's family reminiscing our Schenectady days. I had the pleasure of meeting many of his neighbors and friends who were all high ranking Navy officers. Teoman had bought the beautiful single family house he was living in and decided, as it was fashionable in those days, to convert it into a multi-story apartment building. He subcontracted the construction work while he was supervising the entire job himself. He and I spent a lot of time going to Izmit, the next big town, to buy all the construction materials, cement, reinforcement iron, bricks,etc. The building, which was right by the water, turned out to be very beautiful. Years later on August 17, 1999 when the big devastating earthquake hit the Izmit-Gölcük area, most of the buildings were leveled and thousands of people died. Ironically Teoman's house on *Yüzbaşılar Mahallesi* was the only building left standing. It was because he constructed it right by using the proper materials without stealing, which is what many contractors had done causing all the destruction, collapse of the buildings and death to thousands of people from the earthquake.

After five months of separation, during the New Year holiday of 1969, Ilkay flew into Istanbul. My father and mother came to Istanbul to meet her for the first time. I convinced them to wait in the hotel since the arrival time of her chartered flight was not definite. I spent one and a half days waiting for her at the airport. During the wait I even welcomed Tony Curtis, who was well known in Turkey with his movie "Trapeze" where he co-starred with Burt Lancaster and Gina Lolobrigida, another gorgeous Italian. In spite of a terrible flu Ilkay had, she looked very lovely and most presentable in her fashionable blue dress. My parents were very happy to meet her and tried their best to make her feel welcomed. The next morning we all took the bus to Izmir and got Ilkay settled with my parents. I spent the next couple of days in Izmir showing Ilkay my "old proving grounds". It was very nice walking together with her along the *kordon* in spite of the terrible smell. Again the Turkish saying *Sayılı günler çabuk geçer*, (numbered days pass swiftly) was most appropriate for my situation. I had to rush back to Gölcük to complete the remainder of my training before graduation from Reserve Officer School.

Teoman was trying to get me assigned to the Naval Academy after my graduation. He had his friends at the Navy headquarters in Ankara check on my file to see if they could help. While they were looking through my file, they noticed an anonymous letter mailed from Izmir to the Office of the Commander of the Navy informing them that I was married to a foreigner. The informant, further, gave all the details of my marriage to Hatice Ilkay Tuncel. I was shocked that anyone who knew us so well would do such a despicable act. They had nothing to gain but the satisfaction of seeing me serve as a soldier rather than an officer. It could only be a jealous and vile person who could do such an outrageous and devastating thing. All of a sudden my frail world was turned upside down. In the short time I was in Turkey I had to overcome so many hurdles and now I had to deal with another deplorable problem that could have profound consequences in my life. In difficult times like these, people always dwell thinking the worst possible scenarios. My mind kept on drifting to the unbearable thoughts of my not qualifying to be an officer in the Turkish Navy. Trying to explain logically that Ilkay was a Turkish Cypriot and a Moslem would have no influence on the military. Our school's commander Hikmet Bingöl had stated on the first day of school, "Once you pass through these doors the logic stops." We decided to take our chances and continue our lives as we had planned and hope and pray for the best. My nerves were completely shattered. Sometimes in frustration I would ask myself what the hell was I doing here? I had given up a gratifying career with all the money I needed and a very comfortable life. I was not looking for an adventure when I came here. I had come to serve my country and do something useful, not to live in fear and in uncertainties. Over the years, however, I found out that in Turkey adventurous incidences always find you even if you are not looking for it. I reassured myself I would overcome this also, so I continued attending my duties until the end of the Reserve Officer's School.

As the days were approaching towards the end of our school term, preparations were being made for the graduation ceremonies. Because of the informant's letter, I did not know whether I was going to graduate or be shipped to a far corner of the country as a soldier. I shared my dilemma with my friend Talha Dinibütün and he assured me that the military could not do anything like that. I was somewhat relieved. A couple of days before graduation we were to find out where we would be assigned for our officer duties during the next eighteen months. The entire student body was assembled and one by one our assignments were handed out. The Merchant Marine graduates were all assigned to various ships around the country and those boys of influential families got themselves assigned close to Istanbul. I still had not gotten my assignment yet. My heart was pounding and my stomach was in knots. After everyone got their assignments, the names of the three candidates with Ph.D's were read: Özcan Tuncel, Talha Dinibütün, Öner Arıcı. We were assigned as teachers to the Naval Post Graduate School (*İleri Hizmet Okulu*) in Derince. Derince was located directly across the bay from Gölcük, next to Izmit. The commute to Derince from Istanbul by bus would take about an hour. I felt relieved that I was graduating and I had a good assignment given to me.

Graduation day was on 31 March 1969, and my parents and Ilkay came to the graduation ceremony. After a few speeches our diplomas were given out and as a group we marched through the streets of the base following the Navy band to Atatürk's monument. After a brief ceremony and laying a wreath at the monument, the graduation festivities came to an end. We were now First Lieutenants in the Turkish Navy. My father was beaming and so proud to see his son as an officer.

Turkish Navy's Post Graduate School

Derince was a small village next to Izmit, situated on the beautiful shores of Izmit Bay, about 70 km from Istanbul. It seemed like the shores of Izmit Bay was an extension of Istanbul's industrial arm where shipyards, manufacturing complexes, petrochemical industries and summer resorts were intermingled with no serious urban planning. Even in its early days before the industrial mega complexes expanded around its periphery, the beautiful clean waters of Izmit Bay was rapidly getting polluted just like Izmir Bay was. At the shores of Derince a small undeveloped port was used to handle the excess load the port in *Haydarpaşa*, Istanbul could not service. There was no major road going from the Istanbul—Izmit highway to the port but a narrow village road. The noise from the trucks going to the port would spoil the tranquility of this beautiful village with lush flower gardens and fruit orchards.

Sometimes ships coming from far distances would wait for days in the middle of the bay until they could unload in this small port which did not have much equipment for the load handling. Across from Derince, the Navy's Gölcük Base and the shipyard could be seen with all the Navy ships lined up and tied to each other. In the middle of this pack stood the famous mighty ship *Yavuz*, also known as the Goeben when the Ottomans had accepted it from the Germans during the First World War. *Yavuz* was now a showpiece with no military use.

Next to the Derince port, tucked away along the shores of the Bay were nicely designed buildings housing the Turkish Navy's Post Graduate School (*İleri Hizmet Okulu*). The Post Graduate School was primarily established to give additional education to the Navy's young officers with the ranks of Second Lieutenant and Captain. The school was so successful that they expanded the services to Petty Officers and even to Iranian Navy personnel.

In addition to the usual Navy staff, a small group of select Reserve Officers were assigned to the school with responsibilities varying from teaching to guard duties. Most of the professional courses were assigned to the Reserve Officers to teach. The Turkish Navy had quite a few high speed boats furnished with General Electric gas turbines for propulsion systems so they were very much interested in gas turbines. This time my GE background came handy for a change when I was asked to teach a course on the principles and operations of gas turbines. At every opportunity the school's commander would assign us more courses to teach. A few months later I was assigned to teach another course on Applied Mathematics. For sure the Navy was now utilizing us very effectively and I was happy that I was doing something useful for my country.

Most of the students were young officers with a few years of service since their graduation from the Naval Academy. In fact they were all younger than me. One day when we were going to the lunch room one of the officers who was only one rank above me stopped and scolded me for not saluting him. I did not think we needed to salute on the school grounds every passing officer, all day long. I think he was trying to show off. After lunch it was time for my mathematics class and the young officer who scolded me was in my class. Not long after the class started I asked him to the blackboard and asked him to solve a tricky problem in differential equations. To his embarrassment he could not answer any of the questions in front of all his fellow officers. I, naturally, made it sure he could not and in certain terms I reminded him that he should be, as an officer in the Turkish Navy, more responsible with his school work.

We were working quite hard in school and the Navy was getting their money's worth. The pay was a mere 950 Turkish Lira a month ($95 at the time) which did not even cover the rent. All the other expenses were out of pocket, diving deep into my rapidly dwindling savings. One of my superior officers, Colonel Ahmet Ateş took a business trip to Germany with a group to review some of the torpedo boats the Germans were building for the Turkish Navy. When he returned he was very pleased and excited about his trip. He called me into his office and showed me all the machinery instruction books he had brought back from Germany. I told him the books were in English, not in German. He happily assured me that he brought these books for me so that we both could translate them into Turkish. His English was not that good but he informed me that the Turkish Navy was paying for translations per page and he would share the money with me. I needed the money and besides he was my supervisor whom I did not dare cross. I unwillingly accepted the offer. By now I was getting to be one of the best technical translators in the Navy and my Turkish was rapidly improving. I started writing the translations into Turkish at every opportunity I had and gave it to Col. Ateş who had one of the sailors type them. He himself spent time arranging the results into a nice format to be submitted to the Navy Headquarters. He repeatedly assured me our payment would be a good sum. Oh, how I could use that money. Unfortunately, maybe even not surprisingly I never got a dime out of that work.

During the weeknights we could stay in school whenever we chose to. Some weekends we had guard duty and had to stay in school. This meant we were in charge of the entire complex and the students that were in school. It was a big responsibility. On one of the weekends when I was on duty, my father, mother and Ilkay came to spend Sunday with me at school. I had the sailors prepare a nice lunch for us which we ate outdoors under the shade of a large oak tree. I was fully dressed in my white Navy uniform with a sword hanging from my waist. During the flag raising ceremonies I was performing with my sailors, my father came and stood next to me like a sailor himself, very proud and touched. I think that made him much more happy than my educational accomplishments.

On another weekend when I was on guard duty again, my school's commander informed me that there was a ship coming from America and he would be at the school to meet the ship. I knew from the Petty Officer students in school that in those days their entire dream in the Turkish Navy was to go to America and "get a ship". Based on NATO agreements the American military was giving all kinds of hardware to the Turkish military as military aid. The Turkish Navy periodically would get a ship from the American Navy left over from WWII. The old ship would go through an overhaul and get upgraded in one of the American shipyards. A full crew of the Turkish Navy personnel would be sent to the United States to take over the ship. After the official transfer ceremonies the ship would sail to Turkey under the Turkish flag. The crew had the opportunity to buy anything they wanted from the base store at very low prices and bring them to Turkey. The Petty Officers would buy as many boxes of American cigarettes as they could and sell them in the Turkish black market for huge profits. Other Officers would buy electronic goods which had high tariffs and get them into Turkey duty free. The Customs Office did not have jurisdiction over the military and ships from overseas could come in without any inspection. During this period in Turkey, because of shortages of many goods and the country's policies of not being open to the outside world, many things were sold at very high prices on a thriving back market.

That Saturday morning when I was starting my guard duty, I could see a big ship in the middle of the bay across from the school deep in the water all the way to the top level indicator. I knew right away that was the ship that had come from America my commander was referring to. This made me think about my home in America, my friends and co-workers at GE. Before long, early in the morning the school's commander showed up and took charge of the activities. The small boats *iskampanya* were ferrying all day long between the ship and the school's dock carrying all kinds of goods and loading them onto trucks. The commander made it clear that in no terms did he want me around the dock. The unloading continued into the late hours of the evening and the sailors worked feverishly. If only the dock workers would work like this in the Derince commercial port there would be no ship back ups. The rumor was that they even brought a car from America on that ship. The next morning I checked out the big ship and it was way up in the water almost to the lower level lines. I wondered how much goods they had carried out all day and night. The following Monday our school duties commenced without a single word about the weekend activities.

Kızıltoprak, Istanbul

Across the Bosphorus on the Asian side of Istanbul, the city was rapidly expanding with apartment buildings sprouting everywhere. *Kadıköy* and *Üsküdar* were the two historical neighborhoods anchoring the Asian side of the city with ferry boats to the European side of Istanbul. Baghdad Boulevard was the main road extending parallel to the Marmara Sea, connecting beautiful quaint towns such as *Suadiye*, *Bostancı*, and *Fenerbahçe* to each other. During the Ottoman period these towns were the popular country resorts of Istanbul's rich and famous, with exquisite mansions *(köşks)*, situated in the middle of lush gardens full of honeysuckles, gardenias, lavenders, jasmine and roses. Now all these beautiful homes were replaced with monstrous apartment buildings with no architectural appeal. It seemed like the architects copied the designs of these buildings from Turkish government handbooks similar to dull looking Turkish school buildings. During this significant transition from single family dwellings to multi-family concrete jungles, the corresponding electrical, sewer, road and transportation services were never improved, just like in Izmir, causing arduous chaos.

Kızıltoprak was situated at the beginning of Baghdad Boulevard close to *Kadıköı* and to all the communities. Ilkay and I started looking for a rental apartment and found a reasonably priced one in *Kızıltoprak* on the first floor of an apartment building. It was a newer building with a good size yard around it. One of the residents, who enjoyed gardening, had planted flowers on one side of the building and vegetables on the other. We liked this because it reminded us of our home in America we had left behind. A moving truck brought all of our belongings from Izmir and in no time we were settled in our new home.

A few steps from the *Kadıköı* ferry terminal was the shopping district we frequented. The open air bazaar was lively, colorful and a delight for us. There were fresh fish, butcher shops, and fruit and vegetable stalls filled with wonderful produce lined up along the cobble stone streets. We spent a lot of time at this bazaar either browsing or doing our weekly shopping. A short walk from this area was the neighborhood of *Moda* which had exclusive shops and boutiques. *Fenerbahçe* was another nice neighborhood we occasionaly walked to.

Sometimes things were not as good as they seemed from the outside. Ilkay and I were very concerned about the military police or jandarmes coming to question the neighbors to find out about our marital status. I still had a long eighteen months of service to complete and I was sure during this period the Navy Headquarters would follow up on the informant's letter. I did not know what they would do or know what would happen next, but whatever it was would be devastating. We were very scared. At our apartment Ilkay always kept the curtains closed and did not socialize with the neighbors. No matter how discreet we were, our Turkish neighbors were very curious and nosy checking on everything we were doing.

During the week I would commute to Derince by bus from Kadiköy and depending upon the duties at school I would sometimes stay overnight. My commute would start from Kızıltoprak to Kadıköy with a *dolmuş*, a shared taxi. They say "necessity is the mother of invention". Turks are very innovative people. Since there was not sufficient means of public transportation in rapidly expanding and crowded cities, *dolmuş* would supplement the public's transportation needs. After school had started and our teaching duties were identified, our lives turned to normal. I could handle my teaching responsibilities readily with time to spare. Since the salary I was getting from the Navy was not even sufficient to pay the rent and with daily expenses increasing and the reserve savings diminishing, I had to find another job for additional income.

The country at the time had very few higher educational institutions, which were not meeting the ever increasing demand of the large youth population. Again Turkish ingenuity and entrepenurship met this challenge by opening many small private higher educational institutions. These schools were accredited by the Turkish Ministry of Education. Işık Engineering School (*Işık Mühendislik Okulu*) was such a technical school, training engineering students. Because there was a large shortage of trained teachers for these schools, when I appeared at *Işık's* doors for a job, they were very pleased to hire me. My first course was "Strength of Materials", which was a simple and basic course to teach. The problem I had, however, was not the technical contents, but rather the corresponding technical terminologies in Turkish. Since all of my engineering education was in America, I did not know any of the technical Turkish terms. I rapidly overcame this problem by using the Turkish translation of Timoshenko's textbook which we had used in college. I prepared my lectures and learned my technical Turkish while I was commuting back and forth on the bus to *Derince*. People sitting next to me were always staring and wondering what I was doing. Since the classes at Işık Engineering School were in the evenings, during my return home from Derince I would first go to school and then go home to Ilkay very late at night. Unfortunately, Işık Engineering school was located in *Beşiktaş* across from *Üsküdar* on the other side of the Bosphorus, an unrealistic commute for anyone. When I got off the *Derince* bus, I had to take a dolmuş to the *Üsküdar* ferry terminal. The *Kadıköy-Üsküdar* dolmuş vehicles were all ancient, large Russian automobiles that looked like limousines with converted three row seats. When the cigarette smoke filled car crept to the top of a hill, the driver, a sweaty, smelly man with unshaven beard and ever present mustache, would shut off the engine to save gas and let the Russian piece of junk roll all the way to the *Üsküdar dolmuş* stop at an ever-increasing speed with no braking. The *dolmuş* was packed with people and was running through the narrow winding roads of *Üsküdar* at a trecherous speed with continuous honking of it's horn to warn pedestrians to get out of it's way. As I held on to my seat, I wondered nervously if the driver would be able to stop this junky vehicle at the end of this roller coaster ride.

At *Üsküdar* I had no time to wait for the ferry boat to cross the Bosphorus to *Beşiktaş* since I did not want to be late to my class. Similar to *dolmuş* cars, *dolmuş* boat services continuously ran between *Üsküdar* and *Beşiktaş*. The boats were very small, fishermen's boats challenging the big waves and strong currents of the Bosphorus. It was a dangerous means of transportation but I did not have any other alternative. On my return, late at night, again with a *dolmuş* boat in the middle of the rough waters of the Bosphorus, I felt like George Washington crossing the Delaware. I was exhausted but happy because I was earning some extra money.

Even though our lives continued in fear, we were now in a routine which by itself was a temporary relief. We did not have too many friends and family members in Istanbul and we did not dare make new friends and expose ourselves to the outside world either. We tried to keep ourselves very obscure and discreet. My cousin Meral and her husband Mustafa were my only relatives nearby, living in Suadiye, whom we occasionally saw. Our closest friends in Istanbul were Professor Michael Green, his wife Sylvia and their four lovely young daughters. I knew Mike when we were both young engineers at GE in Schenectady. Mike had left GE to get a Ph.D. and go into a teaching profession. When he was in the American military, he was stationed in Incirlik-Adana, Turkey and had loved the country very much. While there they had their four daughters whom they named in Turkish. After receiving his Ph.D. he and his wife decided to move to Turkey and work there. He was now teaching at Roberts College in the Mechanical Engineering Department. Mike and Sylvia loved being in Istanbul and they were both fluent in Turkish. On weekends Ilkay and I would go to visit them in their lovely home on the shores of Emirgan overlooking the Bosphorus. At other times we would all go picnicking at *Pendik*, *Kartal* or *Büyük Ada*, one of the Princess islands.

One day we realized it had been six months since Ilkay had come to Turkey and her visitor's visa would soon expire. There was no way to renew her visa except for her to leave the country and re-enter. That summer her parents were going to Cyprus for a visit and then coming to Izmir and Istanbul to be with us. I decided to send Ilkay to Cyprus also to visit her relatives whom she had not seen since she left as a little girl. Thus we secured a new visitor's visa for her for another six months. Ilkay was now pregnant and due the end of December. Summer passed swiftly and my routine had not changed. Although we did not have classes, I was still commuting to Derince for other duties and teaching summer courses at Işık Engineering School. Before long another six months was approaching for another visa renewal for Ilkay. I could not afford to send her out of the country again just for this purpose. My friend Mike proposed an interesting plan for taking Ilkay across the Greek border by car and return with a renewed visa. Ilkay, my cousin Meral from Izmir who was visiting us at the time, and I boarded Mike's stationwagon together with his entire family and started driving towards Edirne. After four hours of driving, we arrived at the Greek border just outside of Edirne. Meral and I got out of the car on the Turkish side where we saw nothing but cabbage fields as far as our eyes could see. Mike continued driving the car into the Greek side. We could see the border guards across from each other with the Turkish and Greek flags of the two countries fluttering in the wind. Too bad the relationship of these two neighbors was not amicable. An hour later Mike drove back into Turkey with another renewed visa for Ilkay and lots of goodies they had purchased at a local store such as instant American coffee, chocolates, cereal and some Greek cognac, Metaxa for me.

Back in Istanbul schools had re-opened. On a couple of occasions Mike invited me to Roberts College to lecture at seminars. At other times I met many members of the Istanbul Technical University staff through Talha Dinibütün. The class work in Derince had also started. In the morrnings I would wait for Talha who was coming by ferry from *Fatih* and we continued our commute together.

Nükhet Is Born

As the time of delivery of our baby was approaching, my mother and father arrived at *Kızıltoprak* to be with us and help out. It was a very exciting period of our lives. Sometimes when we were at the beautiful movie theatre Kent in *Kızıltoprak*, which was only a walking distance from our home, Ilkay would let me feel the baby's kicking. It was an undescribable sensation for both of us. We were very happy with Ilkay's obstetrician Dr. Ayhan Öner, who had trained in America. All we had to do now was wait for the arrival of our baby.

My parents and Ilkay passed their days by shopping for a few necessities for the baby. One day Mother disappeared for a few hours which concerned Ilkay. When she came home she had a baby tub in her hand. She was tired and exhausted. She had started walking to *Altı Yol*, which was a few miles from home, thinking it was closer. Carrying the tub back in her hands had tired her out. She would talk about this escapade of hers for many years. On Tuesdays there was a huge bazaar in *Kızıltoprak* and they would go shopping for our weekly fruits, vegetables, cheese and even grocery items. These were some of the happier times in our lives since my return from America.

On December 23,1969 early in the morning Ilkay told me it was time for me to take her to the hospital. Luckily it was the weekend and when I frantically rushed to *Bağdat Caddesi* to get a taxi, I did not have any trouble finding one. I was panic stricken and I told the taxi driver we had to rush to the hospital because my wife was having a baby. When he stopped at a gas station to make sure he would have enough gas, I was exasperated that he was wasting precious time. He assured me, since he had seven children, that babies do not come out that fast. We somehow made it to *Zeynep Kamil* Hospital in *Üsküdar* and a few hours later our beautiful baby girl was born. We named her Nükhet Naciye.

Because Ilkay's milk was not sufficient and not nourishing enough, the baby was constantly hungry and crying. The doctor prescribed a baby formula, SMA, similar to Similac which was sold only on the black market. We were living in a period in Turkey where everything from electronic equipment to cigarettes and even baby food was sold in a flourishing black market at exuberant prices. After combing the entire Asian side of Istanbul, I found the baby formula on the European side.

We were very happy and busy with our newborn baby in our apartment. Ilkay was looking after her little companion and I was continuing my commutes to Derince and Beşiktaş. As Nükhet was growing, whenever people saw her in her stroller or in our arms, they would always comment how beautiful she was. Her wavy blond hair, blue-green eyes and overall feautures looked just like my mother. My mother and father stayed a long time with us and helped out around the apartment. They enjoyed being with their first grandchild. When my father started getting bored, they decided to return to Izmir where he had more friends and neighbors.

I found out at school, where by now everybody including the school commander knew my situation and were watching out for any suspicious signal to warn me, that the Navy Headquarters was following up on the informant's letter. I was told an inquiry letter was sent to the Istanbul Jandarme Headquarters to check on my marital status. Our calm world was about to be turned upside down again. I had completed eighteen months of service and had only six months left. We immediately decided to move and loose our track. We found a beautiful apartment at *Duvardibi, Üsküdar* and got settled rather quickly. Down the road from our apartment was a historical site which dominated the skyline of the Asian shore, Selimiye Barracks (*Selimiye Kışlası*). The Selimiye Barracks was originally built at the beginning of 1800's by Sultan Selim III to house his soldiers. During the famous Crimean War of 1853-1856 when the British and the French fought on the Ottoman side against the Russian Empire, the Barracks were used as a military hospital. The British nurse, Florence Nightingale took charge of the medical services at the Selimiye Barracks and worked tirelessly saving hundreds of lives. Part of the Barracks was established as a museum recognizing Florence Nightingale's heroic contributions. We felt more secure at our *Duvardibi* apartment since no one knew us there.

One day when we were together with our friends Teoman and his wife Semra, I briefed them about the Navy's letter to the Jandarmes. Semra suggested that her brother Riza Abi, who was retired from the Jandarmes as an officer, could help me. All the high ranking officers in the Jandarmes were Riza Abi's classmates and were close friends. Riza Abi was well known and a very much liked selectman (*Muhtar*) of Emirgan. I immediately went to see him and explained my dilemma. He smilingly assured me not to worry about it. He and I took the bus from Emirgan to the Jandarme Command Headquarters in Beşiktaş, only a few blocks from Işık Engineering School where I was teaching. When Riza Abi and the Commander started embracing and wholeheartedly greeting each other, I felt relieved. They seemed like two close buddies who were happy to see each other once again. Their conversation and reminiscing the old days went on for a while as I nervously sat next to them without saying a single word. Towards the end of our visit, Riza Abi told the Commander we had a problem and needed his help. He told him there might be a letter questioning my marital status. The Commander asked his orderly to find my file where the letter from Ankara was inquiring about my marital status. After reading the letter, the Commander ordered his subordinate to respond to Ankara that they investigated the situation and there was no such thing. Thus the matter was closed and our nightmare was over. The next day I visited the Commander with a box of chocolates thanking him for his help. Sometimes the kindness of a stranger can make a significant difference in a person's life.

Ilkay and I were feeling very relieved and we decided to finally enjoy ourselves and our beautiful baby without any worry. We took walks along the Üsküdar shores until we could see Leander's Tower *(Kız Kulesi)*. This well known Bosphorus landmark, left over from the Byzantine period, always reminded me of the legendary princess who was confined there because she was warned that she would die from a snake bite. In spite of all the security imposed by her father the Emperor, the snake duly appeared from a basket of figs and struck the fatal blow. Ironically I thought to myself with a sense of relief, we got away from the snake this time.

Everytime I was in a *dolmuş* taxi I could see the driver struggling in handling the change with all the coins thrown in a bag or spread out on a small piece of cloth on the dashboard. I also felt this was causing additional risk in difficult driving conditions. I thought a coin exchanger used in buses in America would be very useful for *dolmuş* drivers and if I manufactured them I could even make some money. I ordered a sample from America and modified the design to a simpler configuration. I used aluminum tubes to store the coins and designed the other parts to be manufactured in presses at my cousin Necdet's factory in Izmir. I had to make quite a few trips to Izmir to get the press dies prepared and parts to be pressed. Ilkay and I had the arduous task of assembling the finished product in our apartment. I called my product Tik-Tak Money Exchanger (*Tik-Tak Bozuk Para Makinası*). Unfortunately, by the time I was ready to market this product, my military service was coming to an end. By then I had neither the energy nor the interest in continuing this project. All I could think about was finishing my military service and returning to America as soon as possible. I sold all the items at cost to a taxi driver and got out of the money exchanger business.

On September 30, 1970 my Navy duties as a Reserve Officer in the Turkish Military came to an end. I got my discharge papers upon successfully fulfilling my duties. I was done with the military and the mission was accomplished. We moved our few belongings with a truck back to Izmir to my parents house. Before I left Istanbul I had job offers to teach at Roberts College and another one to head the Mechanical Engineering Department of the new Research Facilities of the Turkish Government called TUBITAK in *Gebze*, outside of Istanbul. By then I was ready to return to my job at General Electric and nothing could entice me otherwise. Since I had exceeded the two year limitation on my Green Card, the US Consulate in Istanbul wanted a letter from General Electric. Ray Dickinson, our Department's Human Resources representative responded immediately with a letter stating," . . . . We are anxious to have him return to the position which we have continued to hold open for him while he fulfilled his military commitments." I renewed my green card and left Istanbul.

In Izmir as I was preparing to return to America, I ran into another problem. After I had paid all of my father's siblings for their interests in our house, we had it repaired and upgraded. It was very nice and presentable now. During the two year period I was in the military, the value of the house like everything else in Turkey due to high inflation had increased. The greedy siblings of my father decided they did not get enough money for their shares and demanded more. At this point we still did not have the deed to the property because of one missing share owner and technically they were still all owners. They were not shy about reminding us of that fact. Although we had notorized papers in our hands showing that they had already received payment for their shares, in the Turkish courts those papers were not acceptable. I could never understand the Turkish Judicial System. I was disgusted with my father's screwy family members. I consulted with a lawyer and started a court case to get the deed with the understanding that I would pay additional money to my uncles and aunts when we got the deed to the house. This case would eventually break up the remaining family ties and continue about 15 years with significant lawyer and court expenses. In the end we were never able to get the deed to the house at No. 36.

I was now all done with Turkey. We packed all our belongings into one luggage and decided to travel thru Europe on our way back to America. We assured my parents that we would visit them more often. It was sad leaving them behind but we felt that we had to get on with our lives.

Ilkay and I, with Nükhet in our arms, flew to Rome. I still remembered all the sights I had visited 14 years ago when I was first going to America. In Rome I had the contact name and address of an Italian neighbor who owned a share of the empty lot next door to my parents house. I found this neighbor and made arrangements to buy his share of the lot. In one day I got all the sale papers prepared, notorized by the Turkish Embassy in Rome and mailed them to my mother. With another petition case (İzalei-Şuu Davası) we were later able to buy the rest of the lot.

From Rome we took the train to Venice. Since this was October, the weather was raw and damp. We bundled up Nükhet with a wool blanket and strolled thru beautiful Venice for two days. From there we went on to Paris. When we arrived in Paris we could not understand why all the stores, museums, and other establishments were closed that day until we noticed the front page of a newspaper that Charles DeGaulle had died. After a few days of visiting the usual touristic sites in Paris, we left for Amsterdam. It was very tiresome for us to be carrying 10 month old Nükhet in our arms all day as she would constantly try to hop. We completed our mini vacation with a final stop in London where we visited Ilkay's uncle Turgut and his family. After completing our 21 day much deserved tour, we were on our way back to America.

Meeting Ilkay, 1964   At our engagement

Our wedding at the Washington mosque with Fazıl Erdoğan, May 7, 1966

Graduation from Brooklyn Polytechnic, 1967

Students at the Turkish Navy's Reserve Officer School, 1968

Lieutenant at the Turkish Navy with Ilkay, 1969

At the Turkish Navy's Post Graduate School
(Talha Dinibütün second from left)

End of the Navy duty, 1970

12

Returning To America

Back to Schenectady

I thought to myself, happiness is being back in America with my family: lovely wife and beautiful baby; in my own house with my gratifying job at General Electric; away from fear, stress, uncertainties and not knowing what tomorrow would bring. In our lives in America, there was a sense of security and stability, with some guarantee for the future. I had missed that very much and I was happy that we were leaving Turkey and coming back to that life style again.

Towards the end of November 1970, our European mini vacation ended up in Baltimore at Ilkay's parent's house. We immediately contacted Selma and Boris Wundt to see how they were doing. Selma surprised us with the pleasant news that she had saved quite a bit of money for us from the rents she had collected from our two-family house. They had been looking after our welfare just like our own family. That was a refreshing and encouraging news. Our next task was to buy a used car to take us back to our home in Schenectady. We found out a family friend of my in-laws, Dr. Ibrahim Türek, was selling his used Ford Mustang. We were excited that we would get a classic Mustang, a dream car which every young person wanted to own. We thought that since Dr. Türek was a well to do doctor and a family friend, he would sell the car to us for less. We must have been very naive. He did not budge a penny from his price. Since we did not have too many options, we agreed to buy the yellow colored Mustang. The car turned out to be just like its color a real "lemon". It turns out Dr. Türek had not done any maintenance on the car, not even having an oil change for a long time and soon after we bought it every component in the car started breaking down causing me a big hardship of paying for many repairs.

In no time Ilkay and I got settled into the routine of our married life in the downstairs apartment of our house at 1039 Gillespie Street that Selma had gotten ready for us. On December 1, 1970 I reported to work at General Electric to my old job. Nothing much had changed at work or at GE. I felt like I had never left the place. The turbine business was still booming with a lot of new orders and everybody was extremely busy. I was welcomed to my old group by our Unit Manager George Fischer with a new position as the Technical Group Leader of all the bucket development programs at a substantially higher salary. Of course anything was better than what I was getting in Turkey during my military service which was next to nothing. I was off to a good start with a lot of responsibilites. I was in charge of the technical aspects of some critical turbine components. A few days later on December 23, 1970 we celebrated Nükhet's first birthday and soon after that we happily observed her putting one step in front of the other walking on her own for the first time on our snow covered porch in front of our house.

It did not take me long before I took charge of my group. At the beginning of 1971 we started tackling stress and vibration problems of the steam turbine buckets. I was given the freedom to hire a few more engineers. I hired George Schlottner, Don Sturges and a Danish engineer Horst DeLorenze into my group. Not only did I give them work assignments but I also put a lot of effort training them to be successful in their endeavors. A few years later, after I left Large Steam Turbine Department, they all moved to key positions making significant contributions. Throughout my General Electric career I was happy to train many good engineers for the Company.

In mechanical engineering field it is a known fact that in the rotating machinery, whether it is a steam turbine, gas turbine or jet engine, the blades or the buckets are the most critical components which are very susceptible to fatigue failures. Any blade failure would cause a costly "forced outage" of the turbine. It was therefore our job to master the vibratory behavior of turbine buckets under operating conditions. A blade running in a turbine has a "vibratory signature" just like a human heart beat. One of the main jobs of a turbine bucket development engineer was to understand this behavior both analytically and experimentally. The vibratory behavior of blades was characterized simply by a "Campbell Diagram" for each individual type of blade. A Campbell diagram was like an electrocardiogram of the turbine blade. Wilfred Campbell who was born in 1884 in England was hired into General Electric in 1908. In 1919 when Wilfred Campbell was in the Turbine Engineering Department, he was in charge of investigating turbine vibrations of all sorts. In May 1924 he presented his research findings at the American Society of Mechanical Engineer's meeting which became a major breakthrough in turbine technology. He was a rare genius devising an ingenious method of analyzing the cause of failures of large turbine wheels and buckets. Even in the early period when proper instrumentation was not available, he had made everlasting contributions to the industry and his work has been used to this date by engineers who worked on any kind of rotating machinery. A Campbell Diagram of the blade is simply a frequency-speed diagram showing the variation of frequency with speed. An important criteria in a steam turbine bucket design has been avoidance of the superposition of the natural frequency of the bucket with the excitation frequency coming from the stationary nozzles which could cause a resonance hence a fatigue failure. A Campbell Diagram was a simple way of illustrating this phenomenon. Since I was in charge of the bucket development work at General Electric, the giant of the turbine industry, I had to master the understanding of Campbell Diagrams. After so many years of working on bucket designs, bucket vibration frequency charts and Campbell Diagrams became a second nature to me.

As the country's power needs increased so did the size of steam turbines. A 500,000 to 600,000 kilowatt turbine was then a standard size. With increased turbine size all the components became larger with the new 33 ½ inch last-stage bucket we designed, being extensively used as a successful "work horse". Our challenge was now directed to the utilization of steam turbines in nuclear power plant applications. With Westinghouse and General Electric in fierce competition, two types of reactors led the way to very large power plants. The Pressurized Water Reactors of Westinghouse and the Boiling Water Reactors of General Electric pushed the power plant sizes requiring as big as 1,200,000 kilowatt turbines. The length of the last stage buckets in these applications was 52 inches (for lower speeds) and the wheels carrying these buckets were so large that they had to be assembled at the power plants because of shipping limitations. The Tokyo Electric Power Company (TEPCO) became our biggest customer ordering many nuclear power plants. As bucket designers we were challenged with all kinds of new design issues such as bucket tip erosion because of excessive moisture content in nuclear steam, as being one of the major problems. My old work and expertise on erosion came handy to tackle with this issue. The ever expanding turbine business and continuously increasing turbine sizes, made our jobs very demanding and challenging. The 1970's was one of the most exciting and dynamic periods in steam turbine business at General Electric and I was happy that I was in the midst of this action.

Our family life became routine with no excitement. I certainly had enough excitement when I was in the Turkish Navy and I did not need any more. Ilkay started going back to Russell Sage College taking evening classes while I was at home with my beautiful little baby Nükhet. As we were getting our family situation into a happy and stable condition, news that followed from my parents in Turkey were not good. Again my father's siblings, led by my one armed uncle Cevat, had ganged up on my parents demanding more money for the inherited house. It seemed like they could not get enough money from me. The more I gave the more they wanted. Years later I speculated with many justifications, that the culprit who wrote the infamous letter to the Turkish Navy regarding my marital status was my uncle Cevat. My frail father took the behavior of his brothers and sisters very hard. They never came to visit him and even their children turned against my poor parents. They were such money hungry and greedy people. My father was very much saddened and depressed and soon after at the beginning of 1972 he had another massive stroke. This time he could not pull through. After his stroke, my father who was once a strong, towering man, became a little crippled helpless individual looking at my mother for help. She took very good care of him, even under the most difficult conditions. In addition to paralysis of his arm and leg, he also had paralysis of the throat which made him choke every time he tried to eat.

Ilkay and I immediately made plans to go to Turkey that summer. We had decided she would go with Nükhet ahead of me and stay with my parents a few weeks longer than I since I only had two weeks vacation. On July 1, 1972 Ilkay and Nükhet arrived in Izmir only to find out my father was in the hospital and in a coma. She immediately called me and urged me to rush to Izmir. The next day with my heart full of fear and anxiety I made it to Izmir with three flight connections. At the hospital I saw my father lying in the hospital bed comatose. I spoke into his ear, with tears running down my face, telling him I was there next to him. I think he acknowledged me with a gentle squeeze of my hand but he did not get up and give me his usual hug, squeezing me with "*oğlum benim*" cries. His strong arms and erect, powerful body was no more. He was dying but I think he was waiting for me to arrive. I knew with the unspoken words that the strong ties between us was keeping him alive until I arrived. On July

3, 1972 in the afternoon, my father passed away. He was only 62 years old and it was too soon. He was too young to die but he was gone. He was no longer going to be around to go to the movies with me, give me bear hugs or see and enjoy his grandchildren.

My father lived a happy and a sad life. He was happy with his wife and his only son and he was happy living with his mother. He did not have much of anything but love towards us. He was a proud but lonely man. He would invite people passing by the house to come in and show them proudly his son's family photos. He was however sad that his siblings were no good, abandoning him when he needed them the most. He was also sad because he lived far away from his only son for so many years with deep yearnings for him as a big load in his heart all those years. His being gone left a big emptiness and void in my heart. I wished I could have been together with my father more and spent more time enjoying each other's presence. Alas that did not happen. I consoled myself thinking that my beautiful baby daughter would fill the emptiness left in my heart.

Life goes on. I could sense that my mother had readily accepted her fate and she was well resolved in her mind to continue life as it was. But she was always much stronger than I was. My maternal grandmother Pembe moved in with my mother to keep her company and at the same time they could look after each other. I made all the financial arrangements for them so that they would not have any concern for money. At this time my mother and I vowed not to have anything to do with my father's siblings anymore. It was an unfortunate but sad ending. Towards the end of July we returned back to the United States from Turkey. As we were flying back I rested my head against the airplane window and thought in vain how much I would miss my father.

Materials and Processes Laboratory

After our return from Turkey my friend Russ Chinoy who was then the Manager of Measurements Engineering group in the Materials ans Processes Laboratory asked me to join his organization. I was interviewed and hired as the Manager of Project Engineering Unit. In November 1972 I transferred to the Materials and Processes Laboratory and this was the beginning of my management career at GE. During the next thirty years I would work in various management positions in different organizations within General Electric Company.

The Materials and Processes Laboratory (M&P Lab) initially was dedicated to product development and applied technology devoted exclusively to improving the reliability and efficiency of steam turbines and generators. The M&P Laboratory which was a part of the Large Steam Turbine Department conducted applied research, development and evaluation of materials, processes and related measurements in the fields of chemistry, insulation, metallurgy, welding, electrical and mechanical engineering and non-destructive testing. The testing capability and services were later extended to other General Electric Departments: Mechanical Drive Turbines, Gas Turbines, DC Motors, Jet Engines, Nuclear Equipment and Transportation Systems (locomotives). The Laboratory was funded by these departments and there was always more funding and "work requests" than we could handle. Some of the technical work done in the Laboratory was new advancements in technology. Based on these studies many technical papers were being published by the Laboratory staff. I was very impressed with the Laboratory when I saw creep test specimens in the Metallurgy Laboratory being subjected to varying loads at very high temperatures of over 1000 degrees continuously for as long as ten years. The Laboratory was always challenged by the product departments to meet their needs and demands to keep up with ongoing advancements and technologies. I thought this was a good opportunity for me to broaden my scope beyond the turbine buckets and rotors. I would also learn new technologies besides turbine bucket design. In addition I was going to be challenged with management responsibilities in which I had no experience. Although I felt confident about handling technical aspects of the new position, I was nervous about the dealings required to manage a group of technical staff.

When I started in the Project Engineering Unit I had 28 people reporting to me. Most of the testing we were doing were routine tests on turbine buckets in the "wheel box" test facility, a subject I was very familiar with. With an ever-expanding application of turbines in the fields, we needed to perform many field tests to acquire data. I got interested in developing equipment and data acquisition techniques for field applications using telemetry techniques, data loggers and data recording equipment. Telemetry tests on turbine buckets fascinated me. We could get bucket vibration data in a turbine operating under steam loading from a strain gage attached to the bucket and vibration signals were transmitted on an FM radio frequency. From the frequency receiver we could tape record the data and later analyze it in our Data Reduction facility in our laboratory. With plenty of funding available I was busily buying new and advanced test equipment into my organization. In a very short time with very successful tests and good service we were giving, other departments besides the Large Steam Turbine Department came knocking on our door. I kept on hiring more engineers and technicians and continued purchasing more equipment to meet the increased work demand. Within two years after I started in the Laboratory, my organization grew to 68 people. I had even hired a Turkish engineer to my group. My Laboratory business was booming and in many instances on big projects, I accompanied my engineers and technicians to the field, observing their work and getting involved with the technical aspects of the job. I was a hands-on manager.

During the next couple of years I travelled to every corner of the United States supervising or running tests on fossil or nuclear power plants, steel mills, gas turbines, heat exchangers and manyothers. Field tests on gas turbine transition piece was very challenging where our instrumentation had to survive excessively high gas turbine combustion temperature and our data acquisition with data loggers was very difficult. During this period it was fashionable in the Laboratory to publish technical papers. Based on the development work we did, I published a number of papers in the Society of Experimental Stress Analysis (SESA) on the subjects of high temperature strain gage developments, residual stress measurements and on other related subjects. Also during this period I was very active in technical societies of ASME and SESA and I was the Chairman of the Regional Society of Experimental Stress Analysis. Although these kinds of technical activities were secondary to the jobs we were doing, they helped to get proper recognition among our peers within and outside of the Company as a significant contributor in the fields we worked on.

One of the "work requests" we received from the Gas Turbine Department was to go to Saudi Arabia to find the cause of failures of the gas turbine nozzles. In March of 1977 my technician Tom Mayer and I flew to Dhahran on the eastern shores of Saudi Arabia where the ARAMCO (Arabian-American Oil Company) headquarters were located. This was the location where all the Saudi Arabian oil production was controlled and most of the oil was shipped from. The ARAMCO personnel living quarters in Dhahran, for mostly American and English staff, were very exquisite. I was so impressed to see how green the grass was in front of their homes in the middle of the desert. The houses were beautiful and the living quarters had everything they could possibly want. Obviously they were very well taken care of. Besides many restrictions, we learned women and foreigners like us without a work permit could not drive in Saudi Arabia. Women did not have much of any rights. I wondered how they could contribute to the well being of their society if they were so invisible. Saudi men however, were no great drivers either. The sides of the roads in the desert were cluttered with abandoned vehicles after accidents. Saudis preferred to buy new cars instead of repairing them. There were no repair shops anywhere that we could see. We were driven everywhere including into the desert. As a precaution, everytime our car was parked, a colorful plastic cone was placed behind the vehicle. Before backing out the cone was removed while it was throughly checked to make sure nobody was under the vehicle. Because of the excessive heat of the desert, many Arabs were taking naps under the vehicles causing many fatalities.

We were driven to Uthmaniyah in the middle of the Saudi desert three hours distance from Dhahran. Here GE gas turbines were pumping water into the ground to pressurize the oil which was forced out to the surface from another hole to be separated from water by centrifugal separators. We instrumented one of the gas turbine nozzles with high temperature strain gages which we had developed in our laboratory. We tried to start the test to acquire data with our data loggers but because of the hot desert temperatures and additional heat coming from the gas turbines, the electronics of our data loggers would not work. When we explained our dilemma to the ARAMCO personnel, in no time a portable room with an air conditioner was flown with a helicopter to our test site in the desert. That quickly solved our problem. We found out the Saudi Arab operators were accelerating the gas turbines at a faster pace than allowed, in spite of the restrictions given to them in the operational manual, causing thermal stresses on the nozzles and hence failures. We then installed limitations on the acceleration control of the turbines that the Arab operators could not override. This solved their problem.

In the middle of the desert at a distance I could see a Japanese petrochemical plant processing the oil right in place with cheap energy available locally. The oil pipes in groups were running in all kinds of directions. The desert was not an empty, desolate place as the name implies. At nights the excess gas burning everywhere lit the desert into a bright, festive site. As we were being driven back to Dhahran near Huffuf our English driver, with a cynical and sarcastic attitude, pointed out to me an old, rundown, dilapidated fortress in this oil-rich land which belonged to the Ottoman Turks. He didn't have to remind me the period in history when the English helped the rebellion of the Arabs against the Ottomans to take this land away from the Turks and transfer them to the Arabs. The Saudi Arabs continued even to this date destroying in their lands everything that was Turkish so that it would not remind them of the five hundred years of Ottoman rule. On the way back we spent a couple of days in Dhahran and observed the Arab men lazily sitting around at the coffee shops, smoking their *nargile* (waterpipe) while the women, covered in black head to toe, were shopping in some exclusive stores. After staying in the desert for almost a week, Tom and I were happy to be in the city seeing the Saudi women eventhough they were completely covered in their *abaya or chadour*. With the light hitting them from behind, we could see some of them had nice shapely legs and were wearing mini skirts under the transparent black outfits. This reminded me the time when I was 14 years old looking at Nermin's legs in Izmir. We were extremely dicreet in our observations however, since we did not want the risk of being stoned to death in a market place by Saudi Arabs just for looking at their women. At nights our invitations to ARAMCO management homes to have non-alcoholic cocktails and lavish dinners were wonderful and a welcomed change.

After Tom Mayer returned to America, I directed my way to Tehran to visit Ilkay's sister Zekiye and her husband Morteza and their two children. They had recently moved there from America. The Shah of Iran was spending a lot of his oil money on the country's development as well as building his military with American equipment. He was an arrogant, self righteous individual. Of course we all know what happened to him and to his country in the end. On the way back from Tehran I flew to Izmir by way of Ankara. While I was flying over Mount Ararat in Eastern Turkey I strained myself to see if the remnants of Noah's Arc were still at the peak of this rugged mountain. Needless to say I did not see anything. In Izmir my mother and grandmother were very happy to see me. Once again I spent some quality time with them and then continued my journey back to America.

Between January 1972 to May 1974 I returned to teaching at Union College. After I returned from Turkey, Professor Ketchum, the Head of the Mechanical Engineering Department once again asked me to teach Mechanical Vibrations graduate course as an Adjunct Associate Professor. This time I expanded the course into two semesters as "The Vibrations of Discrete Systems" and "The Vibrations of Continuous Systems". Before I went to the military service in Turkey, I had always wanted and planned on writing a book on Mechanical Vibrations, thinking my book would be different than the standard text books since it would include "real-life" problems as examples based on my actual engineering experiences. The military service and my unpleasant and stressful experiences in Turkey had drained my initiative, my spirit and my energy and drive. Unfortunately that never happened when I gave up on the idea.

During 1973 when I was teaching the Spring Semester at Union College, the energy crisis in America started with the Arab Oil Embargo. The Arabs were boycotting the American policies in the Middle East by not pumping enough oil to be delivered to the United States. There was a significant shortage of gasoline with long lines waiting at the gas stations. Because of the energy crisis, my two evening classes of two hours each were consolidated into one four hour class. After working all day at GE, lecturing and writing equations on the board for four hours was very exhausting. After 1974, with my family growing and my work responsibilities increasing, I had to give up my evening teaching job at Union College.

Doğan Is Born

While I was busily enjoying myself working at General Electric and at Union College with all kinds of technical challenges, in May 1973 Ilkay accomplished the task she had started by graduating from Russell Sage College with a Bachelor of Arts Degree. I, her parents and Nükhet, who was three and a half years old attended her graduation ceremonies.

Now that I had a taste of being a rental property owner and a landlord, I pursued to purchase the 4-unit building that was for sale across the street at 1046 Gillespie Street. Turkish people always liked owning properties and holding onto them. In an everchanging and inflationary economy and with unstable governments in Turkey, Turks always found security investing in real estate. Their interest in real estate was not speculation but rather long term income and security. I reasoned that could be one of the reasons why I was buying properties. I then looked into purchasing a two family building next door to my house but I realized with all my work load the burden would be too much. A dear family friend, Gil Ogilvie, one day came to our house with a street sign which read "TUNCEL STREET", proposing to change the street name since I was attempting to buy all the homes on the street.

We decided living with the tenants was not easy nor enjoyable. Again I asked Selma Wundt, whom I started calling my "Jewish sister", to find us a nice single family house. Through Preisman Realty, where by now we knew the entire Preisman family, we purchased a new construction at 1260 Cranbrook Court in Niskayuna, a town adjacent to Schenectady. Right after Ilkay's graduation, we would move into our new home. That summer my mother had come to the United States to be with us. On a nice Saturday a few of my friends from work and I moved our belongings into our brand new house. That evening when I was asleep Ilkay woke me up because she heard noises coming from the kitchen below. I nervously walked downstairs to look around and saw a big skunk in the middle of the kitchen rummaging through our garbage bags. I could not close any of the doors since they were removed from their hinges while we were moving the furniture. The skunk had marched into our house through the partially open garage door. I was afraid that the skunk would spray into the kitchen penetrating a terrible smell into our brand new home. I did not know what to do. After a few minutes observing the animal and putting all the doors back on their hinges quitely, I got the courage to walk by it and open the sliding door directly across from it. The animal did not budge one bit. To direct the skunk out of the sliding door opening I clapped my hands and it ran out of the open door. That was a very scary experience for me. My mother did not know what to make of this incidence since she had never seen a skunk before.

Not long after, Dr. Nihat Önderoğlu, his wife and two sons came to visit us. My mother was very happy to see them since she considered Nihat Abi her other son. My cousin Necdet Itmeç and his business partner Ismail Bey also came to visit us. When I saw them I realized how much I missed my family members and thought about returning to Turkey and settling there.

During these activities the delivery time of our second child we were expecting was approaching. One evening Ilkay very calmly told me to take her to the hospital because she felt it was time. We did not know whether the baby was a girl or boy. I rushed her to Ellis Hospital while Nükhet stayed with Ilkay's grandmother who had come from Baltimore to help out. I chose to wait outside and not go into the delivery room. The waiting room was a small space only a few paces wide. I started pacing it back and forth with anxious and determined steps as if I was going to make a difference to the delivery efforts. I felt like a caged lion rapidly moving back and forth. As time passed, my steps slowed down but did not stop until the doctor came to give me the good news. He said, "It's a boy!" I thought my heart had stopped beating. Because of my excitement and happiness, I immediately hugged the doctor and kissed him on both cheeks just like we do in Turkey. He did not expect it and did not know what to make of it. In any case, on January 22, 1974 I became the proud father of a beautiful little boy whom we named Doğan, a popular and well respected name for a Turkish boy. We had another urgent matter to take care of and that was his circumcision. After my difficult and painful experience with my circumcision I was not going to subject my son to the same dreadful experience. We talked with Dr. Metin Kölüksüz, a Turkish doctor in the hospital, to perform the surgery. He was more than happy to do it. Ironically the surgery took place one day before Ilkay was released from the hospital on a Friday, the Moslem holy day. I reminded Dr. Kölüksüz to say some Moslem prayers first before the surgery.

In the summer of 1974 we had made plans to go to Turkey and Cyprus but on July 20th a war broke out in Cyprus between the Turks and Greeks. We therefore could not make our annual visit to Turkey and Cyprus that year. It was an unfortunate and devastating war. If some of the leaders of the countries and the people supporting them were more reasonable, generous and forgiving in their hearts, wars would not happen.

The independent Republic of Cyprus on the island was established in 1960. The Greek Cypriots and the Turkish Cypriots with the approval of England, Greece and Turkey developed a constitutional framework that established a bi-communal state for the Greek and Turkish Cypriots. In addition, a Treaty of Guarantee was entered into by England, Greece and Turkey that established Cyprus as a sovereign independent state; and union of Cyprus with Greece, Turkey or any other state was forbidden. Not long after the establishment of the Republic, in 1963 the Greek Cypriots irresponsibly declared the Constitution null and void and ousted the Turkish Cypriots from the government. Greek Cypriots monopolized the government without a single representation from the Turkish side. For many years Greek Cypriots refusing to recognize the rights of Turks to live in security and freedom in their own land of Cyprus, systematically plotted schemes to annihilate and in the end to completely wipe out the Turkish population from the island. These plots of intimidation, destruction, terrorism and murder were staged in hundreds of Turkish villages and in the Turkish sections of larger towns from 1955 onwards, when the terrorist organization EOKA began its operation. Turkish villages were left without water and electricity. Turkish Cypriots were continuously harrassed, terrorized and subjected to discrimination. Pictures of Turkish Cypriot families, murdered in their homes were in all the newspapers in Turkey and Europe. Archbishop Makarios' government did nothing to control the spread of this bloody terrorism. In 1974 when the Greek Cypriot terrorist leader Sampson, with the backing of the Greek Colonels Junta who were then in power in Greece, toppled the Makarios administration in Cyprus and proceeded with his plans to annex Cyprus to Greece, Turkey had no choice but to safeguard the lives of the Turkish Cypriots. Turkey exercised its international treaty rights by intervening and separating the Greek and Turkish communities with its military forces. This was the 1974 Cypriot War.

From 1974 to 1983 negotiations between the Greek Cypriots and the Turkish Cypriots did not deliver a just and equal solution for the Turkish community forcing the Turkish community to declare an independent Turkish Republic of Northern Cyprus on November 15, 1983.

Since we could not go to Turkey and Cyprus in the summer of 1974, we decided to take a mini vacation in the United States. Ilkay and I, together with our two children, first drove to Baltimore. We left Doğan with Ilkay's parents and together with Nükhet we went to California. After enjoying Disneyland, we visited San Diego and completed our tour with a visit to San Francisco.

Back at home I started a vegetable garden as a hobby. I enjoyed watching all my plants grow and picking my own tomatoes, cucumbers, peppers, beans and squash. In September Nükhet started kindergarden. Although she had been going to nursery school for the past two years, this was actually the beginning of her school attendance. It was exciting watching her get on the school bus for the first time by herself.

I was making a good name and reputation for myself throughout General Electric. One day Don Janis, who was my student at Union College and later General Manager of Moisture Separators and Reheaters for nuclear power plants, offered me the job of Manager of Engineering in his group in Portland, Maine. For as much as I was getting tired of Schenectady, I turned down this wonderful opportunity. It turns out to be a right decision because not long after that General Electric got out of the nuclear reactor business.

At the beginning of 1975, General Electric was facing a big dilemma, trying to decide what to do with its Nuclear Reactor Business. The industrial leaders in manufacturing nuclear power plant equipments were Westinghouse and General Electric with Combustion Engineering and Babcock & Wilcox as smaller players. General Electric had selected the Boiling Water Reactor (BWR) concept for its simplicity in design and controls. The BWR nuclear system was a steam generation system;

consisting of a nuclear reactor core and other internal structures assembled within the reactor pressure vessel, with auxiliary systems to accommodate the pressure vessels and corresponding controls, instrumentation and safeguard devices. Water was circulated through the reactor core, producing saturated wet steam which was directed to the steam turbine. Between the high pressure and low pressure turbines a moisture seperator-reheater was utilized. The steam from a boiling water reactor was slightly radioactive. During the shutdown maintenance the BWR steam turbine, condensate and feed water components would still show small remnants of radioactivity which would be a major concern. Westinghouse, however, used Pressurized Water Reactor (PWR) concept with the main difference of having an intermediate heat exchanger between the reactor and steam turbine. The steam turbine and condensate cycle would then be free of any radioactivity. The United States Nuclear Navy uses the Westinghouse PWR concept.

Although General Electric established the nuclear power equipment business in 1955, growth of the business was slow. BWR design concept evolved very slowly and since it took as long as seven years for the power plants to be completed, new designs were not readily tested and proven. During the 1960's and the first half of 1970's General Electric had 66,000 MW of nuclear plants in operation. After mid-1970's the nuclear business came to a standstill with the government not encouraging and not favoring nuclear power. More and more utilities were switching from the nuclear option in favor of coal-fired stations or to gas turbines. General Electric decided to set up a "Nuclear Reactor Task Force" to decide what to do with its reactor business headquartered in San Jose, California. I was asked to be in the Mechanical Design section of the Task Force together with the well known engineers Charlie Elston of LSTG and Marty Hemsworth, Chief Engineer of Aircraft Engines. We were asked to review the design limitations and make recommendations for the future of GE's nuclear business. In January 1975 Charlie Elston and I travelled to San Jose and spent days at a time for a couple of months to review the designs. I was always pleased to see my old boss Don Rubio who was then the General Manager of the Reactor Design Group. After Schenectady's cold and dreaded snowy winters, San Jose weather was heavenly. The work of our task force and many other components task forces continued for months while we commuted to San Jose periodically. After lengthy reviews based on the Task Force recommendations General Electric decided to get out of the nuclear reactor business.

Doçent Dr. At İTÜ

In the summer of 1975 we travelled to Turkey. Since one year had passed after the war in Cyprus, we decided we could safely visit there and Ilkay's relatives. With my mother and our two little children Nükhet and Doğan, we flew to Ercan Airport near Lefkosa (Nicosia) in Cyprus. We were welcomed by most of Ilkay's relatives at the airport. The island of Cyprus was a beautiful place with the Mediterranean Sea surrounding it all around and green mountains rising towards the broad blue sky. The buildings however, whatever was left behind after the war, were riddled with bullet holes. The unfortunate signs of the war could be seen at every corner. When we walked to the landing site of the Turkish forces on the northern shores of the island we could see the grave sites of the heroic Turkish soldiers who gave their lives during the initial landing. It was a sad moment for us. At Ilkay's hometown Magosa, after visiting many family members, we ventured towards the beaches. The exclusive hotel district *Maraş* was completely closed. *Maraş* was kept as a bargaining chip by the Turks. However no bargaining ever happened and this beautiful hotel district over a long time crumbled under the heavy weight of neglect and severe weather. We then went to Salamis Bay where we found the pristine sandy beaches to swim and enjoy. My favorite location however was Girne at the northern shores of the island which was the beautiful fertile region between the blue Mediterranean and green mountains. Ilkay's cousin Tokay and her husband Dr. Mustafa were very hospitable to us and showed us around the quaint city of Girne. The Turkish Cypriots were happy that they were free from the Greek atrocities and ongoing harrassment. They were free to direct their own destinies and to make their own free choices. They were eternally grateful to Turkey for the sacrifices that the country had made for them to make and keep this little homeland free.

On my return to Schenectady I started feeling lonely and desolate. When another unbelievable wintery cold weather came from Canada and snow storms piled up coming from the lakes district by way of Buffalo, I was ready to get out of Schenectady and I felt I had to do something. The dream of returning to Turkey was always haunting me. I thought if I returned to teach in Turkey it would be my starting point therefore I decided to apply to Istanbul Technical University, my old school, for the Doçent exams. Doçent positions in the European educational system was equivalent to the Associate Professorship in the United States. In Turkey in order to achieve the Doçent title we had to submit a thesis and successfully complete the qualifying exams. It was unusual to apply for Doçent examinations from outside since the school preferred internal candidates who had been laboring through the hardships and trying environment of the school. My friend Talha Dinibütün, who was then in the teaching staff at İTÜ, encouraged me to apply saying that there had been some candidates who applied from outside and received a Doçent degree.

I started working on my thesis based on some of the original work I was doing on vibration testing. In a short time I completed my thesis and submitted it to the faculty of Mechanical Engineering at Istanbul Technical University. Naturally the thesis had to be written in Turkish and my teachings at Işık Engineering School during my military service came handy to prepare it. The thesis was entitled, *"Frekans Tarama Hızının Titreşim Yapan Sistemlerin Cevabı Üzerindeki Etkisinin İncelenmesi ve Türbinlere Uygulanması"* (The Effect of Frequency Sweep Rate on the Response of Vibrating Systems and Application to Turbines). The thesis was reviewed and accepted. Towards the end of 1975 I travelled to Istanbul for the language exams and happily passed them. The road was now clear for the general qualifying exam. During the wintery months of 1976 I spent the evenings getting ready for the İTÜ exams. It was ironic because this was the second time I was studying for İTÜ exams, the first time being in 1955 for the entrance exams after high school. At times while I was studying, my mind would drift into the past to the cold damp nights in Izmir when I was studying under the dim light of my kerosene lamp. It seemed like all my life I had been studying and taking examinations. The more it snowed outside in Schenectady, the harder I studied.

In April 1976 I was again at Istanbul Technical University in front of the faculty members being subjected to questions on general engineering subjects. In the second day of the exams I was asked to lecture for one hour on the subject of my own choosing just like I would lecture in a classroom full of students. This time the students were the faculty members. I chose "The Energy Methods in Engineering Analysis" as my topic. This was a subject I had written a small book on and used in the Advanced Engineering Program at GE. Of course the lecture was in Turkish also. The next day I was pleasantly informed byProfessor Mustafa Gediktaş of the Mechanical Engineering Department that I had passed all the requirements and had received the Doçent Dr. Title at Istanbul Technical University. This was great!!

During that period I went to Izmir to visit my mother and grandmother. Ilkay and the children had also come to Izmir to join me. While I was in Izmir I visited my friend Orhan Erdil who was a well known architect and builder who was building a beautiful office building in the heart of Izmir called *Yeni Asır İş Hanı*, named after Izmir's Yeni Asır newspaper. I bought an office condominium from him thinking it would be a good rental income for my mother. A few years later upon my mother's insistence that she could not deal with it, I regretfully sold the office. Orhan Erdil was my friend from Namık Kemal High School and also my friend in New York City during our bachelor days. Our parents were also good friends. He was an excellent architect but he had a very difficult personality. Thus people in Izmir did not care for him. In fact, when he was running in one of the elections for Mayor of Izmir, some of the statements he made were most unpleasant and controversial. Needless to say he did not win the election.

Upon our return to the States I went to the 1976 Olympics in Montreal with our family friend Gil Ogilvie who was from Montreal and stayed with her family. Ilkay did not want to come because of the children. This was a one in a lifetime opportunity and I did not want to miss it. I had a wonderful and memorable time.

Work at the Laboratory was very excessive and I was involved with many other activities also. I was able to go to many SESA conferences and present and publish papers on the work we were doing in the Laboratory on high temperature strain gages and on residual stress measurements. In November 1976 General Electric sent me to Princeton University for the Doctoral Recruiting for the entire company. When one of the applicants, Dinçer Özgür, who was Turkish, sat across from me nervously found out I was Turkish, he could not believe it. I put extra effort to bring him into GE and placed him in the Materials and Processes Laboratory where I was working.

Müge Is Born

The winter of 1977 was the coldest winter ever recorded during the last 200 years. Schenectady, being located next to Canada in the north and to the lakes District in the west, was always subjected to the flow of penetrating cold and piles of snow coming from these regions. For as much as I had enjoyed my early professional years and accomplished many of my goals in Schenectady, it was no longer fun being there. Although my job was very gratifying, I did not care for the Schenectady winters. I felt I had to do something to get out of this area but I did not know how. There was not much to do in Schenectady in the winter time. We were busy raising our two beautiful children and enjoying every minute we were with them. I always took Nükhet who was then 7 years old to ice skating either at the

Edison Club or to a frozen pond close by in Niskayuna. We enjoyed our two children so much that we decided to have another one.

When the cold and dreadful winter came to an end in May, I rushed to my vegetable garden to begin planting. The garden was located next to a small brook which ran along my backyard. I prepared the soil very nicely with plenty of peat moss and cow manure and started planting all kinds of vegetables. I planted peas and beans first and added different types of tomatoes, cucumbers, peppers, eggplants, squash and even pumpkins. On the side Ilkay also had an herb garden. After sitting in the office all day and "walking the shop" from time to time, I looked forward to going home and working in my garden. This was a very relaxing hobby for me which I thoroughly enjoyed.

During the lunch time of June 8, 1977 my technician Kathy Wadsworth excitedly informed me that Ilkay had called and wanted me to rush home immediately. At a record time of fifteen minutes I was inside our home. We left Doğan with our neighbor Rose Daley and rushed to Ellis Hospital in Schenectady. This was the same hospital Doğan was born at. We checked into the hospital at 1:45pm and at 3:27pm our beautiful baby girl was born. At 4:00pm I got to see the baby and we named her Müge which meant beautiful little white flowers, lillies of the valley. She was just like her name, a little white flower. When we brought Müge home, Nükhet and Doğan were anxiously waiting by the door for her arrival. From there on Ilkay was busy raising the three children.

The winter of 1978 started again with another terrible and cold weather. I was concerned about my family's future and was trying to decide what to do next. We were ready for a change away from the unbearable winters of Schenectady. 1978 turned out to be one of the worst winter periods which followed with the infamous "Blizzard of '78" in the metropolitan Boston area. The city was completely burried under snow and a State of Emergency was declared all around Boston. Nobody was allowed to go out for a week until the roads were completely cleared. At least in Schenectady we missed that blizzard but the winter was still dreadful. It seemed like all the accumulated moisture in the Lakes district always poured its excessive snow over Buffalo, NY to Schenectady. On January 22nd Doğan had just turned four years old. The entire family was anxious for a change from Schenectady's snowy, cold winters.

We seriously entertained the idea of moving back to Turkey where with my new Doçent degree I could get a good position at any university. In 1978 the country still did not have enough Ph.D.'s for rapidly expanding educational institutions. But the situation in Turkey was extremely dismal. The incompetent, weak coalition governments in Turkey for many years were ineffective in dealing with economic and social problems. The country's political system was paralyzed because of stalemate between the two major political parties: The Republican People's Party under Bülent Ecevit and The Justice Party under Süleyman Demirel. These two leaders had terrible personality conflicts and deep animosity towards each other which reflected in their parties' positions. The two parties refused to cooperate in forming a strong coalition government. Instead they formed coalitions with small, extremist parties which could not govern effectively. These political leaders failed in every respect, paralyzing the parliament and allowing the country to fall into the hands of anarchists. Turkish people have a short memory for politics and are easily forgiving. It was unbelievable to me how the people of Turkey many years later again brought these same politicians back to leadership positions to lead the country. It was with great dismay and frustrations however where in recent years I watched history repeat itself, when the two leaders of the major parties, Ms. Tansu Çiller and Mesut Yılmaz, because of their personality conflicts and dislike of each other, not agreeing to a major coalition, dragged the country into chaos ending with an Islamic leaned government. The increased polarization of leftists and rightest was accompanied by a wave of terrorist killings, reaching more than 25 a day by late 1980. Schools and universities almost ceased to function as they became the focal point of terrorrist activities. Journalists, politicians, businessmen and judges, together with their families were under constant threat from either left or rightwing terrorists. Inflation had reached 130% and the country's industry was paralyzed with ungoing strikes. Management at the work places were under constant threat because workers were killing them or the business owners. At the universities students were attacking the professors. There was no security or stability in the country. I found out that during this period my friend Ali Üstünol Ernas who had come to America with me as the top student in our group was killed by revolting workers when he was trying to resolve a dispute between the workers and the management. Those people who could financially afford to leave the country found safe haven in Europe and in America. In these conditions it would not be realistic for us to go to Turkey to settle there. For the time being we dismissed that idea.

    In Turkey things continued to get bad before they got better. As the living conditions were deteriorating rapidly and the country was crumbling under the terrorist activities, General Kenan Evren, the head of the

Turkish Joint Chiefs of Staff and his military led a peaceful coup d'etat on September 20, 1980 bringing peace to the country. A temporary ban on political activities of the former party leaders and members of the central executive commitees of the parties was imposed. In the years that followed, the National Security Council, composed of the commanders of the four services and headed by General Evren, restored law and order, stamped out terrorism, and made great economic progress and eventually through free elections with a new constitution, civilian rule was brought back to Turkey.

In the spring of 1978 I was surprised with a pleasant invitation from Mel Prohl who was Manager of Turbine Engineering in Medium Steam Turbine (MST) Department to Lynn, Massachusetts for an interview. Although I had not applied for any job in MST Department I was very pleased for the opportunity. I knew of Mel Prohl who was a well-known engineer when I was at Lehigh studying mechanical vibrations. He had found a new calculation system for turbine blade and shaft vibrations using "lumped parameters approach". This unique technique was named after him as "Prohl-Myklestad Method" and had been used throughout the industry and was taught in schools. I had met Mel Prohl over the years when we were all involved on the Bucket and Rotor Symposiums held quarterly by all of GE's turbine departments in order to exchange technical information. I was very happy and excited for this unexpected invitation. The interview with Mel Prohl and Gil Wozney and many other engineering staff members went very well. As a result I was offered the position of "Manager of Turbine and Heat Recovery Steam Generator Development Engineering".

The Medium Steam Turbine Department, located in Lynn, was a part of General Electric Company's Power Generation Business. Lynn was an old industrial, blue-collar workers city located only 15 miles north of Boston. Of course Boston was very well known as one of the most beautiful, culturally and technologically advanced cities in America. It was obviously much better than Schenectady. The job offered to me was very responsible and challenging. It involved working on the marine and industrial steam turbines as well as heat recovery steam generators (HRSG) used as boilers at the exhaust of gas turbines in combined-cycle power plants. The job had very broad application fields with a lot of diversity and management responsibilities. This was a wonderful opportunity and I felt I was very lucky to get such a job offer. I accepted the offer immediatelyand started making arrangements for our big move. It was not long after on July 5, 1978 I started my new job in the Medium Steam Turbine Department in Lynn, Massachusetts.

13

Changing Times

Lynnfield, Massachusetts

It is said that "the only thing that remains unchanged is change itself". It was time for us for a big change. The exhilirating new job offer was very timely and uplifting and we were more than ready for it. The entire family was very excited that we were moving to Boston. The children were young enough that they could easily adapt to a new environment and to a new school system. Selling our home and buying another one was not easy however and it was very frustrating. As I started my new job I was feverishly looking for a house in the surrounding towns north of Lynn in the North Shore area. During this period while we were trying to sell our house in Schenectady, I was commuting there every weekend. After six months of searching for a house, I bought a building lot in one of the exclusive neighborhoods in the town of Lynnfield and started building our new home. The construction delayed the family's move out of Schenectady until December. By then our house in Schenectady was sold also. All I had left behind was a four unit apartment building which I sold a few years later.

We moved to Boston and spent a few weeks at the Lakeview Motel in Beverly, Massachusetts while our new house was rapidly being completed. We entered the New Year of 1979 at our efficiency motel room. We had enrolled Nükhet at Huckleberry Hill Elementary School which she started right after New Year's. Every morning Ilkay would pack up the children and drive Nükhet to school in Lynnfield. Again she would go back in the afternoon and pick her up. We were excited and extremely happy that we were starting a new life in Lynnfield in our brand new home. At the end of January 1979 we moved into our beautiful home at 18 Wildewood Drive and started a satisfying period of our lives while raising three wonderful and very active children.

Lynnfield was a beautiful, quaint town completely covered with greenery and woods only 15 miles north of Boston. It was an exclusive, well-to-do town, home to many professionals and businessmen. The town of Lynnfield was a traditional New England residential community with an open town meeting form of self government. Many members of the community were devotedly involved in many boards of the community. The town officials have always been committed to maintaining the high quality of life to all of its residents. The center of the town was graced by the Common, a small green area bordered by historic structures including the Lynnfield Meeting House built in 1714 and the Lynnfield Public Library, which was built just before the Civil War. The town provided a spectrum of recreational facilities with sport fields and parks. The residents enjoyed the small town feeling while being located within a short commute of Boston's cultural and technological opportunities. Lynnfield bordered the city of Lynn where General Electric was located. During the next 25 years my commute to work would be an easy short distance. For me being in the greater Boston area surrounded with its beautiful sea shores had another significance since it was reminding me of Izmir's Bay.

Boston had an important place in American history from its early beginnings. Boston evolved into an international center for finance, trade, culture, the arts, medicine, technology and education. Boston maintained its historical charm and beauty while blending the past and the present. Each year tourists flock to Boston to explore America's historic origins while thousands of students, many foreign, fill the city to get a higher education from the city's hundreds of colleges and universities. Cultural centers such as the Boston Symphony Orchestra, the Boston Pops, the Museum of Fine Arts and the Boston Ballet are among the world reknown treasures that keep the visitors coming and the residents happy to live there.

We spent a lot of time visiting Boston and trying to get to know the city. We started with a walking tour along the famous Freedom Trail learning some of America's historic origin and continued to the oldest part of the city, Beacon Hill. Beacon Hill was beautifully maintained from its 18th and 19th century presence with its red brick sidewalks and cobblestone streets, ancient mansions and rowhouses. The Back Bay area was the most desired and exclusive section of the city overlooking the Charles River. Everytime

I visited this area I thought of Alsancak and how beautiful it could have been if they had maintained its old appearance without destroying it with ugly haphazard concrete constructions. As we visited many historical sites I got a better insight to the American history. The King's Chapel, built in 1754, reminded us of the English rule in America. The house of John Adams and John Quincy Adams in Quincy, Paul Revere's house in the North End, Faneuil Hall and Quincy Market Place, and the Bunker Hill Monument in Charlestown were all parts of America's historical landmarks we enjoyed. It was exciting for me that years later my daughter Müge would be living across the street from the Bunker Hill Monument where the Battle of Bunker Hill was the beginning of the American Revolution in Charlestown.

Just a short trip across the Charles River from Boston, Cambridge is a vibrant city where academic, political and high technology history has frequently been made. As home to such distinguished institutions as Harvard University, the oldest in the country and Massachusetts Institute of Technology, where major scientific and technological advancements were born, Cambridge has earned the reputation as one of the foremost academic and cultural centers in the world. The greater Boston area was the place to be at and we were happy to be a part of it.

As we got settled in our new home, Nükhet continued her school and got involved with sports and piano lessons. Doğan had also started school and in a few years Müge followed as well. Their educations were completed in a very pleasant environment without much stress and anxiety. While in school they made some wonderful friends with other Lynnfield children. Besides normal class work, cultural activities and involvement in sports was a part of their school activities. We as parents did not experience any of the difficulties, anxieties and the financial burdens parents in Turkey experience to educate their children.

Right after we moved into our home, my friend Teoman Uzkan who had retired from the Turkish Navy came to visit us. We started looking for a job for him in the United States. With his excellent educational background from Stanford University he had no problem finding jobs. We found him a job at GE but he instead accepted a position with International Harvester in Chicago and later moved on to General Motors' Diesel Locomotive Division. He and his family have stayed in Chicago to this date.

In March 1979 my friend Fikret Atahan came to visit us, also looking for a job. I had met Fikret and his wife Aynur with their three lovely children in Schenectady. I got a job for Fikret at GE in my department. Fikret stayed with us for the next six months while he saved enough money to have his wife and children join him from Turkey. Fikret and I commuted to work every day and spent the evenings together as well. During this time Ilkay not only had to care for her three young children but had to take care of Fikret as well. By the time Fikret's wife and children came, he was financially able to rent an apartment and move out. Fikret's brother Hikmet along with his wife and children also came looking for a job. Since he had no trade or educational skills, I was not able to help him find a job and they returned back to Turkey.

Not long after, my friend Teyfik Kısacık, who was from a well established family in Adana came and joined us looking for a job. His educational background in Textile Engineering from Germany, easily landed him a job in Camden, Maine working for a company making robes for the designer Ralph Lauren. During this period Turkey was still in chaos with terrorism and anarchist activities causing havoc in the country. I could see many of my friends were gradually leaving the country. It was so sad that Turkey was experiencing a significant brain-drain while the political leaders of the country were insistently fighting to keep their "chairs".

In the years that followed my mother came to America a number of times to be with us. She enjoyed being with her three grandchildren, playing games with them and even kicking the soccer ball around with them. On many occasions we travelled within the United States, visiting Ilkay's family in Baltimore and driving to Florida to enjoy Disney World. We also made sure, that at least once a year in the summer when the children had vacation, to visit my family in Izmir. We had a close bonding with my mother, my grandmother, my aunts and with other family members in Izmir. Our annual visits to Turkey helped my children to understand the Turkish culture, our religion and be fluent in the Turkish language.

Medium Steam Turbine Department

General electric's Power Generation Business consisted of the Large Steam Turbine-Generator Department in Schenectady, New York, Medium Steam Department in Lynn, Massachusetts, Mechanical Drive Turbine Department in Fitchburg, Massachusetts and Gas Turbine Department in Schenectady. Each business was decentralized at GE and the individual departments operated independently from each other. There were invisible boundaries among the departments. I knew for instance that technical exchanges among the departments were done through quarterly symposiums. Technical communications among the engineering staff of individual departments were on per-request basis with everybody trying to protect their own turf. Design procedures and design philosophies were different. Each department expanded their business based on their own technical capabilities.

General Electric's Medium Steam Turbine Department, located in Lynn, Massachusetts along the shores of the Saugus River, had a very long history. The building complex, known as the Lynn River Works, was originally the headquarters of the Thomson-Houston Electric Company. In the 1880's the Thomson-Houston Electric Company was one of the electrical manufacturing giants of its time. On April 15, 1892 the Edison Electric Company and the Thomson-Houston Company formed the General Electric Company in New York. After the merger, the General Electric Company in Lynn rapidly grew to be the largest employer in the North Shore area of Boston. As the power generation business grew so did the Lynn River Works complex adding new buildings one after another. Just like in the Schenectady plant, every component of the turbine was manufactured in the Lynn plant. The steel foundaries with open-heart furnaces, the pattern shops, extensive machine shops and all kinds of manufacturing and testing facilities were located within this complex. There was no job out-sourcing. The generator and transformer manufacturing and gear manufacturing added diversity to the turbine business in the River Works plant. It was a "city within a city". As the demand for electrical generation increased, a new and the largest building, Building 64, was added to the complex in 1918 to build the ever-growing turbine and generator components.

The Medium Steam Turbine Department's scope was designing and manufacturing turbine-generators for industrial and utility applications through 250 megawatts, and turbines for a wide range of ship propulsion applications. This department also offered STAG (Steam Turbine and Gas Turbine) combined cycle power plants with ratings ranging from 67MW to 600MW. The product line in the Lynn plant had a wide range of steam turbine-generator equipment, heat recovery steam generators and gears.

General Electric's Medium Steam Turbine Department was supplying turbine-generators to utility companies for power generation in the United States and worldwide. The same product line was extended in applications to industrial companies where power and process steam was produced from the same fuel source as cogeneration. Almost all of GE's industrial sales in the United States has been cogeneration applications. In addition, combined—cycle power plants blend the best of gas turbine and steam turbine technologies to provide more efficient electric power. The Medium Steam Turbine Department took the lead in combined-cycle plants where the exhaust heat from the gas turbine was recovered to produce steam for the steam cycle with no additional fuel input. This arrangement made the combined-cycle the most efficient plant in power generation systems. These plants were more fuel-flexible, had low capital costs and could begin generating electricity in as little as 12 months from the date of an order. Medium Steam Turbine engineers were challenged to design and build the heat recovery steam generators (HRSG) which were basic boilers. For turbine designers this was completely a new field but they met the challenge.

At every opportunity Medium Steam Turbine Department engineers found challenges in utilizing their turbines in different applications. Geothermal power generation was one of those cases where the geothermal steam coming from the ground after being separated from the moisture was directed to low pressure turbines for power generation.

Prior to World War II, General Electric had built a world-wide reputation in the design and manufacturing of quality gears. The GE River Works had produced gears for many applications, for the textile industry's loom motors, gear sets for railroad steam and diesel engines, for aircraft superchargers, for mechanical drive applications, pumps and compressors and for merchant marine and Navy ship-propulsion. In 1941, with the war rapidly escalating in Europe, the US government selected the GE Lynn River Works as the location to build a gear manufacturing plant. Many gear sets were designed and manufactured in the Gear Plant to support the war effort. After the war, the Gear Plant was bought by GE from the government to continue manufacturing state-of-the-art gears. GE has designed and built steam turbines, gear propulsion equipment and turbine electric drive systems for more ships than any other manufacturer in the world. GE's Medium Steam Turbine Department was one of the main suppliers of steam turbines, high performance gearing and their support systems for the US Nuclear Navy, SSN and Trident submarines and aircraft carriers. Most recently the high performance gearing and its support system for the DDG-51 class, Arleigh Burke Series of the new class of AEGIS destroyers, were designed by the Medium Steam Turbine Department engineers and built in the Gear Plant in Lynn. During this time, for an engineer looking for a diversity of engineering challenges, the Medium Steam Turbine Department in Lynn was the place to be.

Turbine Development Engineering

In the summer of 1978 I started working in the Medium Steam Turbine Department in Lynn. I was very excited that I was moving into a department where I knew I was going to face a lot of new challenges. I felt quite confident that I was well prepared and ready to meet these challenges. I was bringing with me relevant experiences I had in the Large Steam Turbine Department and in the Materials and Processes Laboratory. I also had good educational references and a well established engineering reputation. I thought my coming from outside would bring new approaches to the solution of engineering problems.

Right after I arrived at the Medium Steam Turbine Department, a big organizational change took place with Gil Wozney as Manager of Engineering and Mel Prohl as consultant in the new organization. I was given the sub-section manager's position of "Turbine and Heat Recovery Steam Generator Development Engineering". There were four engineering units reporting to me. Bucket and Rotor Engineering with Alex Rotsko managing a large group of engineers was one of the units. The design calculations of all the orders and the development work for new buckets, rotors and bearings were done in this group. My ex-boss George Fisher in the Large Steam Turbine Department who had left Schenectady was now a Senior Engineer in this group. The structural Design Unit was headed by Dr. Mark Little whom I hired into our group when he graduated from Renssalear Polytechnic Instuitute. Years later Mark moved to Schenectady and became Vice president of all the Power Generation Technology group. He then became Senior Vice President of GE's Global Research. Mark's Structural Design group was in charge of the design of the stationary turbine components, casings, foundations and design of heat recovery steam generators. The Fluid Mechanics Unit was headed by a dynamic young engineer, an MIT graduate, Russell Shade, who also later became Vice president of GE's Power Distribution Systems Business in Virginia. Lastly, the Materials and Processes engineering was headed by Al Melilli. This group was in charge of supporting all the factory manufacturing processes. In essence Turbine and HRSG Development Engineering was responsible for all the components of turbines except for controls and generators.

Development Engineering worked very closely with the Materials and Processes Laboratory in Lynn which was headed by Dr. Merrill Cohen, a brilliant chemist. Since most of the funding of the Laboratory was coming from my Development Group, I had a very close working relationship with the Laboratory and very friendly ties with Merrill Cohen. Every Friday morning Merrill and I had our "doughnut meetings" while reviewing our common projects. Our relationship became a close family friendship that continues to this date even after we both retired.

Parallel to my Turbine Development Engineering, Turbine Design Engineering was headed by Tony Rendine. Design Engineering had the responsibility of the turbine hardware and design of all the individual units being built in the factory. Tony Rendine's organization's design work started with thermodynamic calculations performed by Bill Printup's unit and hardware design and drafting was done in the Design Engineering organization. The Turbine Design and the Development Engineering groups had excellent working relationships and we were very supportive of each other.

During the next few years Development Engineering was given some of the most challenging and critical problems we had to work on. Since I was a hands-on engineering manager, I was personally involved in some urgent projects. My introduction to these projects started with the heat recovery generator noise problem. GE had been supplying heat recovery steam generators since the early 1960's and we had more than 150 HRSG units in the field for gas turbine applications. General Electric's HRSG is basically a steam generating boiler without any fuel. It is a counter flow heat exchanger with convective heat transfer. Hot exhaust gas from the gas turbine passes upward through a series of finned tubes, first through the superheater bank and then through the evaporator and economizer banks. Cold water from the boiler feedwater pump generally flows in a downward direction and is progressively heated. Water emerges from the steam drum in the vapor state and passes through the superheater into a steam turbine for additional power generation with no extra fuel. When the hot exhaust gas was passing through the horizontal banks of finned tubes a loud noise was generated that reverberated at a 10 to 20 mile distance. In locations such as Indiana, because of flat lands, the noise could be heard as far as 50 mile distance. At night people living in the surrounding areas could not sleep in their homes because of this continuously disturbing noise. Since many communities were vehemently complaining, we were asked to solve this urgent and critical problem as soon as possible. We identified the problem to be due to sequencing of the tubes inside the boiler. The noise was amplified inside the tube banks as the gas was flowing between the tubes generating eddy currents and the distance between the tubes increased the effects of these eddy currents into a loud noise. I resembled this problem to a group of soldiers marching over a bridge all in the same step, increasing the vibration and hence the possibility of collapsing the bridge. If the tubes were not at equal distances in the tube banks, this problem would not occur. Since we could not replace all the tubes in the boilers in the field, we had to come up with a more practical solution. Dr. John Eskeson from the Laboratory and I set up a laboratory test set-up duplicating the noise but could not find a solution other than moving the tubes around which was not an acceptable field solution. For weeks John and I sat down in the test facility trying to eliminate the noise. In the end we realized we could disrupt the uniformity of incoming flow into the tube banks and eliminate the reenforcement of eddy currents. We accomplished this by putting one row of blank tubes in front of the finned tube banks and disrupted the uniformity of incoming flow which eliminated the noise. This was a great solution and we implemented the fixes in the field. I traveled to a number of power plants measuring the noise before and after the fixes were implemented. The noise was eliminated and the problem was solved.

At the beginning of 1980 the Medium Steam Turbine Department was facing a major turbine problem. The last-stage buckets of the turbines in the SSN nuclear attack submarines and later the last stage buckets of the Trident nuclear missile submarines were experiencing fatigue failures. Obviously the news of broken turbine buckets in a nuclear submarine was a devastating concern for the US Navy and a grave responsibility for General Electric since we had supplied the machinery. The problem occured when the US Navy asked General Electric's Medium Steam Turbine Department to increase the speed of the turbines, and hence the power and the speed of the submarines. Based on analytical calculations, without supporting experimental data, GE agreed to the increase of turbine speed, causing last stage buckets to go into resonance at the next per rev point hence bucket fatigue failures. Turbine Design and Development Engineering were urgently assigned to solve this problem with the US Navy watching over us. I felt I was very well prepared with my many years of bucket design and development experience in Schenectady's Large Steam Turbine Department and my experience in testing in the M&P Laboratory to handle a problem of this importance. The approach was very simple; we first had to verify the cause of the problem and then find a fool-proof solution. I felt very confident I could help to solve this problem. I took charge of running a test on a complete turbine under actual steam loading with water-breaks carrying the load. Instrumentation of buckets, in a steam environment, to measure vibrations was never done in Lynn before. I brought the test group from my old organization in Schenectady's M&P Laboratory. This group had a lot of experience instrumenting buckets with strain gages and collecting data through telemetry even in a harsh steam environment. Previously we had performed these types of tests in many power plants in the field. In a short time, our tests proved the cause of bucket failure to be what we suspected. I traveled to Washington DC periodically making presentations to the Navy explaining our progress on this project. The solution however did not come easily and the many alternatives we brainstormed would not work for certainty. After doing extensive literature research I realized the concept developed by Westinghouse would solve our problem. The concept involved coupling the buckets into long-arc groups to suppress or cancel the energy input into the grouped buckets at that per rev location where the failure occured. We had not used the long-arc coupling before at GE and it was difficult to convince everyone, especially the Navy's capable engineers, that the energy cancellation concept would work. After many reviews of our proposal internally and by the US Navy, where I had proven analytically to everyone that this solution would work, the decision was made to implement the "fix" on our test turbine. Our next telemetry test utilizing long-arc coupling of buckets clearly showed that what was a significant resonance on the last stage buckets was now completely suppressed. The problem was solved successfully. Unfortunately, to make these changes on a turbine inside a submarine required cutting the hull of the submarine, removing the two turbines, and bringing them back to the factory. In 1984 I published this work in a technical paper entitled "On the Long Arc Coupling of Steam Turbine Buckets" and presented it at York University in York, England at the vibrations conference of the International Institute of Mechanical Engineers. I was very pleased and gratified to be able to present my work at an international conference.

I used the same concept of long-arc coupling of buckets to solve the next major bucket failure in India. The US Government, over the years through the Marshall Plan, had given India about twenty 50 MW GE turbines whose last stage buckets were failing in the field after more than thirty years of operation. Product Service represantitive Ken Sullivan and I were summoned to New Delhi and later to Hyderabad, India in the winter of 1982 to solve this problem. The charts in the power plant showed me that because of the increased demand for power, the power plant operators had increased the loading on the turbines for as much as 10 to 15 percent causing a speed drop, hence bucket resonance and fatigue failures.

Before returning to Boston, Ken and I visited the Taj Mahal in Agra which was only 200 km south of New Delhi. Taj Mahal was built by a Mosem, Emperor Shah Jahan in the memory of his dear wife Queen Mumtaz Mahal. Taj Mahal, with its mystic and splendor, was a precious jewel in India. Like other tourists, I took a ride on an elephant and even watched a cobra come out of the basket when the "snake charmer" played his flute. I was assured the poisonous fangs were removed from the snake but I did not get close enough to check them out. As we were leaving the site, I saw a man kneeling down on the pavement with a mangoose tied next to him. I excitedly said,

— Isn't that a mangoose?
— Yes.
— They fight snakes don't they?
— Yes. Do you want to see?
— Oh, Sure!

He pulled a five foot black snake from the basket and a fierce fight between the mangoose and the snake started. After ten minutes the mangoose won the fight with the big snake lying dead on the ground. I gave him ten dollars and thanked him for the show. As we were walking away the man with the huge snake in his hand started running after us yelling,

— Sir, sir. Ten dollars.

I responded,

— I just gave you ten dollars!
— Oh, that was for the show. Ten dollars for the dead snake.

Ken and I returned back to GE to prepare a proposal to fix this problem in India. In my next visit there, I attended many meetings with the Indian Government officials in New Delhi and later with the utility personnel in Hyderabad presenting them our proposed solution in coupling the buckets into a continuous long-arc. It was not easy to convince them that the solution would work, especially when they were facing a hefty bill from General Electric. This meant that I had to run a wheel-box test to prove to them my proposal would work. In 1983 I was back in India showing them my test results. At each visit to India, I made it a point of extending my flights to visit Bangkok, Hong Kong and later to Egypt.

Bangkok, known as "Venice of the East" was a very interesting place. The many shrines and the Royal Palace were very colorful and ornate. The people who lived along the canals did their daily chores of laundry, taking baths, and washing their dishes and food in these dirty waters. In the floating markets cooking was done on the boats. Floating vendors would sell their goods in little boats on these waterways. This was quite interesting to see but was not very sanitary.

On my next stop in Hong Kong I was pleasantly surprised when ten Chinese and their children met me at the airport with a big sign:

"Welcome Dr. Tuncel"

I had asked my Chinese engineer, Steve Chan, whose family lived in Hong Kong, to have his brother make a hotel reservation for me. The Chinese are just like the Turks, very friendly and hospitable people. In the next four days Steve's family took upon themselves to show me every corner of Hong Kong. Hong Kong and Kowloon were very exciting, colorful and a jubilant place. The skyscraper buildings forming the skyline of Hong Kong were more modern and beautiful than any I had seen in the United States. At the time, there was a big concern in everyone's mind of what would happen to Hong Kong after Communist China took over.

In Egypt, however, I found 4000 years of history at every corner. The Cairo Museum was filled with the precious artifacts and mummies discovered in many tombs left behind during the golden age of the Pharaohs. The artistry in their jewelry and the scientific knowledge in their mummification was mind boggling. To this day I am still trying to figure out how the ancient Egyptians, with that period's technology, built those magnificent pyramids. At the footsteps of the Giza pyramids I decided to ride on a camel; another touristic activity. I assured the camel driver, that since I was Turkish, I knew all about camels. As I was settling on the camel, it started to stand up, first lifting the hind legs up, then the front. When the camel lifted it's hind legs up, the slope was so steep that I found myself on the ground with my mouth full of desert sand. I was intact, but my pride was hurt in front of the Arab. Outside of Cairo, a magnificent mosque with its distinct Ottoman style of thin and long minarettes adorned the hillside. This was an impressive reminder of the Turkish ruling of Egypt during the Ottoman Empire. I was very impressed that Egypt had so much history to offer the world.

On my trips to New Delhi I became close friends with GE's India Representative Mr. Bakshi who once took me to a very interesting and colorful Zoroastrian wedding. As I learned more about India's incomparably rich culture and Indian people, I formed warm feeling and understanding towards them. When I saw a street sign in New Delhi, "KEMAL ATATURK ROAD", I was especially impressed with India's recognition of our great leader just like their own great leader Ghandi.

On my fourth and last visit to India I found out all the fixes we implemented on their turbines were working without any problem. As we were leaving Hyderabad Airport I observed a Saudi Arabian man of about 50 years old with a 15 year old Indian Muslim girl going to Saudi Arabia. The little girl looked frail, scared of the unknown, and confused. She was sitting on the floor with all her personnal belongings wrapped in a little bag waiting for the next motion from the Saudi man. My friend Mr. Bakshi explained to me that these Saudi men were always coming to Hyderabad, and in exchange of a *başlık* (dowry) of about $100-$200, they were buying these Muslim girls from their families and taking them to Saudi Arabia. Mr. Bakshi further explained to me that these men, after a few years of "using" these girls, would bring them back to Hyderabad and leave them stranded in a hotel room, making them the Indian Government's problem. Since they were considered "used goods", their families would have nothing to do with them. I looked at the Saudi man with disgust. He looked aloof, indignant and indifferent to his surroundings. I was ready to walk over and give him a piece of my mind but I realized it would be to no avail.

On a similar bucket problem in Korea, I traveled to Seoul, Korea in February of 1984 to make presentations on the continuous coupling of buckets. Korea was a newly upcoming country striving to excell in technology. I was surprised to see how diligent and hard working their people were. To reach their goals, the country and its people were making a lot of sacrifices. Even the conference rooms of a major Korean company where I was making presentations were freezing cold because they were economizing on the fuel that they imported. After the Koreans accepted my proposals, GE's Product Service group implemented the changes I presented.

During the period I was heading Turbine Development Engineering, besides being a trouble-shooter, I had the opportunity to travel extensively making marketing presentations within the United States to our industrial customers. At that time we were competing against the Japanese manufacturers whom we had taught how to make turbines. I also had opportunities to represent General Electric by presenting a paper in Berlin Techniche Hochschule on the comparison of diesel engines to steam turbines on ship applications. In August 1981 when I presented my paper in Berlin, I had Ilkay and the children with me. While I attended the meeting, Ilkay took the children to the Berlin Zoo. The next day we took a bus tour to go to East Berlin. The tour first started by showing us the Turkish Ghetto alongside the infamous wall. We felt saddened that our hard working countrymen were living in ghetto conditions. At a lookout point we saw the Berlin Wall all enclosed with barbed wire. During the entrance and exit at the Brandenberg Gate to and from East Berlin we were subjected to exhaustive searches. Our bus was inspected thoroughly including the bottom which was scanned by mirrors. East Berlin was dull, quiet and colorless. The buildings were all gray, old and soot covered. The automobiles on the streets were small, beaten down junks. It was a boring place compared to vivid, dynamic West Berlin. The last stop in our tour in East Berlin took us to the Bergamum Museum. I did not know what to expect, but what I saw was most disgruntling. All the antique excavations that ever existed in Turkey's ancient Bergamum (*Bergama*) site were given to the Germans by the Ottoman rulers. The Germans had carried the entire ancient city to this location. I was extremely saddened and upset with what I saw. When we returned to Boston, Doğan who was six years old at the time, could not stop talking about our visit to a large jail where thousands of people were all enclosed by a big wall.

One of my memorable and fun trips was in the Spring of 1984 together with Dr. Merrill Cohen and Dr. Sam Toney of Lynn M&P Laboratory to the geothermal fields in California and in Mexico. Our low-pressure steam turbines, used in the Pacific Gas & Electric's (PG&E) Geyser Mountains behind Napa Valley, outside of San Francisco, were clogging up due to geothermal steam deposit formations. The three of us: a chemist, a metallurgist and a mechanical engineer, set out to visit the plant up on the mountains but found ourselves stopping and tasting wines at every corner in the beautiful Napa Valley. The California wines were just starting to be in competition with the French wines and were exquisitely delicious. By the time we reached the Geyser Mountains I suggested we were in no condition to check steam turbine buckets and should get a hotel room. The next morning we drove up the winding roads to the top of the Geyser Mountains to see large steam pipes carrying geothermal steam from many wells opened at different locations on the mountain. After evaluating different alternatives to solve the clogging and possible bucket failure problems, we came up with a simple solution of having the buckets replaced every five years. On our return to San Francisco we visited the beautiful town of Sausolito and decided to brown bag lunch in a park right under the spectacular Bay Bridge. We decided to buy a nice bottle of California wine to go with our sandwiches. We had a very memorable lunch with a breathtaking view of San Francisco. Since drinking wine in the park was illegal, Dr. Cohen said it would make scandalous headlines in the newspapers: "Three GE Executives Got Caught Drinking Wine In The Park", if we ever got caught drinking by the police. Luckily that did not happen. Our next stop in our geothermal tour took us to Mexicali, Mexico where the Cerro Prieto geothermal field was generating more than 200 MW power and selling it to the US. In the plant I was amazed to see a spare Toshiba turbine rotor built to our GE design and most likely sold at a lower price to the Mexicans. The technology transfer we did to the Japanese some years ago had already caught up with us.

Turkish Students

Now that I had done my military service, there was nothing holding me from going to Turkey and visiting my family and friends. Ilkay and I made it a point every summer to take our three children to Izmir to visit my mother, grandmother and relatives. For as much as it was an expensive ordeal for me, it was still worthwhile and enjoyable for everyone involved. We were especially happy to see our children adapt to the Turkish customs and the Turkish language. Eventhough the distance was far and it was difficult to travel with three little children, we felt it was important for them not to forget their Turkish roots and grow up learning the Turkish culture.

In May 1979 right after we settled in our new home and I started my new job, we decided we needed a break from a very tiring house and job transition and decided to go to Turkey. At that time my friend Fikret Atahan was still staying with us. We left the house and our cars to Fikret and went to Turkey. It was nice to get away from it all. One day in Izmir, my cousin Necdet summoned me to his factory to meet two of his friends, Kemal Baysak and İhsan Özkan. Their two sons were in England at the time finishing an English Language School and they wanted to send them to America to get an engineering education. They wanted my help to do this. I told them that as much as I would like to help, since admissions to schools had been closed months ago, starting school in September would be next to impossible. However, I promised them I would do my best to get the boys into a school when I returned to Boston.

Upon my return in June, after searching and being turned down by many engineering schools in the Boston area, I eventually convinced the Admissions Officer at Salem State College to accept the two boys as non-matriculated students for a year with an option to transfer to an engineering school the following year. This way they would not loose a year waiting around. I quickly sent their school acceptances and affidavit of supports that I signed for both boys to Izmir so they could get their visas. Abdullah Baysak and Cüneyt Özkan came to Boston the beginning of September 1979. When Ilkay and I went to greet them for the first time at Logan Airport, they looked scared and lost. After staying with us for a few days, we got them registered in school and found them an apartment in Salem close to the school. They very quickly adapted to their new environment and to their school. When Kemal Bey came on a surprise visit in February, he was pleased with their schooling and the progress they were making in such a short time. We were extremely happy to have these boys around because they were like big brothers to our children and we felt like they were also part of our family.

In October 1979, one month after Abdullah and Cüneyt had come, my cousin Necdet's son Nihat Itmeç also came to Boston for schooling. Since language schools were extremely expensive, Ilkay enrolled him in the Lynnfield High School first where he would sit in the classrooms but did not have to participate. He could improve his language and at the same time learn the American way of life. No better way could this be accomplished than at Lynnfield High School where the students were very friendly and helpful to Nihat. He later told me that this was the best period of his life.

Salem State College's Admission's Officer was so pleased with Abdullah and Cüneyt's performance that he readily admitted Nihat also for the next semester. Nihat stayed at Salem State College until he graduated in 1985. Abdullah and Cüneyt transferred to Lowell University in their second year into the Mechanical Engineering Department and they both graduated from Lowell and returned to Turkey in 1985.

In September 1981 Meram Birsesli came to us to go to school for a Master's degree. Her father was known as *Kömürcü Mustafa* (coalman) and was a friend of Kemal Baysak. I sent her an affidavit of support and an acceptance which I obtained from the English Language School in Boston. After staying with us for a few days,we got her settled in the school's dormitory. She attended this school for a few months to improve her English before she began her classes at Lowell University.

In February 1982 when I was returning from a business trip from India, I stopped in Izmir to visit my mother. At a dinner invitation at Kemal Baysak's house I told them I would take their daughter Ayşın with me to America if she wanted to go. She was thrilled and begged her parents to send her. The next day we obtained a visa for her from the American Consulate in Izmir and we were off to Boston. Ayşın also briefly went to the language school with Meram. In June 1982 Meram finished the language school and we transferred her to Lowell University. Ayşın in the meantime moved back with us.

While waiting for school to start in September, Meram had moved into an apartment in Lowell with an American girl. One day when I called Meram to see how she was doing, I learned that she was very sick. I quickly drove to Lowell and rushed her to a hospital where our family friend, Dr. Donald Green gave us the bad news that Meram had a brain hemmorhage. I realized, for as much as it was nice to bring students to the United States to get an education, there were other responsibilities towards these young people. That evening we moved Meram to the Intensive Care Unit of Harvard University affiliated Mt. Auburn Hospital and later to the New England Medical Center.

I urgently called and notified Meram's family in Turkey. Within a week her step mother and older sister came and stayed with us. The prognosis from the doctor was a 50/50 chance of survival. Although it was a difficult decision we chose to have the critical surgery done. Her very dangerous brain surgery took 13 hours and was performed by an excellent Chinese neurologist. For the next two weeks I would go directly to the hospital after work and stay with Meram for a few hours. Since I was the only person she was always asking for and the first person she recognized after her surgery, we felt it was important that I be with her as much as possible. Since the hospital costs were very high and she needed to remain in Boston for another 30-45 days to recover, we decided to move her back to our home and Ilkay would take care of her and take her for her check-ups. The surgery was a complete success and Meram recuperated very well with no side effects from the hemorrhage or surgery. After her recovery, Meram and her stepmother returned back to Izmir. Although I had paid the surgeon and emergency care expenses, Meram's father Kömürcü Mustafa was not an honorable man and never paid the hospital. Needless to say, I never had anything to do with Meram's family ever again.

In September 1980 while my mother was with us in Lynnfield, a group of industrialists from Izmir, along with my cousin Necdet and Cüneyt's father

İhsan Özkan, came to Boston at the end of their "love boat" cruise. One evening they were invited to a dinner party in my home where I met Tonguç Ösen who had come along at İhsan Bey's urging. Tonguç and I immediately liked each other very much and formed a close family friendship that lasted a lifetime. Later through Tonguç I met his brother-in-law and partner at Cevher Döküm Aluminum Foundry, Hüseyin Özyavuz and his family. We also became very close friends with the Özyavuz family.

In 1988 Tonguç's son Berat, along with his high school friend Necip, whose family owned the well known Sevinç Patisseri in Izmir, came to Boston to start the language school. I sent them their school acceptance forms and an affidavit of support for Necip for his visa. After completing the language school, Berat started going to Northeastern University in Boston while Necip went to Texas. Two years later Berat's younger brother Bertuğ joined him at Northeastern University. Sinan Atik, son of Süleyman Atik, owner of Akdöküm Foundry, also came at this time and attended the Business School at New Hampshire College.

This was a period in Turkey where there were not enough schools for students to attend and families who could afford it were sending their children to the United States for higher education. My living in the Boston area where there were a lot of reputable schools and my being able to give their children some direction in their educational endeavors was a big relief for the families in Turkey. After this period both the Turkish Government and many private institutions started many schools throughout the country to meet the needs of the new wave of Turkish youth. Even that has not been enough causing strict competition among the students for admissions to the universities. In order to prepare their children for the entrance examinations families have been subjected to a lot of hardship and big expenses. This was something my family and I did not have to face when I was in high school since our teachers were doing their jobs properly. Today companies called *Dersanes*, that give private lessons throughout the country turned into lucrative money making machines as the fastest growing business sector in Turkey.

In May 1984 Abdullah's mother Pervin Hanım and Cüneyt's mother Betigül Hanım came to visit their sons in Boston. After staying with us for a while, they moved in with their sons in Lowell. During the next three months they got to see many parts of the country together by driving around all the way to Florida with their sons. They were happy to be with their boys, taking care of them and cooking their favorite meals. During this period we had the pleasure and the responsibility of having many Turkish students with us in the United States. We observed them while getting their higher education, transitioning from boyhood into responsible young men's positions. They all graduated from their schools and returned to Turkey to their family business. It has been very gratifying for us to see them in leadership positions in their family's businesses and later seeing them start their own families.

Through them we formed very close bonds with their families who became our friends, looking after us everytime we went to Turkey. It was during this period also that Kemal Bey helped move my mother and grandmother into her new apartment built next door on the vacant lot I had bought from our neighbor in Rome. The new building was built on two adjacent lots at the corner and in exchange for the lot the builder gave us a very beautiful, three bedroom unit that my mother and grandmother enjoyed living in the rest of their lives. During this period also we gave up the court case which had dragged on for 15 years on my father's inherited house at No.36 and abandoned it. The house was sold at auction and the people who bought it could not do anything with it. Sadly now it remains in ruins while holding many memories inside its crumbling walls.

Assembly of Turkish American Associations

At the beginning of 1979 after we got settled in our new home in Lynnfield, I started Nükhet in Turkish classes given at MIT on weekends for the children of Turkish families. It was a commendable undertaking by the Turkish American Cultural Society of New England (TACS-NE) for children to have the opportunity to learn Turkish. During this period I met a lot of Turkish families residing in the greater Boston area. I also noticed in many activities taking place that the driving force behind the Turkish American community was one man, Orhan Gündüz who was the Honorary Consul General of Turkey in Boston. He put all his energy and time for the well-being of the community. He was a very pleasant, considerate person with a fatherly appearance and a friendly attitude towards everyone. He was very much liked and highly respected within and outside of the Turkish-American community. In a short time, Orhan Bey, as I called him, and I became good friends. I visited him often in his store in Central Square in Cambridge near Harvard University. In his store he sold imported souvenir goods from Turkey and some Turkish food. He was barely making ends meet with the income from the store but he was a happy man; happy with his wonderful family and happy for being able to serve the Turkish community. Ilkay and I often visited Orhan Bey and his lovely wife Meral Hanım in their home in Nahant, always enjoying their friendly conversations and generous hospitality. In April of 1979 when the elections were going to be held for the Turkish-American Cultural Society, Orhan Bey convinced me to put my nomination in and I got elected as the President of TACS-NE. Although the Turkish-American community was not large and scattered around the greater Boston area, we still arranged the usual activities that were done by all the Turkish American communities around the country; namely the Republic Day Ball, one or two *Bayram* (Eid) Holiday parties and a picnic to bring the Turkish community together. We initiated, for the first time, a monthly newsletter to inform the members on subjects that might interest them. My experience during this period showed me that the Turkish people in the United States did not want to get involved with issues that would possibly affect them. One would rarely see Turks taking part in American politics and having their voices heard. Most of the Turks were professionals and were doing well in their professions and financially, but they preferred to keep themselves in isolation. There were, however, newly developing problems the Turkish American communities were facing. Problems I never saw before were surfacing and gaining momentum by many anti-Turkish groups. Turks were being subjected to unfair treatments and discriminations by some other ethnic groups, such as the Greeks and Armenians and by their political representatives in the United States.

Realizing a grave need for a unified front by the Turkish-American community in the United States, in light of rapidly growing hostility and criticism from many non-friendly Greek and Armenian quarters, the two Turkish-American Associations from Maryland and Washington DC took the lead to bring their Associations together for a better and unified representation in this country. The new Ambassodor of Turkey, Dr. Şükrü Elekdağ encouraged these two Associations to invite the other Turkish-American Associations throughout the United States to form a nationwide umbrella organization. In 1979, there was a crying need to address the attacks, the distortions of history, and the discriminations the Turkish-American community was facing everyday in their jobs, at schools, and in their daily lives. Individual local Turkish-American organizations could not cope with this massive work that needed to be done nationwide. All the local organizations were invited to Washington DC. Orhan Bey advised me to participate in this first meeting and to represent our community as the President of the Turkish-American Cultural Society of New England.

In November 1979 I travelled to Washigton DC with Ilkay and the children. In a two-day conference, after many heated discussions where I made some forceful suggestions, we came out of the meeting with an agreement of establishing the nationwide Assembly of Turkish American Associations. Washington DC was chosen as the obvious location to be the headquarters of the new organization. On May 17-18, 1980 on my way back from a Florida vacation with my family and my mother, I attended another two-day conference at the Embassy Row Hotel with 120 people representing 24 Associations and 5 Student Associations. The conference solidified the plans for drawing up bylaws for the Assembly and elected the delegates in the coordinating committee. During the second General Meeting of the Assembly, which was held on November 15th and 16th, 1980, by-laws were adopted, officers were elected and Articles of Incorporation were filed. Dr. Ülkü Ülgür of the Maryland Association was elected as the first President of the Assembly. I was elected as the Regional Vice-President and worked in that position for the next four years. During these gatherings I became good friends with Ambassador Şükrü Elekdağ, Director of Information Center Murat Sungar who was one of the earliest supporters of the Assembly, and Dr. Ülkü Ülgür, who was also from Izmir. It was not long before the Turkish voice was heard in the United States band with the members of this Assembly protesting unjust treatments and one sided views of Turkey. We became more involved with the elected officials and the news media informing them about the presence of the Turkish-American communities and trying to set the record straight on distorted attacks on our Turkish heritage. The Armenian community came out with a vengance demonstrating and marching outside of our meeting places and campaigning against us at every opportunity they had. Many members of the Turkish community, with the Assembly's support, responded to the many false allegations that the Armenians were making against the Turks.

1982 started with a sad note when Armenian terrorists assasinated the Turkish Consul General of Los Angeles, Kemal Arıkan in the United States. Since 1973, twenty seven Turkish diplomats and members of their families had been killed throughout Europe. Armenian terrorism was wide-spread in Europe, killing more recently a Turkish diplomat in Brussels, followed the next day by the bombing of a Turkish Airlines counter at Orly Airport outside Paris in which seven people were killed and 56 wounded. The wife of a Turkish official was also slain in Lisbon. The Armenian terrorism had now started in the United States. The Armenian underground murderers claimed responsibility for all the killings, insisting they were avenging the deaths of 1.5 million Armenians allegedly occurring between 1915 and 1923 at the hands of the Ottoman government. This view has been rebutted by the Turkish government and by many historians as false accusations and distorted facts.

In March 1982, a group of Armenians were demonstrating in front of my friend Orhan Gündüz's small souvenir shop in Central Square in Cambridge. Orhan Bey knew many of the members of the Armenian community very well and was also friendly with some of the demonstrators. Orhan Bey greeted them cordially and even offered them some hot tea to warm themselves. Although I was very concerned for his safety, he assured me that they were harmless demonstrators and would not harm him. On March 22nd however, the demonstration turned into an ugly violence when his storefront was bombed by the terrorist Armenian group, who claimed responsibility. Though no one was hurt in the explosion, which occurred after the store had closed, the incident left Orhan Gündüz in great financial hardship and difficulty. Although his store was closed for business, I still visited him there to give him some moral support and have a friendly cup of tea or coffee. On May 4, 1982 when he was driving home from his store, on the backstreets of Cambridge, an Armenian terrorist dressed as a jogger brutally murdered him in his car while he had stopped at a red light. They had evidently followed him for several days and knew which route he took to go home. The killer was never apprehended.

This was a devastating and frightening blow to the Turkish community in Boston and throughout the world. He was the fourth victim of terrorism in the United States and the twenty first case worldwide of a Turkish displomat or representative attacked and killed by an extremist Armenian terrorist group linked to international terrorism. The press articles described Orhan Gündüz as a "kind and gentle man" and "honorary uncle" to the Turkish community. Anyone who had known him had been touched by his kindness. He was a good friend to me and I knew he would be deeply missed by the people who were fortunate to have known him.

Since I was still the President of the Turkish American Cultural Society in Boston and I was the family friend of Orhan Gündüz, I took charge of the funeral arrangements. It was a very sad moment for me to go to the funeral home, collect his personal effects including his blood stained glasses and bring them to his beloved wife Meral Hanım. The funeral was very elaborate with representatives from the Mayor's and Governor's offices attending. The Turkish contingency was very large with Ambassador Şükrü

Elekdağ and Mrs. Ayla Elekdağ attending under extremely heavy security. Also attending was the Consul General from New York and several other dignitaries. After many speeches, during the burial ceremony I opened the casket slightly on behalf of the family and put a handful of soil inside as our Moslem religion requires. We bid our final farewell to Orhan Gündüz.

Several television stations wanted to cover the story because it was a major news event. I was interviewed in my home discussing the entire ugly incidence with disdain. I later started receiving threatening telephone calls which made me change my number to an unlisted number and I also changed my travel routes back and forth to work. This was one of the most unpleasant and scary times of my life. To make the matters worse, Mrs. Gündüz, with her young son Doğan, was left in a terrible financial bind. For years our efforts to secure financial help from the Turkish government and from Sakıp Sabancı, one of the richest men in Turkey, never materialized. During a visit to Boston one year, Sabancı had made us some loose promises of help which never materialized. We took the lead of trying locally to collect monetary assistance and Mrs. Ayla Elekdağ put in a great effort arranging many bazaars and fund-raising luncheons at the Turkish Embassy with good results to get additional financial help to Mrs. Gündüz. They say time heals all wounds and makes us forget the bitter moments. This case also remained forgotten with heavy loads in our hearts.

I continued attending many of the Assembly's Executive Committee meetings in Washington D.C. while I was working on the US Navy's submarine bucket failure project. My travels to Washington D.C., because of my work, gave me many opportunities to take an active part in the Assembly's activities. In many annual meetings my entire family travelled to Washington D.C. and attended the receptions at the Turkish Embassy where Mrs. Elekdağ would get my children involved in activities. On April 17-18, 1982 I had the pleasure of attending the Assembly's fourth annual meeting in Chicago with my close friend Teoman Uzkan and his wife and my friend Hüseyin Özyavuz from Izmir. Hüseyin Bey was on a business trip in Chicago and I therefore made arrangements for him to join me at this meeting and reception.

The Assembly continued to do some excellent work addressing issues concerning Turkish Americans in the United States and to promote better relations between Turkey and the United States. The colloboration and increased communication among the component associations of the Assembly had markedly improved the representation of the Turkish American community in the United States. Public education, public affairs, civil rights and legal representation of Turkish-Americans were very important activities undertaken and we now had a champion to have our voices heard. I continued working in the Executive Committee two more years after my four-year Regional V.P. position. At that time I turned my attention to my family's needs and let a new generation carry on the Assembly's well recognized efforts.

Çeşme, Izmir

Çeşme is a seaside resort town located approximately 80 km west of Izmir, at the end of a long mountainous peninsula protruding into the Aegean Sea. Although historically it was a small fishing village settled by the Greeks and the Turks, after the establishment of the Turkish Republic the Greek inhabitants left the area and the village grew into a well known resort town primarily for the residents of Izmir. Across from Çeşme, the island of Chios (*Sakız*) can be seen at a very near distance. This quaint, little, isolated fishing village of Çeşme, after being discovered, rapidly expanded towards the beautiful, white sandy beaches of *Ilıca* with prestine, clear waters as if painted into blue-green, turquoise colors, adding more attraction to the splendor of Çeşme. Residents of Izmir anxiously looked forward to running away from their constrained apartment living in the city to their beautiful summer homes. These homes were built in the midst of small gardens filled with many colorful flowers spreading wonderful fragrances with the soft breeze coming from the Aegean Sea. In the summer time, Çeşme was the place to be.

I remember when I was a little boy, one hot summer day our entire neighborhood had gone to *Ilıca* with a rented bus for a fun-filled picnic. It was so much fun that it was still carved in my mind as a memorable moment. However, Çeşme was not a place everyone could afford. I had not been to Çeşme since then, until the summer of 1972, where after my father's death, I decided to take my mother, Ilkay and Nükhet there for a few days. We stayed at a hotel by the beach and had Nükhet, who was two years old at the time, play and frolic in the cool sea waters. After my father died I never neglected my mother and over the years as my children grew, we continued our annual commute to Izmir to visit my family. It was however, difficult for us to stay in my mother's city apartment during the hot summer days. Nonetheless, we learned to tolerate the heat and the children readily accepted the difficulties of city living. Both Doğan and Müge made friends with the neighborhood kids playing on the street, reminding me of my childhood experiences. Yusuf, the corner bicycle repairman, always let Doğan ride on rental mopeds for free. There were not too many cars or any traffic on the side streets at the time. Bakkal Baha Bey's grocery store had been closed for many years and the neighborhood had aged. None of the neighbors were there anymore and I barely knew anyone in Alsancak. I felt like a stranger in my own home town where I was born, grew up, and where I knew so many people. Being at my mother's house always carried me back to the past memories. It seems to me as we get older we yearn for the past memories more affectionatly, especially if we are living in another country far away from home. Yearning for the past becomes more pronounced.

In the summer of 1981 Abdullah, one of my students in Boston had arranged for us to stay at his uncle, Congressman Cemal Tercan's summer guest apartment in *Ilıca*, Çeşme. Our guest quarter, located on a beautiful beach, was overlooking *Ilıca* Bay. The resort was called Venus Vacation Village (*Venüs Tatil Sitesi*). It was a wonderful place for us to spend the summer and enjoy ourselves. Many of our close friends were also in Çeşme. Abdullah's father and mother, Kemal and Pervin Baysak, Cüneyt's father and mother İhsan Bey and Betigül Hanım, my "big brother" Dr. Nihat Önderoğlu and his wife Sevinç Abla, my dear friend Tonguç Ösen and his wife Cavidan, and equally dear friend Hüseyin Özyavuz and Saliha Hanım, and their family members very cordially welcomed and befriended us. We had a wonderful time but we were deeply saddened when our vacation time ended and we had to return back to the United States and to the realities of life: work and schooling. Life in Çeşme was so exhilirating and exciting that on the way back Ilkay and I discussed buying a place of our own in Çeşme.

The summer of 1982, however, kept us very busy with Meram's brain surgery and recuperation period at our home. I had paid $12,000 of my personal savings to Meram's Chinese surgeon who had charged only a nominal fee because she was a student without insurance. Meram's father was billed for $40,000 hospital expenses which he never paid. Although the hospital tried to collect the money he always found ways of avoiding any payments. As for me, I spent the next two years trying to get my money from Meram's father, Kömürcü Mustafa Birsesli who was always looking for ways to swindle me. In the summer of 1984 when Cemal Tercan intervened and secured my money, we were able to use it as part of a down payment for a beautiful apartment we found in the same complex of Venus Village that we loved so much. The corner unit we bought was on the second floor with a breathtaking view of the Greek islands and *Ilıca*

Bay. The beach was just below our balcony and the entire complex became a giant playground for our children. For us a new era began in Çeşme and it became our summer home to enjoy and have lasting memories.

During the following years, every summer we anxiously commuted to Çeşme from Boston. My mother looked forward to being there with us, spending the evenings sitting on the balcony and enjoying the breathtaking view with flickering lights across the bay. In Çeşme it never rained in the summer and the sky was always a cloudless deep blue. During the day the blistering summer sun sparkeled on the continuously fluctuating waves of the bay. In the evenings the hills were ablaze with the gorgeous sunset. We experienced and enjoyed the ever-changing scenery from our balcony every day. Across from our beach an establishment used as a summer camp by the Ministry of Education bussed dozens of students to enjoy the waters of *Ilıca* to swim and to learn sailing. The cheerful sounds of the youngsters jumping into the cool waters could be heard in the distance. Their miniature sail boats propelled by the breeze looked like little white butterflies leaned over under the force of the wind. Doğan and Müge made a lot of friends in their new neighborhood playing soccer, swimming and jumping from the nearby cliffs into the crystal clear waters of the sea. As they got older they enjoyed frequenting the many discos in the evenings with their friends.

The small village of *Alaçatı*, an adjoining town isolated from modern times, was gradually discovered by the summer crowds of Izmir. The village life of *Alaçatı* and its unique appearance with its narrow streets and stone-walled houses attracted many visitors including foreign tourists as it grew into a bustling town. Ilkay and I enjoyed going to the *Alaçatı* bazaar, walking down the crowded isles of the market filled with fresh vegetables and fruits. The shouts of the vendors added more excitement to the vibrant market place. While my mother was resting at a coffee shop in the market place next to an old mosque, which used to be an old Greek church at one time, Ilkay and I browsed around the adjoining antique bazaar that was always filled with large crowds of tourists. A small bay outside of *Alaçatı* lied between two mountains and like a funnel, strong winds rushed over the bay. This phenomenon made *Alaçatı* the "Surfer's Paradise". Surfers from all over the world flocked to this small enclave to enjoy surfing over the waves, back and forth between the two mountains. Recently, *Alaçatı* was discovered by the "rich and famous" crowd of Istanbul who made *Alaçatı* their summer resort. The narrow cobblestone streets of *Alaçatı* are now filled with small attractive boutiques, art galleries and cafés. We looked forward to our vacations in Çeşme where we would visit our dear friends, relax and explore nearby towns. There was always something to do. Çeşme, with its many splendors, warm and friendly athmosphere, was a lot of fun for us.

Back at General Electric work demands were continuously increasing on me and on my development group. General Electric's STAG system for power plants became more popular with many customers preferring combined-cycle to the standard-cycle fossil or gas powered steam turbine power plants. With the improved designs, industrial gas turbines became more reliable and efficient than the previous designs and when combined with the steam turbine, STAG system became a popular choice. The initial investment was lower and the startup cycle time of the combined-cycle plant was shorter than the simple steam turbine plant. All in all, GE's STAG system was a very attractive preferred combination. One of our biggest customers, Tokyo Electric Power Company (TEPCO) came to the Medium Steam Turbine Department with an offer we could not "refuse". They wanted to buy 14 large combined-cycle power plants from us, with the provision of Hitachi and Toshiba each building one of the plants to our blue-print drawings, with GE building the remaining 12. As the STAG system was in its early development phase, the Japanese recognized the future potential of this approach and wanted to get into this business. Once again the Japanese were after our popular and well known new technology with a big "carrot" of buying 14 plants from us.

At the beginning of 1980's GE's Power Generation Business was not doing well. The Large Steam Turbine Department was almost at a standstill since utilities were not building large power plants or nuclear power plants. Combined-Cycle Plant business and the US Navy business were keeping Medium Steam Turbine Department barely employed. When the Japanese offer for 14 large combined-cycle plants came, it was rejuvenating for our MST-Department. We could not afford to turn down such a large order, even though we had to give our technology to the Japanese. We knew it would not be long before Hitachi and Toshiba would be in the market place competing against us with our designs at a lower price we could not beat. After much soul searching and procrastination GE unwillingly agreed to TEPCO's proposal while licensing our technology to Japanese companies. After so many years I found myself once again in the same situation as I was a decade ago in Schenectady, transferring GE technology to the Japanese engineers and giving them our blue-print drawings of the heat-recovery steam generator (boiler) designs together with the corresponding structural calculations we had done. In July 1981 a group of us from my development group travelled to Tokyo for meetings and presentations we made to a large group of Japanese engineers on our design calculations. I found out these engineers had stayed up all night studying and reviewing our presentations and coming to the meeting next morning well prepared with many excellent questions. On one occasion, at the beginning of a meeting early in the morning, one of the Japanese engineers showed me where I had made a mistake in my equations in my previous day's presentation. He had stayed up all night and re-drew all my equations and found my mistake while Dave Skinner and I were at a club having our cocktails in downtown Tokyo. He seemed very pleased with himself, especially when I agreed with his correction. They were certainly getting their money's worth! Meanwhile, Dave and I continued to venture to downtown Tokyo to have our beers, sometimes sitting on beer barrels under the overhead subway rails and eating our chicken shish kebabs. We would then stroll into Karaoke bars to see the Japanese enjoy themselves while singing their songs. This was the first time I heard Karaoke music since it had not yet arrived in the United States. I also noticed the night clubs were full of Japanese men gathering after work in so-called "Gentlemen's Clubs" to have their drinks and enjoy the shows with many large-sized Caucasion, Latin and Black naked women. They did not rush home after work like we all did in America.

The next day's strenuous meetings continued. It was very enjoyable to return to the hotel after the meetings and be greeted by a beautiful Japanese girl at the elevator dressed in her national geisha outfit. After bowing with her usual customary way she would ask me what floor I wanted to go and press the elevator's button for me. When I arrived at my floor I thought this was so pleasant that I pushed the ground floor button to go down and see the geisha again and repeat the exciting experience once more.

Before I returned back to Boston, I was asked to go to Manila, Phillipines to check on a Siemens steam turbine. Filipinos were not happy with the service they were getting from Siemens and wanted us to replace the broken last-stage buckets with our GE design. After examining the turbine, I decided since we did not have Siemens-type dovetails, a one-time design change with a large engineering overhead expense would not be feasible for us to take on this project.

In March 1987, the world's largest combined cycle power plant, with a total generating capacity of 2,000 MegaWatts, owned by Tokyo Electric Power Company, began commercial operation. Of the 14 units, 12 were supplied by General Electric Company. They were fired by liquefied natural gas, delivered directly to the plant by LNG carriers with a capacity up to 130,000 m3, delivering gas from Brunei, Indonesia, Malaysia, Abu Dhabi and Alaska. The LNG was stored on-site in four 66,000 ton underground tanks. The entire plant was located on 287 acres of landfill in Tokyo Bay. This was an extremely impressive accomplishment by the Japanese and I was pleased to be a small part of this extraordinary "Japanese Miracle".

General Electric's Heat Recovery Steam Generators were manufactured in our Durham, North Carolina plant. These boilers with many internal finned tubes were very labor intensive and thus expensive to produce. Before long, we realized with the Japanese coming into this business, we could not compete in the market place. We found a partner, NEM Corporation in Leiden, Holland, just 30 minutes from Amsterdam to take over our HRSG manufacturing business. At the beginning of 1983 I sat up an engineering office in Leiden with Dave Skinner heading the group to work with the Dutch engineers in modifying our designs to their manufacturing processes. That became a viable approach where NEM supplied all the boilers for GE's combined-cycle power plants. I spent the next few months commuting to Amsterdam then to Leiden with KLM Airlines by way of New York City.

In the summer of 1983 while my mother was visiting us, we left the children with her and Ilkay and I went to Leiden. We started our trip from Paris. Of all the cities I visited, Paris has always been my favorite city. After renting a car in Paris, we drove north to Brussels, Belgium. From there we went to Ghent and then to the medieval town of Brugge (Bruj). Brugge is an old and tranquil medieval town north of Belgium's capital city Brussels. To us the canal-lined streets of Brugge with its quiet ambiance was most interesting. The many cobblestone streets led to the centre of the town to the *Markt* where historic old buildings faced a large open square. Durind the day *Markt* was filled with antique stalls and shoppers. This city was known for its intricate handmade lace and there were many shops selling these goods. In the evening we watched a very enjoyable show on the canal representing the medieval times. From here we drove on to Holland. Our first stop was the port city of Rotterdam. We later went to Delft where we were able to see the making of their famous "blue Delft" glazed earthenware.

When we arrived at Leiden I went to work to review the work progress while Ilkay spent her time sightseeing. At night we enjoyed the friendly neighborhoods of Holland especially on the North Sea shores in Schweningen. Leiden was a beautiful historic city lined with canals and filled with museums, fashionable shops and sidewalk cafes. Leiden University was the country's oldest university and was very highly regarded academically. Leiden was also well known as a town where Rembrandt was born and grew up and where the Pilgrims lived before boarding the Mayflower in 1620 to sail to the New World and land in Plymouth, Massachusetts.

Since I was a frequent traveller with KLM, my family and I became good friends with the local KLM representative in Boston, Paulette Russell. For years we spent many holidays together with her family and in the winter time we all travelled together to a winter ski resort near Cannon Mountain in New Hampshire where our children learned how to ski. One year when we took a trip to France, Ilkay and I visited Paulette's parents in Northern France on the Normandy coast, in a lovely little town called *Le Petit Dalle*. We then drove south together with Bob and Paulette Russell and stayed at their summer house in the small town of *Mont Clus*, in the Provence Region in Southern France. Provence has always been one of the most beautiful regions of France. It later became well known throughout the world with the bestseller book by Peter Mayle entitled "A Year in Provence".

We took many side trips to Aix-En-Provence, Cannes, Nice and Monte Carlo. Our most enjoyable trips however, were the local ones where we discovered the Provence culture and its many wonderful vineyards. During one of our local ventures we discovered the world's most famous vineyard, Chateauneuf de Pape. We naturally had to go in and have some wine tasting at this famous winery. We left the vineyard with a case of wine. The countryside was lined with tall grapevines as far as the eye could see. As we were leaving the vineyard I got the brilliant idea of picking some fresh grape leaves to cook our famous Turkish delicacy; stuffed grape leaves *(yaprak dolması)*. That evening while Bob, Paullette and I were sipping our Chateauneuf de Pape wine and relaxing on the patio under a quince *(ayva)* tree, Ilkay was laboring in the kitchen stuffing the Chateauneuf de Pape grape leaves! The meal turned out to be delicious. I thought we should be in the Guinness Book of World Records for being the first people who enjoyed stuffed grape leaves made from the famous Chateauneuf de Pape grapesvines. One summer Paulette visited us in Çeşme and enjoyed the Turkish hospitality of our many wonderful friends. Our friendship continues to this day even after she and Bob retired and moved to Cape Cod.

It seems like good things do not last forever. I was very happy in my job as the Manager of Turbine & HRSG Development Engineering, working on challenging engineering projects, seeing their applications in the field while travelling all over the world. Professionally, my job was very gratifying because I had made a very good reputation at GE and I was well known all over the Company. However, with the business of Large Steam Turbine Department being significantly reduced and since no new large power plants with steam turbines were being built, our new Chairman Jack Welch had other plans for the Medium Steam Turbine Department. In June of 1984 an announcement was made that Medium Steam Turbine Department would go under Large Steam Turbine Department. We knew that this would be the ultimate end of the Medium Steam Turbine Department.

Troubled Period at GE

In June 1984 the announcement of bringing Medium Steam Turbine Department under Large Steam Turbines was very devestating for us. We knew that it would be the beginning of a "slow death" for Medium Steam Turbine Department until it was completely closed and our jobs were eliminated. We, Medium Steam Turbine Employees, did not understand nor agree with the wisdom behind the decision since we had all the technology and the corresponding lucrative business on combined-cycle power plants, industrial turbine business and the Navy projects. We reasoned that the "powers-to-be" were in Schenectady and Large Steam Turbine Department needed our business to keep its plant open. We also knew Jack Welch did not like the Lynn Plant because of its strong labor union which always resisted the Company's many initiatives. It was obvious to us that Jack Welch was out to get the union and the Lynn Plant. It was not long before the engineering staff from Schenectady arranged meetings with us to start transferring our technology to the Large Steam Turbine Department. These meetings were not pleasant for us since we were giving our jobs away to another GE Department. We of course had no other choice but to comply. Meanwhile, there were many new orders coming in and the Navy projects that we had to work on to satisfy our customers. Morale was very low and it was hard to invigorate the personnel.

In 1981 when Jack Welch became GE's Chairman and CEO replacing Reginald Jones, GE was a very big conglomerate, selling everything from power plants to light bulbs. It owned businesses as diverse as mines in Australia, television network (NBC) and financial Service Companies (GE Capital). If one worked at GE during the period when Jack Welch was Chairman, one's life was most likely touched by his far reaching decisions and actions. He came to the top of GE in a period when the Company was big and powerful but needed a good overhaul. After a short duration of evaluating the position of GE, he moved rapidly to change GE and its culture. Jack's biggest skill was his instinct of foresight of the future. He could predict accurately where the economy was going and make business decisions accordingly and take actions immediately. Welch expressed his ideas in very simple terms. He first divided GE's businesses into three circles. He wanted each GE business to be number one or number two in the fields they competed. He suscinctly told us if we were number one or number two, we would be inside one of those three circles, and otherwise we were outside of the circles and would be eliminated. We were then preoccupied to see where we would fall in these circles. We knew he meant business when he sold the housewares division which had been in existence since the formation of the Company. GE appliances were found in almost every home worldwide and we were shocked with this sale. When he said he was going to do something there was no second guessing Welch. Within a few years after taking over GE through divestitures and downsizing, Welch had cut the number of employees from 400,000 to 220,000. At the beginning of each year we all waited nervously for the outcome of the annual Boca Raton Meeting which gave directions to the Company for the year's actions. For as much as GE's performance during the period of Welch's reign had been extraordinary with sales and earnings steadily increasing, he was not popular among the workers within the Company. While the Company's market share climbed and Jack became most popular in the media, the morale inside GE had bottomed out. The employees not only were in fear of losing their jobs but were always being belittled. I remember in one meeting one of Jack Welch's General Managers stating "engineers are a dime a dozen". Engineers at GE had lost the recognition they deserved and the business turned into an MBA run institution. Jack Welch felt that the turbine business had enough technology and did not need any more. Therefore very little money was put into R&D. The turbine business was used as a "cash-cow" by Jack Welch to support his financial adventures in GE Capital. GE was rapidly growing to be a big financial institution.

Jack was not flamboyant like his predecessor Reggie Jones. He spent only a few words to express himself but they were direct and to the point. Even his top management were at "razor's edge" and afraid of him. If they did not deliver the numbers that were assigned to them for their department, they were immediately out. In the process, because of his tactics of laying off thousands of people and closing plants, Jack Welch earned the nickname of "Neutron Jack", the man who kept the buildings standing, but eliminated all the people inside. Jack was not happy with that title and at every opportunity in the media he tried to defend himself. He had a great vision for the future of GE, but he was ruthless in the process of achieving it. He wanted a "boundaryless" company that worked with "Speed, Simplicity and Self-Confidence"; the three S's which were drilled into us. Meanwhile the media continued to immortalize him. The investors liked him since GE stock price was going up continuously together with the rest of the market. He wanted and received the highest salary with many additional perks of any CEO at that time. This did not go too well with the thousands of employees who were loosing their jobs and their livelihood.

In this difficult environment, my Turbine Development Engineering was facing some big challenges. The SLEP (Ship's Life Extension Program) was a big program we had with the US Navy. One of the nuclear aircraft carriers, SARATOGA, was going through a major overhaul, including the overhaul of the turbines at the Philadelphia Shipyard. When the turbines were inspected it was observed that the rotors had stress-corrosion cracking around the dovetail pin holes which were susceptible to rotor failure. Since the turbines were located at the bottom of a seven-floor aircraft carrier structure, the turbines needed to be fixed and installed first before any other work could be done. In case of critical problems like this the normal solution would be replacement of the rotors with new ones. The overhaul however, was on a very tight schedule and there was no time to get new rotor forgings. I was asked to come up with a permenant, fool-proof fix for these rotors. After reviewing different design concepts, we decided to remove the cracked holes from the edges of the rotors and cover them with dovetails without blades. I called them "a pair of pants", since they looked like pants. When Dick Burke, MST General Manager and I travelled to Philadelphia to present our new concept to the Admiral in charge of the ship yard, the Commander asked me:

— Dr. Tuncel, how long will this fix last?

I responded,

— For the rest of the ship's life.

The meeting went very well and the Admiral accepted our proposal. We retrofitted the SARATOGA aircraft carrier turbines with our newly modified design. As soon as the ship's overhaul was completed it went into service in the Mediterranean. The turbine modifications lasted over 20 years without any problem until the ship was recently retired. Dick Burke was very pleased with the outcome of our Philadelphia meeting and not long after that he became General Manager of Aircraft Engines in Lynn. Medium Steam Turbine Department was left without a General Manager and started being managed from Schenectady. The "slow-death" of the Medium Steam Turbine Department was continuing.

The US Navy had given GE's Medium Steam Turbine Department a very big study contract called the IPMP (Improved Performance Machinery Program), for the design of new engine rooms for future submarines. The existing SSN-Attack Submarines and the Trident-Missile Carrying Submarines had extremely heavy engine rooms that were designed and built by General Electric. The engine room, which comprised of two steam turbines, a large reduction gear, and the sub-base which supported the equipment, was a large percentage of the submarine's total weight. The US Navy wanted significant reduction in the total weight of the engine room. This was a major departmental effort. My Turbine Development Engineering group was assigned to the task of design evaluations and analytical calculations. It was obvious to us that most of the weight in the existing design was due to the subbase which was supporting the two turbines and the reduction gear while keeping them aligned. A perfect alignment of the turbines and the gear was most critical. The subbase was attached to the ship's hull with many rubber isolators which had the tendency to creep in time loosing their noise isolation effectiveness. We realized any small design modifications on the existing design would not give us the required weight reduction which was the Navy's primary concern in the evaluation. I had learned in my many years of experience that fixing a design problem in the field, small design changes would not solve the problem. To do the job right, drastic design modifications were needed. In order to win this contract we had to come up with a design concept completely different and unique in reducing the total weight significantly.

I proposed to eliminate the subbase completely and to tie the turbines and the gear with new structural elements that would support the equipment while maintaining alignment. With the new and advanced ANSYS computer programs, we were now in a position to analyze structures like this that could not be done 25 years ago. Eliminating the subbase would give GE significant advantage over our competitor Westinghouse and it would be a unique design concept. The proposal was very well received and we started detailed analytical calculations on the new structure. As a result of this new design concept I received five patents:

"Condenser Integrated Turbine Support"
"Apparatus for Supporting Two Turbines in Marine Propulsion"
"Vibration Isolation System for Marine Propulsion Equipment"
"Support and Isolation Systems for Marine Turbine and Gear"
"Tri-Axial Vibration Isolators for Ship Gearing"

Although with these patents I received a lot of recognition within the Company, there were no financial benefits since the patents were GE property and I was a GE employee. Because of their criticality, the Navy imposed "SECRECY order" on these patents. The Medium Steam Turbine Department put together a very large team, including outside consultants, to prepare the proposal and the total package was then presented to the Navy. After a long evaluation the US Navy gave GE another contract to continue the design. The project however, was never implemented into hardware.

Because of the analytical work I did on the IPMP program and noise measurements I used to do in the Materials and Processes Laboratory in Schenectady, I was considered the "noise expert" in the department. Since noise is a vibration phenomenon, and because of my vibrations background, I tended to get more involved with noise problems. When our department had a gear noise problem in Colombia, South America, I was asked to go there to solve it.

As we were flying into Bogota, Colombia we were warned not to carry much cash or valuables with us including jewelry and expensive watches. People who wandered alone only one block from the hotel to sightsee found themselves with a machete on their throat, threatened to give everything they had or else face the consequences. Outside the hotel, men were trying to peddle green crystals as emeralds to the tourists. It was very uncomfortable to be on the streets of Bogota and we always had to look over our shoulder to see if we were being followed.

General Electric had just installed a gas turbine power plant on the hills of Bucaramanga, Colombia for the Colombian Utilities Company. The sale was a barter arrangement, where our main customer was Sumitomo Trading Corporation of Japan who bought the power plant from General Electric and sold it to the Colombian Government in exchange for coffee and emeralds. I was very impressed with the Japanese who were very creative in their business transactions. The Japanese engineers at the power plant site were very demanding. The General Electric gas turbine, the reduction gear and a generator we had supplied, were generating excessive noise above specification limits and the Japanese and Columbian personnel would not accept the power plant at these noise levels. The noise was eminating from our reduction gear reverberating through the beautiful green and lush hills of the Colombian countryside. Although these hills were relatively safe compared to Bogota, during the mid 1980's when I was there, they became sanctuaries for many drug warlords in the later years and no one could step into this beautiful landscape without the permission of these drug dealers. I spent the next ten days trying to come up with the easiest and cheapest solution for the noise problem by changing the alignments of the generator and the gear box against the gas turbine to optimize the noise being generated with proper alignment. On the hills of Bucaramanga I was thinking of the Optimization Course I had taken from Professor Erdoğan at Lehigh and how I was now applying those concepts I had learned then. Once we reduced the noise to the acceptable levels, we made our presentations to the executives of Sumitomo and Colombian Utilities in Bogota and I was happy to leave Colombia.

After the IPMP program was shelved by the US Navy, all the resources were directed into building the new Arleigh Burke destroyers, DDG-51 Series. The future of the Navy would rely on these high-tech missile carrying destroyers with very sophisticated, advanced electronics. The Navy was planning to build a large number of destroyers which meant big orders for the component manufacturers and the shipyards. For the engine room, General Electric's LM Series jet engines were selected as the prime-mover, but the reduction gears were open for bids. Each ship would have two reduction gears for four jet engines. Since the jet engines were operating at higher speeds than the steam turbines, reduction gear design was more challenging, requiring new manufacturing capabilities for hardening and grinding individual gear teeth. The Medium Steam Turbine Department was desperately in need of a big gear manufacturing contract, since the Gear Plant did not have any other orders. Our initial proposal of supporting the heavy gear box with rubber isolators was immediately turned down by the Navy. Because of creep characteristics of rubber isolators, the Navy was not interested in installing components that required periodic maintenance. Our principal competitor Westinghouse had been successfully using steel tubular isolators in various applications for many years and they had a lot of experience with their metallic isolators. It was very clear that if we did not have very good noise isolators, General Electric would not get the multi-million dollar gear box orders. In many meetings I attended with the US Navy personnel in Washington D.C., for as much as our gear design was superior to the Westinghouse gears, we were always reminded that the noise isolators were the critical components of the total proposed package. Each reduction gear had a "noise signature" over a broad range of frequency spectrum. Isolators were designed to reduce or eliminate the transmission of the noise from the gear casing to the ship's hull. Since water is a very good transmitter, the noise signature could be detected easily by others if not isolated sufficiently.

Since my Turbine Development Engineering was the only subsection in the Department with advanced structural analysis techniques and computer-aided design and test capability, we were assigned the task of coming up with a new isolator design. I realized the isolator design would be a "make or break" of the high precision gear business at General Electric. If we did not get the gear-box orders for the DDG-51 Destroyer program, we would have to close the Gear Plant and lay off hundreds of people. On the other hand, any design similar to the Westinghouse isolators would not give us the required edge for the orders. We needed to do better than Westinghouse's existing design. Westinghouse had published an ASME paper describing their metallic isolators with the analysis and test results given in details. It was an excellent technical work they had done. I studied this design in their technical paper over and over again. Basically in mechanical vibrations terminology, it was a thin and tall tubular section which acted as a metallic spring in a "one degree freedom system" with the gear box being the "mass". Based on my turbine bucket design experience, I came up with a completely novel idea of using a "two degree freedom system" for our metallic isolators. In our new design we would avoid the resonances of our "spring-mass system" with gear-mesh frequencies, and still attain much higher attenuation (noise reduction) than the Westinghouse system.

The analytical calculation work we did showed us that this new approach was a fool-proof concept and it was well received within GE and later by the Navy. We urgently worked on the details of the design and built a prototype. The isolator was tested and exceeded the specifications. We were confident that our support system would meet every noise isolation requirements the Navy needed on the DDG-51. I patented this design under the title of:

"Vibration Isolation in Marine Drive Systems"

This was my sixth patent but again the Navy imposed a "SECRECY order" on it. The Navy accepted our proposal and gave General Electric a multi-million dollar contract for a series of gear boxes with the corresponding new noise isolators. This was a tremendous day for the Medium Steam Turbine Department and the Gear Plant but a big disappointment for Westinghouse. A few years later, just like our Medium Steam Turbine Department, Westinghouse would also fold under and be bought by Brown-Boveri of Switzerland. It would be the end of Westinghouse Company.

Although the Gear Plant business was thriving, the rest of the turbine business in the Medium Steam Turbine Department was gradually being transferred to the Large Steam Turbine Department in Schenectady. My visits to Schenectady became more frequent as we were transferring our work to the Large Steam Turbine Department. In one of our trips, the entire management of the Medium Steam Turbine Department travelled by bus from Boston to Schenectady to discuss ongoing work transfer. On our return trip, we stopped at a restaurant to review the day's events and future plans. Our Engineering Manager, Gil Wozney, realizing that Christmas was approaching very soon, decided to announce:

— Dr. Cohen and Dr. Tuncel will be in charge of arranging this year's Christmas festivities for the Department.

I leaned over and quietly said:

— Gil, do you really want a Jew and a Muslim to be in charge of your Christmas activities!

He then retorted:

— Oh! OK. We'll then have Dr. Eskeson be in charge of the Christmas Party. This reinforced the fact that there was never any prejudice or bigotry within our work environment.

In June 1986, my friend Bob Couchman, General Manager of the Turbine Engineering in the Large Steam Department invited me to Schenectady. He took me to lunch at the famed Edison Club, one block from where I used to live on Union Street when I first started working for GE in 1962, almost a quarter century ago. During lunch he asked me if I would be interested in heading all the turbine development work in Schenectady. Furthermore, my job as Manager of Turbine Development Engineering in Lynn was coming to an end. It was an offer no one in his right mind would refuse and everyone thought I was going to accept this generous and impressive offer. Back at home that evening during dinner Ilkay and I told the children about the offer and our possible move back to Schenectady. They all started crying and told me they did not want to go back to Schenectady. They were very happy in Lynnfield and they had many friends they did not want to leave. Ilkay and I were not much interested moving back to Schenectady either. I regretfully informed Bob Couchman that because of my family obligations I could not accept his wonderful offer. At General Electric Company if you wanted to advance in your career you had to be a "good soldier"; do what you were told and go where you were sent. Otherwise, there was no other chance. Soon after, the Medium Steam Turbine closed and I was without a job.

14

GE Aircraft Engines

Gear Engineering

In 1986 the Medium Steam Turbine Department was closing with the last remnants of the factory equipment being moved to Schenectady. Our large Building 64 looked like a ghost house. Every corner we walked into was empty and quiet, with vacant desks lined up next to each other. All those vibrant sounds coming from each office with people doing their daily duties were gone and all the lights were turned off. It was dark and eerie everywhere. Together with those lights, my dreams were also shattered. This was the place where I worked so hard, made significant contributions and enjoyed myself. This was the place where I was so happy, but now it was all gone. People who were working in these premises started scattering around. Older personnel started retiring immediately: Tony Rendine, Alex Rotsko, Bill Printup, and Merrill Cohen all took their early retirements. Younger staff like Russ Shade, Mark Little, Dave Skinner and many others who were in my group moved to either Fitchburg or Schenectady. In no time, my protégées, Russ Shade and Mark Little became vice-presidents in GE's different departments. I was almost fifty years old, not old enough to retire nor young enough to move to a fresh start. It was a very difficult age for working people. This scenario would be seen throughout the country in the coming decades, as the businesses lost their competitiveness and started laying-off their workers in their most difficult and productive age period. I was given my golden opportunity to go to Schenectady to head all the R&D work but being a free spirited individual and realizing my family came first, I made my choice of not accepting that great offer and I had to live with my decision. When I looked back, I realized I made many critical life decisions on my own; leaving Istanbul Technical University to come to America, changing my major at Lehigh University from Metallurgy to Mechanical Engineering, changing my Ph.D. program to attend Brooklyn Polytechnic full-time and giving up a lucrative job to go to the Turkish Navy. Now I was facing a difficult situation of having my wonderful job completely eliminated and being out of a job.

I decided to take my family for a spring vacation to California rather than despairing about my predicament. We started our memorable tour in San Francisco. After we spent two days roaming the interesting sights of the city, we went to visit my old boss Don Rubio who was then the head of APRI, American Power Research Institute in San Jose. He had left General Electric's nuclear business which had also folded. We reminisced about the time he had hired me as a new graduate from Lehigh into General Electric. It was very nice to see him again after so many years.

Rather than driving on the fast speed freeway, we decided to take the scenic coastal route from San Francisco to Los Angeles. Our next stop was at Carmel, one of the most beautiful towns in California. Carmel was like a storybook town, small, quaint and very affluent. A few years later Clint Eastwood became the Mayor of this beautiful town. After visiting Big Sur and Hearst's San Simeon Castle, we discovered that the scenic route was closed due to recent mud slides. We were forced to climb through the narrow winding roads of the Santa Lucia Range to a main highway. As we inched our way, we prayed to safely make it down the mountain. That climb by itself was an excitement. The single lane road was very treacherous but the view of the Pacific from the top of the mountain was breathtaking.

When we arrived in Los Angeles, we visited Hollywood and Beverly Hills. We had promised the children we would go to Disneyland which we did. One of the highlights of our California trip was rushing back to the hotel in Los Angeles for the "happy hour" that the entire family enjoyed. While Ilkay and I were having our cocktails, the children enjoyed their "Shirley Temple" drinks. Doğan, meanwhile, was busy shooting pool with other adult guests. We completed our tour with a visit to Las Vegas and then to the majestic Grand Canyon. It was a great, memorable and fun-filled family vacation. It also kept my mind away from my job situation.

After our return from California, I learned that the Gear Engineering Manager's position was available. George Sarney, whom I knew from our Schenectady days, gave me that job right away. In June 1986, I took over my new job as Manager of Gear Engineering.

The Gear Plant in Lynn was a unique facility, dedicated to the design, manufacture, assembly, and testing of complete geared propulsion systems. The Gear Plant, which covered 500,000 square feet, was the leading supplier of advanced propulsion systems to the US Navy fleet ranging from massive aircraft carriers, super quiet submarines to small auxiliary ships. At the beginning of the 1980's when the US Navy required high power density gear systems that were 50 percent smaller and 50 percent lighter than the conventional units with equal power output and lower noise levels, the case hardened gear teeth with precision grinding was introduced. The world's most advanced grinding machines were installed in GE's gear plant to finish the gear teeth to tolerances one could not possibly see with the human eye.

In the gear plant large gear components up to 160 inches in diameter and 38.5 tons by weight were handled. When I started my job as the Manager of Gear Engineering, we were building the gears for DDG-51 Arleigh Burke, the lead ship in a powerful new class of AEGIS destroyers which was going to be launched at Bath Iron Works, in Bath, Maine. When the first set of gears were built and assembled together with my patented design isolators, the complete system was fully tested, shipped, and readied for assembly.

In my new job I found new challenges I did not have before. Although I had a lot of turbine experience, I did not know too much about gear design and I had to learn this business in a hurry. Furthermore, I had a lot of gear drafting personnel who were difficult to manage because of their labor union connections. As Computer Aided Design (CAD) was newly introduced into our systems, the drafting union was slow accepting it. The work coming out of drafting was extremely slow and quite contrary to my temperament. In my new position I had to deal with many problems other than technical and also a few issues that had to be attended to immediately.

The gear plant was still manufacturing reduction gears for utility applications for gas turbine and generator packages, similar to the one I had worked on in Colombia, South America. These were standard reduction gears not requiring high quality precision manufacturing. The cost of our utility type reduction gears was not competitive in the market place and a decision was made to get out of that business. Our Purchasing Department found another gear manufacturing source, John Brown Engineering in Glasgow, Scotland for utility applications. We travelled to Glasgow to evaluate their capability and discovered that John Brown Engineering was more than capable to handle our needs for utility gearing. We thus gave them the job of manufacturing utility gears for us. The Scottish people were very friendly and generous and they welcomed us into their homes. They took us to their local pubs to taste many different Scotch malts, which we had not heard of in the United States. Each one of them was tastier and smoother than the other. It seemed like they were keeping the "good stuff" for themselves. Not long after I joined Gear Engineering, we got out of the utility gear business completely.

Another issue that had been dragging on in Gear Engineering which I had to face was a conflict with the Spanish Navy on the turning gear we had supplied them for their aircraft carrier. The Spanish Navy was in the process of building an aircraft carrier with General Electric jet engines as prime movers. It was much smaller than the US Navy's nuclear aircraft carriers. We had supplied the Spanish Navy two turning gears to keep the long propeller shafts continuously turning at a very low speed when the ship was docked, to keep the shafts from bowing. The turning gears, however, because of excessive friction, were not doing the job right and turning the shafts intermittently but not continuously.

General Electric, in its usual arrogance had claimed that there was nothing wrong with our design calculations since we had extrapolated the design from a US aircraft turning gear design which was working without any problem. The Spanish Navy engineers however, had calculated otherwise. As the new Manager of Gear Engineering, I spent long hours studying many files of calculations and data generated by both sides. In the end I realized direct extrapolation, when the designs were different, would not work. I found out when we calculated the design on individual basis, our turning gear design would not be sufficient for the Spanish Navy as they had claimed. After many internal reviews, a Product Service Representative and I travelled to Spain for meetings with the Spanish Navy Engineering personnel. From Madrid we travelled to El Ferrol where the Spanish Navy headquarters and their shipyard were located. El Ferrol was a town located on the Atlantic coast of Spain by the Portuguese border. The shipyard was an ancient historical port, enclosed with walls one meter thick, where the Spanish Armada used to leave from for discoveries of the New World. Five Spanish engineers and their bosses walked into the meeting with files of data and calculations. Representing GE was only the Product Service Representative and I with a few pages of calculations. After the initial greetings, I told them before we discussed all that data and continued arguing each other's positions that I had an announcement to make. I basically told them we had made a mistake at GE in our design calculations and we were here to ractify it by upgrading the turning gears to new ones. My new calculations correlated well with their numbers and we were now in full agreement. Within an hour the meeting was finished and the Spaniards were so happy that they gave me hugs and kisses like the Turkish style. They immediately took me to their Admiral and told him the outcome of the meeting. I got more hugs and kisses from the Admiral! That evening we were treated to a fancy dinner at the Navy's exclusive restaurant. I asked my hosts why they were building an aircraft carrier and they said, "We have islands to protect". I think they meant the Canary Islands by the Northern shores of Africa to be protected from the Africans and Arabs. Our mission was complete and we went back to Madrid where I spent the next two days going to their famous Prado Museum during the day and their night clubs with Flamenco dancers at night. On my return from Madrid I made my flight connection to Boston via Paris, my favorite city. I spent the weekend there enjoying the everlasting beauty and excitement of the eternal city.

Germans historically have always been excellent and superior in machinery design and manufacturing. GE had a long arrangement with a professor from Munich Technicke Hochschule as a consultant to follow the German technology on gear designs. It was a pleasant duty for me to go to Munich to meet with our consultant and see different gear manufacturing facilities and follow up on various research works being done at the University. Munich was a beautiful Bavarian city and the countryside has always been one of my favorite spots in Europe. In the evenings our consultant and I continued our technical discussions at the *Hofbrauhaus* in Munich, the largest and most famous beer hall in the world. I don't think we accomplished much in the very noisy atmosphere with the Umpha Band playing in the background while we were sipping our tasty German beers from large steins. If there was anything I learned from our German advisor, it was not to try to keep up my beer drinking with the Germans.

As gear manufacturing was going well, my gear drafting business was falling behind. It was very frustrating for me to see draftsmen spending the entire day not doing much work. I think Jack Welch was right with his attitude towards the union personnel. Although I had not planned it, one day when Dick Burke, the General Manager of Aircraft Engines in Lynn, whom I had worked with on the Navy's SLEP program, called to ask me a question, I told him about my frustrations in Gear Engineering. He soon arranged interviews for me and within a month I had a new job in GE's Aircraft Engines Division as Manager of Component Development Laboratories.

Component Development Laboratories

General Electric's Lynn plant had some of the country's most reknown engineering staff and the corresponding highly skilled manufacturing capability. It was the obvious place for the US Government to locate the country's first secret jet engine development and production work in the Lynn River Works plant in 1943. America's first jet engine was developed and tested in this plant and Lynn became the focus of America's jet engine development and production center for decades to come. Out of the early research done on jet engines, significant Aircraft Engines Business for General Electric was developed and done in the Lynn River Works plant. Throughout the 1940's and during the following decades, General Electric made significant contributions in jet engine designs and developments evolving many engines in a wide range of thrust power. Jet engines play a powerful role in the world today: from jet aircraft both commercial and military, pumping oil through pipelines, generating energy for factories and utilities, to driving ships across the seas.

Although gas turbine engines are simple in theory, they are complex to build. High operating temperatures mean greater efficiency, so engines must be designed to operate above the metal's normal melting point. Vibration can ruin gas turbines, so perfectly balanced blade assemblies must be accomplished. Internal tolerances must be extremely closed to avoid leakage and loss of efficiency and seals must fit perfectly and last for years. It takes a tremendous amount of commitment to develop such a sophisticated machine. An engine moves from a design concept, to prototype, then to testing, with significant amount of effort and attention paid to details. Individual engine components are tested and proved before they are installed into sub-assemblies and are tested again. Finally, an entire engine is assembled and tested in various simulation modes. An engine designed today may not enter the market for as long as ten years.

As General Electric's Aircraft Engine business grew, because Lynn did not have the space to handle bigger engines, larger engine business moved to Evendale, Ohio, just outside of Cincinnati. Evendale later became the headquarters for GE's Aircraft Engine Business, while Lynn supported smaller military and commercial engines.

In September 1987 I joined GE's Aircraft Engines Business Group in Lynn as Manager of Component Development Laboratories (CDL). This was an exciting experience for me because I was moving into a completely different jet engine technology. I felt confident about my new job because of my prior experience in Schenectady's Materials and Processes Laboratory and a lot of the jet engine components were similar to steam turbine components. The Component Development Laboratories included the Component Test Laboratory (CTL) and the Experimental Mechanics Laboratory (EML). CDL's charter was to provide experimental results and evaluations to jet engine designers using test rigs which would predict or simulate actual engine conditions.

The Component Test Laboratory conducted tests on bearings, seals and lubrication systems as well as air flow tests on models and actual engine hardware. The Experimental Mechanics Laboratory performed vibration surveys, fatigue and static stress tests. The laboratory over the years had accumulated a significant amount of test equipment with many test facilities at different locations within the Lynn plant. CDL had the capability and the know-how to run any type of test needed in the development of jet engine components. One of the most impressive features of the laboratory was its capable staff with many years of experience developed on many different engine types.

I quickly got to know all the members of the laboratory and established an excellent working relationship with every one of them. Some of the laboratory staff members, George Fischer, Dick MackWhorter, Pete Hendrickson, Dr. Abe Assa, Art Lisi, and Mike Campbell were my old friends from previous turbine departments. Together with the other laboratory members, Steve McDonald, Bert Campbell, Roger Lacantore, John Asdorian, Bob Landers, Frank Emmith, Dan Gugger, James Smith, Henry Szymczak, Tom Boyle and others, the staff was an excellent team. Over and over again I realized how proud I was to be associated with such a great team. At the age of 50, I felt very lucky and gratified to find this exciting and diversified job.

After I joined CDL, I started exploring and learning the test facilities we had in different buildings. I was appalled to see how old and dilapidated some of the test facilities were. In fact, a lot of the fatigue tests with shakers were being performed in an ancient unsafe building with water puddles on the floor. I could not believe we were conducting advance technology development in such deplorable conditions. I felt that this was an inexcusable negligence. When I found out a complete lower floor of the building under our Experimental Mechanics Laboratory was being vacated, I immediately claimed ownership to it. I made plans to move all the vibration shakers, large test bed-plates, and lube-system simulator test facilities from many scattered buildings into one location. Although Jack Welch falsely claimed he was investing money into new technologies, there were no funds available to upgrade these facilities. I used all the maintenance budget allocated to the laboratory and went to the Finance Department to convince them for some additional funds to finance my plans. I used non-union outside contractors to complete my new facilities within the planned time and available budget. The union was not happy with my actions and I was reminded of that very emphatically. I did however end up with modern test facilities, with advanced data acquisition systems and with all the environmental and safety features. To the entrance of the facilities I added a glass domed vestibule which made it look more like a respectable test laboratory. I purchased large foliage plants with my own money and decorated this area. Everyone was amazed at how lovely the facility now looked.

With our new and automated facilities our productivity improved considerably. I brought many design engineering groups into our test facilities to inform them of our added capabilities and to improve our communication channels better. Just like in my earlier job in Schenectady's M&P Laboratory, design groups were very happy with our responsiveness and quality of work. We thus received more work requests including some from Evendale. With increased work level, I started hiring new engineers into my group. When I found out our design group was relying only on the analytical calculations in evaluating engine drive shafts, I pursued to buy new torsional vibration equipment. I knew too well that analysis without test data could lead to troubles, like the submarine bucket problems we had experienced in the Medium Steam Turbine Department. I somehow scrounged $200,000 from the design departments and got an MTS-Torsional Vibration Test Equipment and from the day it was installed, it has been in use ever since.

The work in the laboratory was going very well and in a short period we had received a lot of recognition. Every summer I arranged family picnics for the Laboratory personnel and their families to generate an atmosphere of togetherness. We would have grilled steaks and lobster and everyone enjoyed themselves at these outings eating, swimming, canoeing and playing games. Even my mother, when she was visiting us one summer, together with my children, was able to attend our picnic and have fun. She was very proud to see her son had achieved such positions during his career. She told me many times how proud she was of my accomplishments and that I had made the right choice to stay in the United States.

As I had experienced in my lifetime before, good things don't last forever. Again tough times started to follow. At the beginning of 1991 with recession starting to show itself, the aircraft engine business had slowed down considerably. Jack Welch's edict to us, in his usual ruthless approach, was to reduce the work force immediately. The Company's Human Resources Department, which at this time was basically useless, had prepared a matrix evaluation scheme to score individuals from top to bottom and instructed us to lay off the bottom ten percent in the first round. It was one of the worst experiences I had in my professional life. All this time I had always expanded businesses and hired people. Firing them was very difficult for me. It was especially devastating for me when I had to call in a female, single mother engineer whom I had recently hired, to tell her she was no longer employed. Unfortunately, during the first half of the 1990's, lay offs continued year after year, reducing the laboratory as well as the entire Lynn plant to a bare bone operational staff. Even then we continued serving the Aircraft Engines Business both in Lynn and Evendale with diligence, meeting their technical needs with our most capable staff. In spite of all the difficulties, I still enjoyed working in Component Development Laboratories very much.

Of Family and Friends

In 1986 when we decided not to go back to Schenectady, our children were still in school. It was a critical age for them when close ties with many of their friends were very important. All three children enjoyed growing up in a small town community with very warm and friendly environment. They practically got to know everyone in town and through them we met many wonderful families. Nükhet first went through the Lynnfield school system and Doğan and Müge followed her. Their schooling was enjoyable and they graduated without any difficulties. At Lynnfield High School Nükhet took an active part in the social functions including being a solo pianist in the school concerts. In the summer after her junior year, she spent three months near Le Mans, France with a French family as an exchange student. After graduating in 1987, she then went to Boston University and in 1991 she got her bachelor's degree from the School of Management. One summer while in college, she even worked at my friend Tonguç Ösen's company at Cevher Döküm in Izmir while living with my mother in Alsancak. We felt this was an excellent opportunity for her to improve her Turkish, her understanding of Turkish customs and see how the Turks did business.

Doğan and Müge were more active in sports. They started playing soccer at a very young age when I was coaching them in little league soccer.

Nükhet also coached one season. While in Middle School they both played basketball and began track and field. Both children were very competitive and very good in sports. When Doğan decided to play American football in high school, we were extremely concerned that he might get hurt. We would try to attend all of his home games and root for the team eventhough we did not much understand the game. Müge, however, became a star soccer player. In her four years on the high school varsity soccer team, she was a center forward and co-captain of the team. She loved the game so much that on one occasion she played the entire game with a broken ankle. In the summers when we were in Çeşme, she would always play soccer with the Turkish boys. They were amazed how she could play such a skillful soccer since it was unheard of in Turkey for girls to play. When they were not playing football or soccer, Doğan and Müge participated in the school's track and field competitions. Müge in fact held the school's triple-jump record. All three children spent their summers working in many different jobs, just like I did when I was in Turkey. They never had any idle time. After graduating high school, Doğan and later Müge attended the University of Massachusetts in Amherst and graduated in 1996 and 1999, respectively.

As the children were growing and leaving home for college, Ilkay found free time to go to work. She developed an interest in the real estate business and after acquiring her license she started working and became good at her job. Her easy and pleasant approach made her very popular and in-demand with customers. I was, however, her biggest fan and customer. Everytime she had a "good-deal" she would easily convince me to buy a condominium unit from her. Before long I had units in Swampscott, Peabody, Lynnfield and New Hampshire that I had to take care of. I knew too well however, together with the rental properties came the difficulties of dealing with tenants. Because of my many years of management experience at GE, I had no problem dealing with people and difficult situations. I also had a lot of youthful energy and my usual perseverance in dealing with problems. I had learned to become a good handyman in house repair back in Schenectady and there was no repair project that I could not tackle with. Throughout these years Ilkay suffered from persistent headaches and blinding migranes. The best clinics and doctors in Boston could not find any cure for her ailments and she learned to live with the excrutiating pains. She figured by keeping busy with her work it would keep her mind off her ailment.

We never neglected visiting my mother every summer in Turkey and spending wonderful times together with her in Çeşme. Memorable moments are when we share happy times with our friends and families that we love. We visited my friend Tonguç Ösen and his lovely wife Cavidan almost every day in Çeşme sharing great moments together. Sometimes we would go on his yacht and spend the entire day touring around Çeşme. On many of these gatherings Cavidan's brother Ilhan Bozcalı and his wife Deniz joined us where we had some wonderful times together. Ilhan Bozcalı, a prominent lawyer in Izmir, always attended my and my mother's business and he has been like a younger brother to me that I did not have. Quite often when I visited Izmir Ilhan and I spent a lot of fun times together. Tonguç and Cavidan often visited Boston when their sons Berat and Bertuğ were at Northeastern University and sometimes for some medical checkups. Similarly, we were often together with Hüseyin and Saliha Özyavuz, and Kemal and Pervin Baysak and their families and enjoyed their generous hospitality. It was always nice when we were with Dr. Nihat Önderoğlu and Sevinç Abla, and with İhsan and Betigül Özkan. We always got together with Kenan and Mazlume Pelit either in Çeşme or at their famous *Sevinç Pastanesi* (Bakery) in Izmir. All these people and their families were more like family members to us than mere friends and we grew to be very fond of them. We always shared our happy and sad moments together, and we were always ready to help each other. When we were not in Turkey, all these friends looked after my mother as if she was their own mother. Knowing that my friends were always there for my mother made my being far away from her more bearable for us and for my mother.

On 17 May 1988, my grandmother Pembe Hanım, who was living with my mother since my father's death in 1972, died in her sleep. She was 92 years old. She lived a difficult but still a complacent and charitable life. She went through many difficulties during her younger years but later in life she found comfort, happiness and satisfaction seeing all her offsprings very well accomplished. She converted her own house into a condominium building giving one unit to each daughter. It was her final gift to them. I was very saddened by her death because I was always close to my mother's side of the family. After my father had died I never saw any relatives from his side of the family.

In Lynnfield we were equally blessed to have many wonderful friends and neighbors. We spent a lot of happy times together with Erdem and Saadet Amasya and Dinçer and Priscilla Ulutaş. With the presence of our neighbors Guenther and Irmgard Greulich and Elliot and Jackie Kurtz, our neighborhood was more enjoyable. On many occasions we would have dinner parties with our immediate neighbors the Kurtz's and the

Greulich's where Jackie would entertain us with her talented impromptu piano playing. We would accompany her, singing old tunes, and sometimes Guenther would even sing some German songs. There were many other wonderful friends nearby whom we enjoyed being with also. We preferred and tried to be with our friends as much as possible rather than being isolated individuals. When we live far from our families, friends are more like family members and precious to us.

Although I had the opportunity to travel throughout the world because of my job at General Electric, Ilkay and I travelled extensively to various parts of Europe and the United States. It must have been the yearning from my childhood days in Izmir, when I admired all the emblems on Eyüp Köknar's Buick, that I liked travelling. At every opportunity I planned my own tours and on different occasions we drove through Germany, Austria, France, Belgium, Holland, Italy and England. We found each one of these countries very interesting and enjoyable. Similarly, we visited many beautiful and impressive places in the United States as well. I enjoyed travelling so much that I hoped one day after I retired I could continue my travels in a more leisurely way.

Atatürk Organized Industrial Zone
(*Atatürk Organize Sanayii Sitesi*)

As the years flew by rapidly, our parents were getting older and were dealing with many ailments. My mother suffered from emphysema and her lungs had gradually lost their functionality causing severe shortness of breath. Although emphysema and asthma are mostly attributed to smoking, which is a widespread and terrible vice in Turkey, my mother never smoked. Izmir, being located like a crescent around the bay, had been blanketed by dense air pollution throughout the years. During the winter months with coal being burned in all the apartment buildings, the intensity of the smog and pollution became unbearably worst. Doctors attributed my mother's problems to her living in Alsancak, which was in the lower terrains of the city, and breathing this polluted air almost all her life. It is ironic that with the advancement of technology our environment is being destroyed and countries are giving lip service to address this problem. Even when she was very ill, my mother would not tell us she was not feeling well. She was always happy and cheerful on the phone with us. She did not want us to worry about her and she never wanted to be a burden to us. She had an easy going, pleasant personality and everyone enjoyed her cheerful company and lively conversations. She was very much loved by everyone, young and old. She was a great listener and always concerned about the well-being of others. Her biggest hobby was going to the Alsancak Bazaar to do her food shopping from the vendors who were mostly Kurdish and they always tolerated her incessant bargaining. This was also her chance to greet and chat with many neighbors who knew her. Having gone through many difficulties in her lifetime, money was important to her. She was always careful in her spending and always warned us accordingly. It was a big joy for her to go to the bank periodically and watch her accounts grow. On her return from the bank, she would make her usual stops at the butcher, baker, grocer or pharmacy, visiting and having *çay* with the shop owners.

My aunt Ayşe also suffered from many health problems. She fell and broke her arm and later broke her leg. She had high blood pressure and suffered from shingles brought on by severe emotional stress. She never recovered after that. My aunt Hanife also suffered from high blood pressure and back problems due to a herniated disk. Over the years her heart condition got worst and she had angina. We tried to have my aunts together with my mother in Çeşme whenever we were visiting in the summer times. Those were the happy and memorable moments for us. One of the more memorable times was in June 1995 where the entire family was together at my Cousin Necdet Itmeç's daughter Nihal's wedding. The three sisters, whom we called "The Golden Girls" *(Altın Kızlar)*, proudly danced with their sons. I was happy that my three children were able to be at this festive occasion and experience the closeness of our family.

During this time Ilkay had lost her maternal grandmother, who was living with her parents in Baltimore. Her mother had fallen and broken her shoulder a short time later making Ilkay very concerned and worried. She tried to go and be with her parents as often as she could.

With our friends we shared good times as well as bad moments together. Both of my friends Tonguç Ösen and Hüseyin Özyavuz had health problems which we attended to in the United States. When Hüseyin Bey's son Haluk, after a car accident, needed surgery on both hips, I arranged the operation to be done at the Mayo Clinic in Rochester, Minnesota in February 1995. Haluk's surgery was very succesful with full recovery over the years. One of the more memorable moments was in the summer of 2000, Tonguç and Cavidan took us on a cruise on his yacht along the beautiful shores of Turkey's Mediterranean coast. The four of us spent one glorious week together on the boat stopping at many ports along the way. In many trips

I made to Turkey on my own, I spent a lot of time with my friend Tonguç. In November of 2000 Tonguç and I went to Ayvalık visiting some of the locations I knew when I was a little boy. It was very enjoyable to have our dinner at the shores of Cunta Island (*Ali Baba*) overlooking the beautiful Ayvalık Bay and go through the city's marketplace. That evening we even attempted to locate my uncle Tevfik whom I hadn't seen in 30 years. I was saddened to find out that he had passed away. I was also very saddened when in July 2001 I received news that my good friend Hüseyin Özyavuz had died after a long battle with cancer. It was a sad occasion for his family and for the country where he was one of the pioneers in Aluminum casting technology and a major contributor to Izmir's well-being. After his father's death, Haluk Özyavuz took the reigns of Cevher Foundary Corporation and at a young age he did a wonderful job running the business. Because of his mangement skills and business achievements, he received many national and international recognitions and awards.

Alp Türksoy was a close family friend of ours. Alp Abi, as I called him, was one of the earliest, well known architects in Izmir with many valuable contributions in the city's landscape including the NATO Building on the *Kordon*. His sister, Dr. Nuran Türksoy-Marcus, was also our friend living in Boston. Whenever Alp Abi was in Boston visiting his sister, he and I always got together for lunch and had wonderful and stimulating conversations. I always looked forward to seeing him either in Boston or in Izmir. My friend Hüseyin Aktuğ was also working for him. Although Alp Abi was semi-retired, he was still working as a consultant to a well known textile company, SÖKTAŞ in Söke. During one of our luncheons, Alp Abi told me SÖKTAŞ was planning to install a co-generation steam turbine at their plant to generate electricity as well as extract process steam. He introduced me to Halil Fırat and Hilmi Kayhan of SÖKTAŞ and I was retained as a consultant for this power plant. Together with Halil Fırat and Hilmi Kayhan in January 1987, we visited several steam turbine manufacturers in Europe; Bloom&Voss, AEG and Siemens of Germany, and Brown Boveri of Switzerland. General Electric was not in the list since a steam turbine capacity of 8-10 MW was too small for General Electric. Although after many visits and evaluations Siemens was picked as the manufacturer to install the plant, the project was postponed. We however, had the pleasure of being friends with Halil Fırat and his lovely wife Canan Hanım. We got to see them in Izmir and in the summer time Ilkay and I often visited them at their beautiful summer house in Kuşadası. When Nükhet was at Boston University, Halil Bey's daughter Seyda was also a student there. We were thus able to be together with them whenever they were in Boston visiting their daughter. I was grateful to Alp Abi for introducing us to such wonderful people.

Atatürk Organized Industrial Zone, (AOS) *Atatürk Organize Sanayii*, is located in Çiğli, Izmir just outside of Karşıyaka. This newly developed site contains close to 500 small or medium sized industrial complexes that manufacture a variety of products from leather goods, textile products to heavy metal equipment. It was a joint venture established by the members of the Aegean Region Chamber of Industry (*Ege Bölgesi Sanayi Odası*). It was the only large scale investment made in the Aegean region in many years which created employment opportunities for thousands of people. During the early 1990's factories were gradually being built in this location and put into service, manufacturing some excellent products. The electricity to these factories as well as to the rest of the country was being supplied by TEK, Turkish Electric Company (*Türk Elektrik Kurumu*). During the 1980's and 1990's Turkey experienced a population explosion and the corresponding expansion of the country. With the growth, the need for electricity increased but the country did not make sufficient investments in power generation. Many cities and industrial complexes experienced periodic shortages of electricity. At the Atatürk Industrial complex the interruption of the manufacturing process was very frequent with the cut off of electricity. The machinery stopped running and the workers spent the time playing soccer in the parking lots while waiting for the power to return. The overall productivity of these factories was very low. The Association decided to do something about this dire situation and set up a committee of eight people to buy and install their own power plant.

In one of our summer visits to Çeşme, I was recommended to the committee in charge of this power plant, by my friend Kemal Baysak. In my first meeting with them I was shocked to learn they had no idea what they were doing. They thought they needed a small 10-20MW power plant. I explained to them that they needed a combined cycle power plant with two gas turbines and one steam turbine giving a total of 120MW output to meet their overall future needs. I also told them this could be accomplished in steps as their power needs increased. They immediately wanted me to work with them on this project and I agreed to it. I felt this would give me a good reason to visit Izmir more often and be with my mother.

It took a number of short visits for me from Boston to Izmir to work with a group of Turkish engineers to finalize the bidding documents and to write the detailed Tender Specifications. I prepared a long list of turbine manufacturers including General Electric and we sent them our specifications. We invited all the companies to present their proposals and submit their bids. Since I did not have much time and I was using my vacation days, we lined up the manufacturers visits in Izmir one after another. After many long meetings and presentations where I basically alone represented the buyers, we finalized the evaluations. In the end, because of higher fuel efficiency, easy installation, reliable field service and a good financial package, General Electric got the order for a jet engine-generator package. Within a year a 40MW power plant was installed and put into service. Later a steam turbine was added to utilize the hot exhaust gas of the jet engine. The plant is now successfully operating and generating electricity with a profit for Atatürk Industrial Zone. I was pleased to have made a small contribution to my beloved hometown.

Nearing Retirement

During the 1990's, life in the Component Development Laboratories (CDL) was routine with ongoing challenging projects. We were in the process of developing a couple of new engines and yet addressing the many field problems on various older engines in service. The laboratory was highly committed to the development of the F414 engine which evolved from the famous F404 engine. Many extensive component tests and later a lube—system simulation test on the F414 engine stretched the ever-diminishing resources of the Laboratory. The F414 engines eventually were installed on the Navy's F/A-18 E/F Super Hornet aircraft. There was always development work in CDL on Lynn's widely used T700 turboshaft helicopter engines. During the 1990-1991 First Desert Storm War, the reliability of the helicopter engines with extensive sand erosion became a major concern and CDL had to do a lot of evaluations. During the period of 1990's, however, we experienced ongoing downsizing of General Electric manpower while the growth of the company continued with Jack Welch receiving many accolades and benefits. Although Human Resources labeled the layoffs as LOW, Lack of Work, which was not the case, or RIF, Reduction in Force, we continued cutting the work force ten percent at a time while trying to get the job done. The Company had an answer to our dilemma. At the beginning of 1990 we were all assigned to be trained in a program called "Continuous Improvement". This program, which followed the "work-out" process, was presented as a tool to achieve a "culture change" to position the business for the 90's and beyond, through process and quality improvements, team work, removing barriers, employee empowerment and so on. We were told if we could make the cultural adaptation of Continuous Improvement successfully, people would have more involvement in the business scope which would translate to more productivity and enjoyable jobs. Continuous Improvement was presented to us as "Obsession with Quality" yielding a system with no errors, giving big gains in productivity, a "one team" attitude and developing better methods and systems. We studied world reknown management consultant, W. Edward Deming's 14 points of Management Principles trying to apply it to our system. It was ironic that the business world in the United States did not recognize and accept Deming until after he became famous in Japan. Brian Rowe, Vice President of Aircraft Engines summarized "the purpose of our Continuous Improvement and Work-Out efforts is to improve the quality and service we provide to our customers, and at the same time develop a team for the 90's that operates with speed, simplicity and self confidence". At every opportunity we were constantly reminded of Jack Welch's 3 S's: Speed, Simplicity and Self Confidence Principle and an "informal" and a "boundaryless company" concept. Meanwhile, as the lay-offs continued at ten percent at a time, we were down to the bare bones minimum staff with only the excellent performers left behind. I could not possibly bring myself to lay off any more of those hard working, capable people. All the secretaries and technicians were already gone and we were doing our own secretarial work. There was still demanding work on some critical engines which had to be done. Although GE was collecting all kinds of accolades as the Number 1 Company in the world, the work environment was not pleasant. Employees were so preoccupied and nervous about their jobs that productivity was very low. Although the Continuous Improvement claimed to enhance the overall job security, it did not happen. The 1990's was a very difficult period. When the year 2000 was approaching we were distracted to get ready for the new Millenium and address the possible Y2K concerns. The year 2000 "problem" was simply switching the computer programs from utilizing a two digit year into the year 2000 as the two digit year 00. We put a lot of effort to make sure the transition into the new millenium went without any trouble.

By the time we moved into the new millennium, Continuous Improvement, the concept that would save the Company and make everybody happy, was all forgotten. The new saviour of the General Electric Company was going to be "Six Sigma". General Electric's Six Sigma inititive started in 1998 when it was adopted from Motorola's Statistical

Process Control methods. Six Sigma refers to a process that produces only 3-4 defects out of every million opportunities. In basic terms, Six Sigma methodology identifies the processes that are off-target with some variation and then improves and controls the process to achieve Six Sigma quality. General Electric organized a Company-wide initiative to implement Six Sigma in everything we did. Every employee in the Company was trained to learn about the four phases (Measure, Analyze, Improve, and Control) of Six Sigma methodology. To further ascertain the implementation of these methodologies, individuals were trained to be Master Black Belts, Black Belts or Green Belts, and to use the statistical methods available in many computer programs. At the beginning of 2000 almost all the sections of the Company were run by a group of statisticians called Black Belts. In fact, in order to get a promotion one had to be a Black Belt, independent of his/her engineering or relevant technical capabilities. This created much unhappiness among the highly qualified engineers and manufacturing personnel who were doing excellent work in their day to day jobs. The atmosphere at General Electric once again was very discouraging. We continued doing some excellent work on the very few development engines the Lynn Plant had. Most of the Laboratory's work became vendor quality control. The manufacturing of a lot of engine parts was "farmed-out" to various outside suppliers. In one case, we even supplied an air-flow test rig to a manufacturing vendor in Tunusia to make and test jet engine swirlers for engine combustors. Every time GE's purchasing agents found a cheaper vendor, they switched the manufacturer and we had to check the quality of their products in our Laboratory for final approval. Many good paying manufacturing jobs at General Electric were being eliminated and these jobs would never come back. It was a sad period for General Electric and a sad period for the country's manufacturing sector. During the period I was in the Lynn Plant, 1978 through 2002, I was very dismayed to see the work force gradually diminish from 20,000 down to 5,000.

By the year 2000, the top management of the Lynn Plant had moved to Evendale. The same thing had happened to the Medium Steam Turbine Department when its management had moved to Schenectady before MST Department found its demise. Again history was repeating itself. During this time I was also reporting to the Evendale management that was always looking for ways to consolidate the Laboratories but could never figure out how to do it. Most of our staff meetings were through telephone conferencing since GE was trying to reduce the travel expenses. The atmosphere at General Electric was not the way it used to be. The happy work environment, where we devoted almost all our working lives to make some significant technical contributions, was replaced with indifference. It was a day to day operation run by people who cared for the bottom line at the end of each quarter. Engineers had lost their recognition and respect they deserved plus they were replaced by business people, statisticians and purchasing agents. Very little R&D work was being performed. I was now approaching an age where I started thinking about retiring.

Sometimes my mind wandered back and I felt happy and satisfied that I had made significant contributions and some new innovations during my 40 year career at GE. Out of the 40 years, I held engineering management positions in many different organizations for 30 years. Throughout my career I worked for one company and practiced real engineering work utilizing all my educational training. It was the most gratifying career I had at GE and I was lucky to be in departments where many new developments were happening and businesses were at their peaks. I was very grateful to GE for giving me opportunities and responsibilities to carry on my work without any discrimination and bestowing me much recognition. I had come a long way, but now I was approaching towards the end.

In Turkey, my mother's health was deteriorating rapidly. She was no longer the strong woman she once was. She could not climb the stairs in her apartment building or go for her routine visits and shopping in her favorite Alsancak Bazaar. She never, however neglected to go to the bank to check on her accounts. Her visitors continued coming to see her and to be with her. Her two sisters, whose healths were also deteriorating, periodically ventured to come to visit her. When Ayşe Teyze's health completely deteriorated and she could no longer make her periodic visits, my mother waited for me anxiously to take her to her sister. It was very sad for me to see all three sisters so frail with many health problems. Their affection and bonding towards each other never subsided. In April of 2001 when Ilkay was visiting my mother, my aunt Hanife Teyze, died during a by-pass heart surgery. It was a terrible blow to the entire family. She was a great lady with her usual cheerful and upbeat demeanor. She would be missed very much by everyone who knew her. One year later, after struggling with many health problems, in July 2002 Ayşe Teyze also died. It was another terrible blow for my mother to lose both sisters.

It must have been her strong family upbringing and a lifetime of challenging experiences that kept her resolve with a positive attitude. My mother continued living a lonely life sitting at her balcony or by her window watching strangers walk by. In the evenings her television programs kept her busy and entertained. Her two sisters being gone left an unbearable emptiness in her life, and everytime she thought of them in her quiet, lonely moments, tears welled up. My cousin Meral never neglected my mother, always attending to her needs. We had a young girl, Aysun, to stay and help my mother. We continued our yearly routine in the summertime going to our apartment in Çeşme with my mother. Those were the happy moments for us. I, more than before, recognized my mother was getting old with shorter time left for us to enjoy togetherness. There was nothing I could do but cherish the moments that I was with her. She was a brave and dignified lady, smart and sensitive. Although her breathing problem was getting worse her mind was still very keen and active. I noticed now, at the age of 88, she had less energy and stamina. She had to rest more often, but she was still determined in mind and body because she loved life and people that she knew. This gave her a strong will to live and be together with the people around her. She enjoyed their happiness and cherished their concerns. She wanted the best for them and for their families. People who got to know her loved her as if she was their own mother. Naciş was everyone's mother. I was always very proud of her, even at her old age. I looked forward to the times when my mother and I together with Ilkay had our coffee in the mornings overlooking the beautiful Ilıca Bay from our balcony in Çeşme. Every Saturday morning we continued our ritual to go to the Alaçatı Bazaar and after seating my mother under the shade of an acacia tree at the courtyard of the coffee shop, we would go buy all kinds of fresh vegetables and fruits. It was always difficult to leave Izmir and my mother thinking with fear that I might not get to see her again.

As we approached the new millennium, all our three children were on their own. Nükhet was in California, married to a wonderful young man, Tim Malone. Doğan had just started his own web hosting business, Spider Web Hosting Company in Boston and Müge had just graduated from college. Our beautiful grandaughter Molly Ayla was born on June 25, 2000 and the following year Nükhet, Tim and Molly moved back to Boston, eventually settling in their home in Lynnfield.

At the beginning of 2002, in order to avoid the cold and wintery Boston weather, Ilkay and I went to Ft. Lauderdale on vacation. While touring around the palm tree lined, canalled neighborhoods, we decided to look at a few properties for sale. An agent at one of these properties offered to show us a few condominiums on the market. Within two days we saw and fell in love with a beautiful unit in Pompano Beach just north of Ft. Lauderdale and we decided to buy it. This place would be my winter getaway. By the middle of 2002, after much procrastination, I decided to retire although it was a difficult decision. I was very concerned and nervous about what I would do with all the free time I would have after working at General Electric so many years. I started planning all the things I would do that I never had time for when I was working and as I started thinking about retirement, the idea of being retired appealed to me much more. It was time to go.

"The Golden Girls", Naciye, Hanife and Ayşe with their mother, 1975

Nükhet, Doğan and Müge in Schenectady, NY, 1978

Data Reduction Center in GE's M&P Lab. 1978

Manager of Turbine Development Engineering, 1980

In front of our house in Lynnfield, 1982

India trip, Taj Mahal, 1982

"KEMAL ATATURK ROAD" in New Delhi, 1982

Family on top of the "twin Towers", New York, 1982

At the Chateauneuf-du-Pape vineyards in Provence,
France with Paulette Russell, 1983

Children with my mother in Çeşme, 1990

Doğan, Nihat, Abdullah, Cüneyt in Izmir, 1994

With my friends Ösen, Baysak and Özyavuz in Kemalpaşa, Izmir, 1996

GE Aircraft Engines Lube System Simulator test in CDL

Four generations with Molly in Çeşme, 2004

On Tonguç Ösen's yatch in Çeşme, 2004

My family, 2004

EPILOGUE

On December 31, 2002 I retired from General Electric after 40 years of service. I was 65 years old. As I moved on to retirement I hoped and prayed that it would be a smooth transition and I would be able to continue to do things that would provide a sense of accomplishment. I now had more time to do things I wanted to do and be together with those I loved. At every opportunity I looked forward to being with my children. My granddaughter Molly, filled my and the rest of the family member's lives with joy. I started living my second childhood with Molly since I had never really had one. Ilkay and I spent the winter months in our Florida apartment avoiding Boston's cold and snowy winters. It was a good opportunity for our children and Ilkay's parents to come and visit us in sunny Florida. We have enjoyed Disney World in Orlando several times with Molly which we otherwise would not even visit. One of the more memorable moments we had was when Tonguç and Cavidan joined us in Florida and with our German friends we went on a Caribbean cruise. It was one of the most enjoyable holidays we had, filled with sweet memories.

I visited my mother in Turkey quite often and spent a lot of quality time with her. Her health was deteriorating but she still had grace and dignity in her appearance. In the summer of 2004 Nükhet and Molly and later Doğan, Bernadette, Müge and her two friends, Stephanie and Sandra all came to Turkey. My mother was so happy to be with her grandchildren especially Molly. Molly and my mother, whom she called *nine*, had an immediate attachment to each other. Molly, even at the age of four, would look after my mother by bringing her her medication and always giving her hugs and kisses. I knew deep in my heart this would probably be the last gathering of my mother with my children. I think my mother also knew that. I always harbored a fear that something might happen to prevent me from seeing her again. After that summer her health deteriorated very rapidly. In March 2005, I received the ever-feared phone call in the middle of the night from Izmir and I rushed back to Turkey. My mother was in the intensive care unit of *Şifa Hospital*. She was happy to see me and instantly asked me about the children and Ilkay. It was as if she was waiting for my arrival. I grieved to see my mother so weak. A few days later on March 18, 2005 my mother quietly passed away and we burried her the next day alongside my father. A long era was finished. She was 89 years old but still too soon for me. She was a simple but a great lady. She left a big emptiness in my heart. She would be missed by everyone who knew her and loved her so much. I certainly will never stop thinking of her and missing her. Sleep well Naciş; sleep well *güzel anneciğim*, my beautiful mother.

In September 2005, Ilkay and I went to Izmir. We were in my mother's apartment; a lonely and quiet place with unbearable emptiness. Her loud television was now shut off and her kitchen did not have all those wonderful foods she used to prepare for us. Wherever we turned, we were reminded of her but she was not there any more. We felt a terrible loneliness in that apartment. Even Çeşme was not the same without her.

Ilkay and I visited my dear friend Tonguç quite often in Çeşme. His fight with cancer was taking a big toll on him. He was very frail but still full of zest for life. When we saw him for the last time on his yacht, we hugged and kissed and waved our goodbyes as if we knew it was the last time we would see each other again. I thought this was just another sign of our fragile mortality. On December 29, 2005 Tonguç Ösen died. I felt a great loss but my life was ever richer for having known him. It was a huge loss for the country. Not only did he grow a small business into a mega-complex company with his entrepreneurial spirit, he was also a philanthropist helping tomorrow's youth through generous contributions to various schools and scholarships. I know he will be missed by his family and everyone who had the pleasure of knowing him. I know I will miss him a lot.

They say, "Life is a journey, not a destination". In my life's journey I had the pleasure of having the love and support of my family and knowing so many wonderful people. I had the most gratifying career, and happy and satisfying life. I hope to enjoy my remaining days and continue to question, learn and grow while making new friends and cherishing old ones. It is most important to stay well and enjoy the golden moments during the rest of our lives.

SUCCESS

To laugh often and much; to win the respect of intelligent people and affection of children; to earn the appreciation of honest critics and endure the betrayal of false friends; to appreciate beauty, to find the best in others; to leave the world a bit better, whether by a healthy child, a garden patch or a redeemed social condition; to know even one life has breathed easier because you have lived. This is to have succeeded.

Ralph Waldo Emerson